Hn Hh

Korean Vet camrads Hellan Kops

A Fortune
Teller's Blessing

—

The Story of
John Alan Adams

Semper Fi'

By Charles Hughes

Charles "Doc" Hughes

HK
Hell Kreek Book

Hell Kreek Productions Mountain View, Arkansas

ISBN: 1450500625
ISBN-13: 9781450500623

From responses to and reviews of Hughes'

Accordion War: Korea 1951—Life and Death in a Marine Rifle Company

"Bought the book. Read it. Couldn't put it down. . . . I'm normally a slow reader but I savored this one. Didn't want it to end.

John Simpson, Marine rifleman, Korean Vet.

"Accordion War is a quality read. Your descriptions of that era are like paintings without the sounds, however, your recounting of the artillery barrages was deafening."

Bob "Doc" Wickman Navy Corpsman, Korean Vet

"Your book is great. If you had done it 20 years ago, I believe it would have become one of the key reference genre chronicles of that war and era. I hope it still can. Stay safe... Semper Fi"

Nick the BAR-man USMC Korean Vet {Jim Nicholson, MD}

I have read many books and articles on the Korean War. This book by Charles "Doc" Hughes is by far the best. It should be on the shelf of every school library."

Jean Moore, widow of Wadie Moore Marine rifleman, Purple Heart Korean Vet.

"This is a gripping work and a must reading. . . . The present day overview/perspective ties the decades together and makes sense of the cost of war as well as the 'why's' of warfare..."

Korean War Project Newsletter

"Hughes, who is professor emeritus of English at Henderson State University in Arkadelphia, Ark., is a gifted writer. . . . This book is hard to put down. The writing is terrific. . . . Well done, Doc."

Leatherneck Magazine of the Marines, Sept 2007

"This is one of the rare books that begs to be read in one reading. . . . the reader can smell both the gunpowder and the kimchi. . . . Well done, Doc."

Military Writers Society of America

www.accordionwar.com

About the Author

Through the years Charles Hughes has published poetry and fiction along with works of literary scholarship on various topics, but his two recent books, *Accordion War: Korea 1951—Life and Death in a Marine Rifle Company* and *A Fortune Teller's Blessing—The Story of John Allen Adams* explore a common theme—war and courage. The books, however, approach that theme from different directions. In the first we see the young Marines Hughes served with face death from an implacable enemy in the rugged mountains of Korea under the harshest weather conditions. In the second we see a man who has overcome a devastating injury join with anti-war friends to confront their own government and many of their fellow citizens as they speak out against a war they believe immoral and unjust, receiving for their efforts public censure, hostility and sometimes imprisonment.

Today Hughes is professor emeritus of English at Henderson State University in Arkadelphia, Arkansas. He graduated with a BA in political science from the University of Texas at Austin in 1957 and for the next nine years worked in communication intelligence for the National Security Agency at Ft. Meade, Maryland, and later the Air Force Security Service as a cryptanalyst (Russian), instructor of cryptanalysis, technical writer (cryptanalysis), technical editor, and finally as the Chief of the Editing and Publications Branch of the USAFSS School at Goodfellow AFB, San Angelo, Texas.

He left that position in 1966 to attend graduate school at Texas Tech University at Lubbock where he received an MA

(1968) and a PhD (1971) in literature and linguistics after which he was hired by Henderson State where he taught up to and after his retirement in 1996, serving for five of those years as Chairman of the English and Foreign Languages Department.

* * *

Preface

On the second page of the 1938 Arkadelphia High School yearbook, *The Ark*, are pictures of three students. Smiling at the reader from the center of the page is the honorary editor, one of the most remarkable students ever to attend Arkadelphia High School, a school which has through the years produced more than its share of distinguished citizens.

John Allen Adams is that smiling young man whose clear eyes are looking toward a bright and promising future. But when that picture appeared in *The Ark* John Allen had been lying in bed for over a year, paralyzed from the neck down from a football accident suffered when Arkadelphia played a rival high school from the neighboring town of Malvern in October of 1936. In one of the bitter ironies of life, that game was to have been his last, for he had promised his Aunt Bessie he would drop football and focus more on piano. He had early on demonstrated musical talent and his aunt had become increasingly unhappy seeing her young charge come in too tired and weary to focus on his piano practice, particularly because she saw great promise for him in music.

Honor student, president of his class every year, a letterman in football and track, an Eagle Scout, John Allen was most importantly a kind and generous friend to his classmates and everyone he came in contact with. So when the news spread of the tragic accident the whole town rallied in support of one of its most popular and respected youths. Arkadelphia grieved for this young man, and in those hard Depression days people dug down and helped John's family pay the costly medical bills, for the intensive care required just to keep him alive.

John Allen was indeed an outstanding young man, but it's not his early distinction that makes his story one that needs to be told. It is the life he lived after his injury that reveals the power of the human spirit and demonstrates the heights one man was able to reach with character and courage.

* * *

Acknowledgements

I regret that many of those to whom I am most indebted for making this book possible are no longer living, principally John Allen's wife Joy Adams, his Aunt Gertrude Horton King, and his Uncle Vernon Horton, all of whom entrusted to me their family papers, photographs and memories. There were also his many classmates and friends, too numerous to name, who shared their John Allen stories with me.

While the two local universities have produced through the years many successful and distinguished graduates, only a few were fortunate enough to matriculate at that other institution of higher learning in Arkadelphia, Adams Book Store. The college students who worked under the tutelage of John Allen Adams received an education that went beyond books and lectures. During quiet moments alone with him in the book store, helping him arrange his papers, shelve his books, preparing his tea and helping him through his daily routine, student workers discovered they had in John Allen a friend who was genuinely interested in them, one who cared about their ambitions, hopes and feelings. In John Allen Adams his acolytes witnessed a living lesson; they saw how the most terrible challenges in life can be met with character and courage, with wisdom and wit, and were able thereafter to go on with their lives with the reassuring knowledge that such a strong, wise and compassionate man lived.

From some of those acolytes—Jim Larkin, Teresa Young, Linda Wells, Sandy Hays, and Sarah Sullivan—I have heard testimonies of their love for and devotion to John Allen. Sara

Sullivan, who today holds a PhD and an MD and is a practicing physician, told me she would not have left her job at the book store if her mentor had not died.

I am indebted to two English teachers at Delight High School in Delight, Arkansas, Mrs. Cyndi Moorman and Ms. Rachel Moorman (who happen to be my daughter and granddaughter) for inviting me to their classrooms to tell their students about John Allen and to discuss the importance of capturing the past in words before it disappears from memory, a process the students are involved in now as they interview their parents and grandparents to produce a historical album for their school. I am also grateful to other members of my family, my wife Marie for being my caretaker and chief proofreader, my Son Chuck for encouraging me to write the book, and his daughter, Jazmin Hughes, for helping me with the title.

Finally I would like to say a word for the citizens of Arkadelphia and Clark County, present and past, who have provided and continue to provide the fertile soil in which the talents and dreams of young people like John Allen Adams can take root and flourish.

* * *

A Fortune Teller's Blessing

The Story of
John Alan Adams

John Allen Adams
August 16, 1919-February 28, 1984

When by some rare chance
or love's green thumb,
the I blossoms freely
and serenely matures and drops the seed,
it is a fine thing, beautiful to behold.
No harm ever comes to such perfectness;
the unrefracted spirit shines through mortality,
and aging is not decline,
nor death an end

Table of Contents

CHAPTER 1

Adams Book Store

———————— ■ ————————

I t was after hours and getting dark, but the sign on the door said "Open" so I crossed the porch, pushed on the door triggering a tinkling bell, and entered a small dimly lit front room lined with books. There was no one in the room, but from behind the facing wall I heard the whirr of an electric motor and then saw a wheelchair back up past the connecting doorway and swing around facing me, and there was John Allen Adams, the proprietor, with a warm smile on his face.

We are all genetically programmed and conditioned by experience to expect others to fit into regular paradigms. If a person is seven feet tall or four feet tall, we notice. When we see a person with a glass eye, or prosthetic leg, or with a port wine birthmark like Mikhail Gorbachev, we notice. We are polite and considerate and certainly don't comment on these anomalies, but we notice. Those who must carry through life such differences learn to deal with the reactions of others, and most do so quite well, like Gorbachev, though others, like Franklin Roosevelt who had been crippled by polio, go to great lengths to conceal their differences for fear of being unfairly judged and limited by others. But John Allen's difference could not be concealed. Being a quadriplegic paralyzed from the neck down, his condition was immediately apparent.

He was held upright in his seat by a strap across his chest which kept his body from slumping in his little balloon-tired motorized chair. The blanket that extended from his lap to his feet did not conceal the contours of his legs which I could see were, like his arms, very thin. He had some use of his arms, but when he turned his hands palm down gravity took over and the hands flopped toward the floor. When I first saw him do that I noticed in his palm a pencil with a slip-on eraser secured to his hand with a broad rubber band, an improvised tool he used very effectively to peck out correspondence and other business on the typewriter which sat on his desk in the corner of the room behind him. When he spoke his voice was soft and whispery, though beautifully modulated and mellifluous. One could see that he had to carefully coordinate his breathing and speech since so much of his upper body was paralyzed.

Thin though he was, his dark eyes and bright expression dispelled any suggestion of sickness. He would have been tall if he could have stood, but he had not been able to stand since his final high school football game, thirty-five years earlier. Though the injury he suffered then cost him the use of his body, it had not diminished his mental acuity or spiritual strength, nor had it taken all his early physical assets. His hair was still thick and dark, his perfect smile that owed nothing to orthodontics still retained its force, and his olive skin, though somewhat sallow from his years indoors, was clear and unwrinkled. His profile reminded me of Michael Rennie, the actor who played the wise and dignified Klaatu in the 1951 science fiction movie, *The Day the Earth Stood Still,* an alien from a more advanced planet who came to earth to warn man not to take his nuclear weapons and warring ways into space, to tell us that there would be terrible consequences if we did not temper our arrogance and learn to control our aggressive impulses. As I would learn over the coming months and years, the similarities between John and Klaatu were more than superficial.

As for carrying the burden of being different through the world, I immediately discovered that for John Allen it was no burden at all; he was completely comfortable with himself and had mastered the skill of putting other people at ease in his presence, though I suspect his was an inborn grace rather than a practiced art. So soon after we exchanged introductions, we were off in a wide-ranging discussion of literature and politics.

John Allen at his Desk

I had recently arrived in Arkansas to take up my new job as Assistant Professor of English at Henderson State University. Since books were my love and the tools of my profession, and since the operators of the college book store saw books, along with T-shirts, beer mugs and sorority pins, primarily as inventories and bottom lines, I didn't find the campus book store with its fluorescent lights and no chairs a comfortable place to hang out. So soon after I got settled I looked around town for a more congenial book store for browsing and perhaps a little conversation. It didn't take long to explore Arkadelphia, a town of ten thousand people, but since it was home to two colleges I did expect there would be some options. There was, however, only one, Adams Book Store, a small white house on the corner of Main and 4th Street, two blocks from the business district and one block from the old courthouse on the street behind.

It turned out that John Allen and I both loved nineteenth-century American literature. I had recently completed my dissertation on Melville while he was a great admirer of Thoreau. The literature and thought of "The American Renascence" as it had been called, or "The Flowering of New England" during the second half of that century, we agreed, had not been surpassed. Man's knowledge had grown, no doubt, and technology had advanced exponentially since that time, but in wisdom, in understanding our place in the universe, we had progressed not a whit. Where are the 20th century figures to equal Emerson, Thoreau, Whitman and Hawthorne?

It quickly became clear to me in discussing literature and ideas with the bookseller that I was conversing with an impressively learned man. But how could that be? His formal education was cut short when his neck was broken at the beginning of his junior year of high school, and following that came months and years of being bedridden, of grueling rehabilitation and painful adjustments to his now restricted life. But John Allen Adams was a perfect demonstration of the truth that when a person has intelligence, curiosity and a real desire to learn, and has available to him resources such as books, family and enlightened friends, nothing can keep him from gaining an education. Conversely, having sat through thirty years of college graduation ceremonies, I can attest to the fact that there are a few dunces in the world with degrees hanging on their walls. As it turned out, when John Allen was suddenly set adrift on an ocean of paralysis, books, family and friends became the lifeline that pulled him through.

Each of us had found a way to turn his love of books into a vocation though we came at it from different directions. While my job would be to talk about books in the classroom, John Allen had chosen to provide students and his fellow citizens with quality reading material. Booksellers and barbers have to be circumspect in discussing controversial topics such as politics and religion since their customers represent a wide spectrum of opinions, some of which are held very dogmatically. John Allen, I learned, had the remarkable ability to converse pleasantly with those whose ideas he strongly disagreed with, hearing them out while gently interposing Socratic questions and comments reflecting his own deeply held convictions. Customers would sometimes leave the store scarcely aware they had been involved in edifying arguments that gently questioned their prejudices, or, when the store patrons were particularly astute, discussions which had risen to the level of genuine philosophical discourse.

Restricted physically though he was, his intellectual interests were wide-ranging. He had a genius for friendship and corresponded with highly literate friends around the country and the world, people whose interests ran the gamut from literature to history to religions of all stripes, from primitive tribal ceremonies to the Judeo Christian tradition as explored by such writers as Tolstoy, to Buddhism and the worship of the Ancient Egyptians. But he was a rationalist, not a true believer. In each of these areas he looked for precepts that he could relate to his own understanding of the universe.

As a businessman, John Allen stocked his store with the books that corresponded with the interests of the town—best sellers, books geared to the local public school and college curricula, self-help books, and a good supply of inspirational and uplifting works on Christian theology, but he also indulged his own interests by including on his shelves works that he loved, books which might sit collecting dust for years without catching a customer's eye. But you can be sure that when someone brought one of those books to his desk for a sales ticket a conversation would ensue that would add one more person to John Allen's world-wide web of friendship and influence.

Readers of all tastes could find an interested and sympathetic listener in John Allen. It would have come as a surprise to many of his customers, however, to learn what a radical he was, to discover that he like Thoreau, the writer he most admired, marched to a different drummer. While many of his good friends and customers made their way each Sunday to the various churches around Arkadelphia with Bibles under their arms eager to hear the good news of salvation and eternal life, John Allen made no effort to lay up his treasures in heaven; he focused his attention on the problems and opportunities here on earth. Surrounded and comforted by his books, more precious to him than gold ingots, he found his spiritual consolation sitting in his little office tapping out with his rubber-tipped pencil warm messages to his many friends and thoughtful letters to newspapers and magazines on various topics, chief among them opposition to militarism and war and arguments in defense of the earth, our natural environment.

Much of his correspondence necessarily involved the ordering and selling of books and, as with any businessman, he responded to the tastes of his customers, but he also indulged his own. While in the early 1970's the poetry of Rod McKuen, the prophecies of Kalhil Gibran, and the psychedelic explorations of Carlos Castaneda were big sellers, John Allen sought firmer ground to stand on. Because he chose to face life directly he was drawn to more substantial writers, to the Transcendentalists, Emerson and Thoreau, and to writers such as Tolstoy and Thomas Hardy whose poetry, while naturalistic and often somber, seemed more truthful. Like Thoreau, he wanted to "work and wedge [his] feet downward through the mud and slush of opinion, and prejudice, and tradition, and delusion and appearance, that alluvion which covers the globe...till [he came] to a hard bottom and rocks in place which we can call *reality*, and say This is, and no mistake." So, as a consequence, John Allen became an honest skeptic of popular tastes and wide-spread religious and political views.

There were many topics worthy of public discourse the year I met John Allen. The decade the country had just come through had been tumultuous. In 1963 President Kennedy had been assassinated; the following year both the Civil

Rights Act and the Gulf of Tonkin resolution were passed; the four years that followed saw a steep escalation in the war in Vietnam and the rise of a wide-spread and vocal anti-war movement. In 1968 both Martin Luther King and Robert Kennedy were assassinated and Richard Nixon was elected president; in 1969 news reached the U.S. that Nixon had begun secretly bombing Cambodia and that in the village of My Lai in Vietnam between three-hundred and five-hundred unarmed civilians—old people, women and children—had been slaughtered by American soldiers. On the heels of this news anti-war rallies broke out across the country, with a massive one taking place in Washington D.C. As I would come to learn, while all of these events were of vital interest to John Allen, he was particularly sickened by the carnage of the war. It was perhaps not widely understood, but Adams Book Store harbored one of the most dedicated political activists in Arkansas, a fearless champion for peace and justice and, long before it became fashionable, an environmentalist, a defender of the earth's natural treasures.

Even though I had experienced combat first hand as a hospital corpsman in a Marine rifle company during the Korean War and had seen directly what a rotten business war is and had by this time concluded that the war in Vietnam was a mistake with no hopeful end in sight, I never gathered the physical energy or the moral resolve to take my opposition to the streets, or to voice my opinions in any significant way to my governmental representatives or to newspapers. I was pretty much content to share my views with my students, with colleagues on campus and friends in the book store. In our Adams Book Store seminars we were all in agreement with John as we dissected the bad news and "body counts" coming out of Vietnam that the war was a tragedy. But most of us directed our energies at the daily business of our lives. "Activists," even for worthy causes, tend to make people uncomfortable, and comfort is what the mass of mankind seeks. So while many of us gave lip service to the anti-war movement, John Allen was the one among us who truly dedicated himself to the cause. As Thoreau says in "Civil Disobedience," "There are nine hundred and ninety nine patrons of virtue to one virtuous man."

Although John's concerns were global, his roots were local. I didn't understand when I first met him how deeply his story and his family's history were interwoven with the history of Arkadelphia and the histories of Clark and neighboring Dallas Counties going back to before the Civil War. I did from time to time spot one member of that family as she floated into view in the hallway from a side door and quickly disappeared into the living quarters at the back of the store. It was Elizabeth "Bessie" Horton, or "Miss Bessie" as she was sometimes called with old Confederate formalism tinged with a touch of patronizing irony.

Aunt Bessie when I first saw her in long faded print dresses from an earlier era, wraithlike and thin as a stick with a bit of a dowager's stoop, was a reclusive spirit like Dickens' Miss Havisham. At her first appearance John told me who she was, but she never came forward for an introduction. It would be years before I would learn her story, before I would understand how this vestige of a once proud family that could have supplied William Faulkner with another lifetime of stories was the repository of a distinguished family history studded with dark and scandalous secrets, a bitter relic of the Horton clan—John Allen's maternal forebears. I did understand, however, that Aunt Bessie was the one who had taken care of John since his injury, the one who had willingly undertaken a lifetime obligation of strenuous physical and emotional care for a quadriplegic, a responsibility which could never offer her a day, a night, or an hour of relief. The fact that she was now in her 80's and growing feeble had been in recent years of great concern to John Allen.

The only other member of the Horton family that I saw sometimes in the book store was John Allen's uncle Vernon who had been, in the first decade of the twentieth century, the curly-headed baby of the Horton clan of eight surviving children, but who was now a six-foot plus portly two-hundred-fifty pounder in his late sixties. John Allen had introduced me to his mother's brother on our first meeting explaining that he was an engineering graduate of the University of Arkansas who had worked on the proximity fuse in World War II. Vernon never said much in conversations when I was present, but it was evident that he, like many others, enjoyed John Allen's company because he could often be found sitting in the store near his nephew. I imagine that when they were alone they sometimes talked of family, of the complex and often dramatic events in their shared history. I don't know where Vernon lived or what the circumstances of his life were then, but from time to time I would see him driving his little Chevy Vega wagon, the seat far back almost in a reclining position to accommodate his ample frame, looking something like a figure from a Dr. Seuss book as he zipped about town conducting his business.

Vernon was the last of the Horton children and Bessie was the first, the proud keeper of family history and the careful guardian of family secrets. She was also a repository of local stories and regional history by virtue of the job she held for years as Linotype operator at the *Southern Standard*, the oldest newspaper in Arkadelphia. A technological marvel, the Linotype machine, labeled by Thomas Edison as the "eighth wonder of the world," made its debut in American press rooms in 1886, the year before Bessie was born. And while the two were strikingly different in build, the Linotype being a seven foot iron behemoth with levers and pulleys and gears that could set letters into matrices, insert wedge shaped spacers to justify the lines then fill the matrices with molten lead to create a "line of type," Bessie was seemingly frail, thin with angular shoulders and a faraway look in her eye. Because of the size and mechanical complexity of the Linotype, most operators were men, but Bessie's appearance belied her inner strength. The Linotype and Bessie shared three important qualities—

Elizabeth "Bessie" Horton

they were strong, dependable and durable, and, like grandfather and his clock, they pretty much came into the world and left it together.

If Bessie seemed reclusive when I first saw her in the book store it was not only because of natural shyness and her advanced age of eighty-four years, it was also because she now had a competitor for John's love and attention. Joy Salisbury, their neighbor who had lived with her husband next door in the old two-story brick building that had served as an armory in the Civil War and later as the Arkadelphia Freedman's Bureau, had been for some time caring for her husband, Tom, who was suffering from terminal cancer. Joy, strong, energetic, gregarious and at times obstreperous, was also generous and big-hearted, so for a time as Bessie's strength flagged, Joy did double duty dividing her time between taking care of her dying husband and helping Bessie with the physically demanding task of caring for her quadriplegic nephew. She relieved Bessie of much of the burden which she was no longer physically able to bear and was also a reassuring presence to John Allen who was surely concerned about the decline of his iron-willed aunt who had cared for him over the past three and a half decades.

Not long after Tom died and shortly after I arrived in Arkadelphia John Allen and Joy were married over the strong objections of his aunt. Now Joy's presence in the living quarters of the book store was bitterly resented by Bessie who knew well how to nurse her resentments, and what fosters resentment more effectively than being dependent on someone you fear is taking your place in the life of someone you love? John's strength was demonstrated, then as it had been many times before facing other challenges, in his willingness to stand up to Bessie and do what needed to be done while showing at the same time the utmost consideration for his aunt's feelings and appreciation for her care for him through the years. From his still chair he was the captain steering the tiny ménage of Adams Book Store through the stormy sea of Aunt Bessie's wrath.

The thought of being abandoned in his helpless state had always haunted John Allen. Some years back when Bessie had been committed to a tuberculosis sanitarium and he was left unsure whether she would ever return, he had tried to escape his nightmare by swallowing a bottle of aspirin. Fortunately it only made him sick and he recovered, as did Aunt Bessie, following which their lives continued on as before.

Bessie had for all those years literally been John Allen's life support, while he in turn provided his aunt with a meaningful and worthy purpose in life. In a letter to his close spiritual friend and fellow peace activist, Mike Vogler, John said that the relationship between him and his aunt was symbiotic, and that description was apt. Just a few years earlier at a time when Bessie was ailing Mike had offered to take care of John Allen but he declined. He told Mike, "The future has a way of solving problems when they arrive." Now the advent of Joy into his life confirmed that faith in the future.

It was some time during that first semester of my new job that I first met Joy. I don't believe I understood then how recently they had married, but I did notice how attentive she was to John and the pride she seemed to take in being Mrs. Adams, even though the two were strikingly different in temperament and world views. Joy's political and religious outlook was conventional, her interests local and domestic. When she would hold forth on some topic John Allen would listen tolerantly and not attempt to challenge her views or engage her in a deeper dialog as he often did with customers and friends. While the central points of their mental lives may have been some distance apart, the compasses of their interests intersected and in that common space where the two circles overlapped, they shared a number of enthusiasms including nature studies, gardening and healthy eating. Joy's boisterous nature required patience from those in close proximity, and since John Allen was a master of tolerance, theirs proved to be a happy union.

After the town chipped in and bought a van for John Allen, for the first time since his injury he was able to escape the confines of the house and the few surrounding blocks he could navigate in his motorized chair and visit the countryside, see the jonquils in bloom, and enjoy picnicking at DeGray Lake. They both needed companionship and clearly enjoyed their

lives together. Joy, strong and capable, gladly took on the chores involved in taking care of John's unresponsive body. The main challenge the two faced in the first few years of their marriage was contending with the smoldering resentment of Aunt Bessie.

Joy Adams, John Allen's bed with lift

Those around John Allen had always loved him and wanted to care for him. His doting mother, Louise, and his father, Al, agreed to leave him with his aunt in Arkadelphia in 1927 only because their itinerant lives as carnival workers made it impossible to provide their son with the stability and education he needed. They knew he would have advantages with Bessie and that Bessie was willing to take on the responsibility. But back then when John was a bright and happy eight-year-old possessed of a preternatural maturity and charm, it's easy to see why he was wanted. Studies show what most of us already know, that the attitudes of teachers (and other adults) toward children are influenced by a child's looks and demeanor, and John Allen was a beautiful and dutiful child. Life is not fair to those less appealing, and it would certainly not be fair to him later on, but his school days in Arkadelphia were for him a golden age. So, as he advanced through school winning admiration from his teachers and fellow students alike for his academic and athletic achievements as well as his modesty and generosity, it's not difficult to see how Bessie could take pride in being his guardian, his protector, and to understand how she could see in John Allen the embodiment of the Horton promise.

After his injury a remarkable thing that set him apart from many other quadriplegics was not that the town rallied around him, for that is to be expected when a young athlete is gravely injured, but that people wanted to participate in his care. There was a huge outpouring of public sympathy and concern after he was hurt, and townspeople were more than generous in providing financial and moral support for the stricken young football player. And the support continued for years with people regularly bringing gifts to John

Allen and his Aunt Bessie. Two of his teachers, Amy Jean Greene, a prominent Arkadelphia citizen and educator, and her cousin Martha Greene were strong supporters. They were frequent visitors who sometimes brought, along with gifts of fruit and flowers, a young relative who became one of the devoted admirers of the handsome paralyzed young man. Amy Thompson, who was eight years old when she first saw him, told her mother that when she grew up she wanted to marry John Allen so she could take care of him.

The desire to care for John Allen was shared by many at that time, but as weeks became months and months gave way to years with no improvement in his condition, the citizens of the town naturally turned their attention elsewhere and Bessie and her nephew, left to cope with their radically changed circumstances, settled into the rigorous physical daily routine that would shape the rest of their lives. But Bessie was up to the challenge; she had confronted family hardships before and prevailed and would again. John Allen's mother, Louise, who loved her son beyond anything, was financially and constitutionally incapable of caring for him, so she once more had to rely on her stalwart sister who had helped her many times in the past, though that help had often been administered with a generous amount of censure and pain.

Bessie not only took pride in her family's history, she was also knowledgeable about local and regional history as well by virtue of the fact that for many years she walked each workday several blocks to the office of the newspaper on 6th Street just off Main where her job was entering local news—births, deaths, social and college events, and calamities of all descriptions—into the ninety one keys of the mechanical marvel which clanked and hummed and sometimes spit out tiny jets of molten lead as it converted her input into lines of type. The *Southern Standard* had been the collector of regional news and local gossip since it was founded in 1868 by two Confederate veterans, James Gaulding and Adam Clark.

Proud of her own Confederate heritage, Bessie studied her family history and worked to preserve local Civil War records and artifacts and family records. She corresponded with other Hortons in the region seeking information of their relationships and their allegiances during the War Between the States. Both she and her sister, younger by one year, Mrs. Gertrude Horton King, a school teacher in Little Rock, could trace their lineage back to the time of the Revolutionary War. The sisters were determined, in so far as possible, to maintain the honor and status of the Horton family.

I knew nothing of John Allen's family history when I patronized his store and little about the history of the region; I only knew that from time to time I found myself seeking his company. I paid regular visits to Adams Book Store, sometimes in search of a book, but always looking for conversation, for personal and political counsel, and for pleasant refuge from the trifling frustrations of academia. John Allen's aura of serenity invited people to open up in his presence. I even a few times found myself sharing my hypochondriacal anxieties with him realizing, even as I did so, how inappropriate it was to be discussing such things with John sitting there strapped in his wheelchair. He always showed concern for my complaints, however, and I'm absolutely certain he perceived no impropriety on my part and took no offense. John Allen was the most truly compassionate listener I've ever known.

* * *

For thirteen years I drew upon the strength, friendship and support of John Allen Adams so I, along with his family and a host of his friends in Arkadelphia and around the world, was grieved to learn in February 1984 that, forty-six years after getting his neck broken in a high school football game, John Allen was dead. We had no reason to be surprised, however. He had beat the odds and lived to be, as far as he and Joy could learn, the oldest surviving quadriplegic in the country, a longevity no doubt the consequence of Bessie's and Joy's loving care and John's dedication to a healthy diet.

In death, as in all things, John Allen was organized and prepared. He had written out detailed instructions for Joy regarding funeral arrangements and family business, and for Arkadelphia he left the following message which was printed along with his picture in the local paper:

Open Letter to Arkadelphia

If a young man happens to break his neck and become paralyzed, there is no better place for the misfortune to occur than in a small town in the South—in Arkadelphia to be specific.

I know; in 1936 it happened to me; and from the first night the town expressed concern. Over the years countless individuals and many church and civic groups gave my aunt and me moral support and a great deal of material support (it started in depression years when no one had much).

So many of the old faces are gone; but we gained new friends along the way. After I married in 1971 people continued to show kindness to my wife Joy and me.

I cannot find words to express my feelings in this matter, but I wanted to give some indication of my deep and long-felt gratitude. May Arkadelphia continue to be a community of caring hearts and minds.

> Sincerely,
> John Allen Adams

After the news of John Allen's death spread messages of condolences, of grief and love, began to arrive from around the state and country attesting to the reach of his spirit and influence. Some responses to John's death appeared in the local paper such as the following:

Dear friend,

You and your book store were an oasis of integrity, a nurturer of peace and compassion and freedom, a center for the arts and sciences, a last "inpost" of enlightenment. Where else and who else in the bright middle of the day, could be found playing the music of Handel, of Mozart or Beethoven, just for the sheer joy of the matter?

Not long after I moved to Arkansas I learned about you. On my first visit to your store I felt frightened and uncomfortable because of your bound and broken body, but you quickly put a stop to that. On subsequent visits we did some buying and selling of books and brown eggs and some trading of absurdities and ideas. You talked of the whole body of Walt Kelly's Pogo works and of the gravity and greatness of Mark Twain's writings. You shared with me your lovingly composed poem that announced to the whole world your appreciation for the man who baked for you his "honest loaf," and after the airing of [Carl] Sagan's "Cosmos," you seemed glad to pass along the good news that, at last, a good use had been found for television. You put me in touch with John Holt and back in touch with Thoreau and on the track of a thousand other understandings. With just a few good words and a knowing sparkle of the eye, you gave me courage to go ahead with "performance of right."

But you've up and died. Do you now tread-tall the great wind-walks of infinity? Does your joyous music now move in time with the love and light of bright wings? John Allen Adams, you were a friend for me and you were a friend for this whirling, hovering, sweet planet Earth. Oh friend, goodbye!

Rebecca Hall Fulmer

Joy continued to receive many phone calls and letters of condolence, and her importance to John Allen was recognized in another letter to the *Daily Siftings*:

Tribute to Romance

Everyone knows John Allen Adams was a man of great integrity, a man truly loved and appreciated by this community; a man whose presence here will be sorely missed by all who knew him.

Everyone knows that John's life has been heroic in the sense of mind over circumstances; adventure in intellect; strength in dignity.

Everyone knows that in a time of extreme need, a wonderful woman came to John and married him in order that she could always be close by to care for him and meet the physical necessities of his life. Everyone THINKS this was self-sacrifice for the sake of human good. They're wrong.

What everyone doesn't know is that this was LOVE in the truest, most romantic sense of the concept. I know Joy Salisbury Adams. I knew her then. She's hard working, driving, energetic, PHYSICAL, FULL OF LIFE. Everyone said, "why would she do such a thing?" I said "she LOVES him." She said, "He reads poetry to me. He sings to me. We share memories of life and times. I tell him of families, jobs, and things that others take for granted in life." She needed him as much as he needed her.

Everyone knows that John Allen Adams' life was fuller and richer the last thirteen years because of things he experienced with Joy. I know that Joy's life has been enriched also by loving John.

Vive'la romance!

Linda Dixon

Of course condolences and praise for the deceased are the norm, even when friends and family have to comb diligently through the departed's past to come up with something positive to say, and often there are unspoken dissenting opinions. But when John Allen died the response was uniform, wide-spread and heartfelt. Without exception, everyone who ever met him and talked to him came away with the same conviction—that they had met an extraordinary human possessed of humor, compassion, wisdom, and remarkable spiritual strength. John had made many friends and his death grieved many people.

One of the first things some of John Allen's friends did after the funeral was to establish a scholarship in his name at Arkadelphia High School where he had been an outstanding student. When we sent out word of the project contributions came in from all around the country and before long exceeded our original goal. Now, for over twenty years, the John Allen Adams Scholarship has been awarded to many deserving students in the name of the bookseller and poet; but for Arkadelphia High students today John Allen Adams is only a name, a plaque on a wall. When they show their youthful exuberance at pep rallies before football games against perennial rivals, such as Malvern High School, no one can expect them to know about a game between those same two rivals during the depths of the Depression when a seventeen-year-old end for Arkadelphia, running interference for a teammate, found himself, after a tackle, sitting on the ground where a player, charging from behind, landed on his neck and changed his life forever.

* * *

CHAPTER 2

Son of My Heart

———————◼———————

Not long after John Allen died Joy called and asked if I would take possession of his papers. When I met her at the book store she gave me several boxes of family correspondence, documents and photographs. He had been fairly faithful in preserving the letters he had received from family and friends and had made copies of some of his own that he had sent out to friends and newspapers on subjects important to him. In addition to his letters, poetry and papers there were records of the Horton family saved by Aunt Bessie who died in 1975. After her death John Allen wrote to his friend Mike Vogler:

> Aunt Bessie died at the age of 88 last year, and several months later, with the help of my wife and students who work for me, I went through the belongings in her small, musty, crowded bedroom to decide what should be kept and what should be given away or thrown away. It was a sad task, of course, the sorting out of a long life's mementos. I kept thinking of Ferlinghetti's phrase, "pictures of a gone world," as we dug into the closets, the cardboard boxes, the

dresser and the large wardrobe with mirrored doors. In the trunk were bundles of letters, some going back to [written in] 1903 when Aunt B. was 16 years old from girl friends, and filled with teenage chat of camp meetings, parties and boys. Many letters were from members of her family—her seven brothers and sisters, her aunts and uncles, her father, her beloved Grandmother Horton. Aunt Bessie seems to have spent her happiest days visiting the farm home of her Horton grandparents. Her grandfather ran a small general store and post office for the community.

Over the next several weeks as I sorted through the old photographs and read family documents and letters, it became clear to me that there was a history in the boxes that needed to be told. Here was the detritus of a remarkable family, the Hortons, whose antecedents can be traced back to the beginning of our country. As for John Allen's immediate family, there were three decades of letters from Louise to her sister, Bessie, postmarked from all over the country as she and her husband, Al, toured with a series of carnivals and traveling shows. And there were John Allen's life-long letters, the earliest from his childhood to Bessie as he traveled the carnival circuit with his parents, and then from his school years in Arkadelphia letters to his still traveling parents reporting on his academic and athletic progress and social activities. After the fateful football game the letters stopped for several years as the family came together and struggled to come to terms with the broken promise of their gifted boy.

After the successful inauguration of the scholarship, I turned my attention once more to the boxes of materials

Joy had entrusted to me. As I shuffled through the yellowed newspaper clippings, the stacks of aging letters and photographs it struck me what a history was here—family heroes and adventurers going back to the Mexican War, the California Gold Rush, the Civil War, and the two world wars. Here also were distinguished educators, doctors and talented musicians, but there were shadows in the family's past as well. In the boxes, it dawned on me, were all the ingredients for a dramatic American story.

In 1985 and 86 I set out in hopes of preserving the story of this remarkable man. Most of those I talked to were eager to share their stories of John Allen. I began with Joy, Uncle Vernon and Aunt Gertrude and then talked to childhood friends and schoolmates. I sent out letters to friends around the country asking for information about John Allen. I visited the site of the old Fairview Plantation and talked to some residents there about the Hortons. I also toured the Sardis Cemetery in Dallas County and Rose Hill Cemetery in Arkadelphia to find Horton family graves.

I filled several notebooks with information from interviews with local family and friends and sent out letters to others seeking information and got many warm and detailed memories of John Allen. Almost all those I contacted were eager to share their memories of him, and all responses revealed a universal admiration and love for the man. But when I asked detailed questions about John Allen's family history from some of those closest to him, some of those who helped him through the darkest months and years after his injury, I got a clear sense that there were doors to his past that were not to be opened. Martha Greene, who along with her cousin, Amy Jean Greene, had been among the most dedicated caregivers

27

A Fortune Teller's Blessing

of John Allen after his injury, who had with Amy Jean been responsible for seeing that his education did not end with his injury, told me that, while she would gladly discuss John Allen's character and accomplishments, she would not answer detailed questions about his family background.

One of his closest boyhood and lifelong friends, W.S McNutt, a polymath—scientist, scholar, artist, satirist, outdoorsman, and philosopher—corresponded with John for three decades. During their formative years they had been boy scouts in their high school principal and Scoutmaster Mr. V.L. Huddleston's Troop 23, and decades later both fondly recalled their scouting experiences in and around Arkadelphia and both expressed an almost reverent admiration for Mr. Huddleston, his wisdom and leadership. The two men remained close spiritual brothers through the decades exchanging ideas on a wide range of subjects.

McNutt lived a full life such as John Allen might have lived had he not been injured. He loved the outdoors—hiking and camping in the Sierra Nevada's while in graduate school in California and skiing whenever he got the chance. He corresponded with John throughout his life, sharing thoughts on his marriage, the birth and development of his two sons, music, books, and life in general, but never talking of his career and accomplishments. He studied science and wound up teaching at Tufts University School of Medicine in the Department of Biochemistry and Pharmacology and published research on biochemistry which can still be found on the Internet.

But when it came to literature and the humanities, W.S looked to John for recommendations, and he purchased those recommendations from Adams Book Store. Under John's guidance, he acquired the great books and read them one-by-one on the commute from his home on Old Road to Nine Acre Corners in Concord, Massachusetts, near Walden Pond to his office at Tufts University. The two men exchanged their perceptive understandings of the great writers at some length, not in academic abstractions, but always in down-to-earth practical Thoreauvian language. There's no way to know whether John Allen's love for Thoreau in any way influenced McNutt's selection of his place of work and residence, but clearly he provided John Allen a vicarious connection to the tramping ground of the writer he most admired.

Having been so close to John Allen for so long, McNutt was one of the friends I was most eager to hear from. But for four years he did not answer my letter of inquiry and when I finally received his response I was left puzzled and somewhat taken aback:

May 11, 1989
Old Road to Nine Acre Corners, Concord, MA
Dear Charles Hughes:

In looking through a box of papers, today, in my study, I discovered, oddly enough, a letter sent to me in 1984, with regard to John Allen Adams. Nothing could have proved more fortunate than my having misplaced your letter by mistake. I could not recall your name or address, most fortunately. What an oddity that this passage of time has been so helpful.

The superficial aspects of John Allen's life do not concern me in the least. What I find so moving is what he has confided in me, letter by letter throughout his life. I have boxes of them.

Such intimate details of his life are not matters he would care to have published, I gather, and which I am certain about. I had no intention, at the time, of sorting through them, page by page, and censoring section after section.

I also received a letter, shortly after yours, from some committee stating that *they* would decide what would and what wouldn't be published, but send it in to *them*. Thank heaven I threw that one out at the time.

What astonishes me, even more, is that there are those there in Arkadelphia who are as stupid as some I have to deal with here in Concord.

Sincerely,
W. S. McNutt

I didn't know what to make of this letter. Clearly McNutt possessed a treasure trove of John Allen's letters, but he, like some I talked to in Arkadelphia, felt protective of his friend and was apparently determined to thwart any attempts to delve into his family and personal past. The letter did strike me as being unnecessarily petulant. When he wrote it he was over seventy, probably retired, and somewhat frustrated after fighting for years the bloodless battles of academe. The letter does, however, reveal the traits that make all his letters highly readable—directness, intelligence, and vitality.

But it was not the above letter or the rebuffs I got from a few of his friends and benefactors that led me to put aside my project on John Allen Adams. I had at that time taken on administrative duties as Chair of the English and Foreign Languages Department at Henderson State and those duties, along with my constitutional tendency for procrastination, led me to set aside the boxes of interviews, letters, and documents and relegate the project to the back of my closet and the back of my consciousness where it nagged at me for years, like a solemn vow un-kept.

Then in 2006, twenty years after I set the project aside, I got a call from one of my ex-colleagues from the English Department, Claire Gherki, who had bought the house on Main and 4th Street, the former Adams Book Store. She was in the process of refurbishing it to open as a domestic craft store—knitting, quilting, crocheting—and told me she found some boxes of John Allen's materials left there after Joy had died in 2003 and wanted to know if I would like to have them.

After I brought the boxes home I retrieved the materials I had stored away and began once more to shuffle through the whole stack of John Allen and Horton family materials. One old newspaper clipping from the *Arkansas Gazette* recording the death of Louis Horton, Louise's father and John Allen's grandfather, caught my attention. It was an account of what appeared to be a murder at the old Horton plantation site at Fairview:

Special to the Gazette.

Arkadelphia, Aug 9, [1914] Louis A. Horton, a planter of Dallas county, was killed and his body cremated in his house, which was burned last night at a late hour. The body was found charred beyond recognition, and investigation revealed signs of violence. Horton until recently resided here. He was making a crop in Fairview and slept alone in one of the farmhouses. No one seems to have any knowledge of the fire, and the smoking embers of the house among which was found Horton's remains, was not discovered by neighbors until after sunup today.

Horton was seen about ten o'clock last night, when a country baseball team returning from some country point passed his home. Members of the team say they saw him reading. Two of Horton's sons heard of the tragedy early this morning by phone from Fairview and immediately set out for the scene, other members of the family following.

A coroner's jury made a full investigation and pronounced the verdict that the dead man came to his death at the hands of some unknown party or parties. The skull of the dead man was fractured.

Aside from a number of conventional family obituaries, most of the newspaper articles preserved in the boxes recorded family distinctions, milestones, and accomplishments. But there was one other reported death from the Arkadelphia *Southern Standard* that jumped out at me.

Jan 5, 1945

Arkadelphia Woman Suicides In Spa Hotel

Mrs. Allen F. Adams, about 50, Arkadelphia, whose body was found in a local hotel room Wednesday afternoon, died from an overdose of chloroform, Garland County coroner Foster Jarrell reported last night in giving a verdict of suicide. Clad in her night clothes, Mrs. Adams had been dead for several hours when found by the hotel clerk, Deputy Sheriff Will Lowe, who investigated, said.

Dr. Jarrell said that Mrs. Adams had left a note, addressed "to whom it may concern," expressing "thanks" to her husband, Allen F. Adams, Kansas City newspaperman and former showman "for kind treatment" and stated "I can't stand the "pain any longer." The penciled note gave no explanation of the "pain," the physician said.

Mrs. Adams, daughter of Louis Horton, prominent Dallas County farmer, registered at the hotel two months ago, the clerk told officers. Whether she was under the care of a physician was not known. The clerk said she had spent some time in the lobby of the hotel with other guests Tuesday evening and that she had retired to her room apparently in good spirits. Officers found nothing in her personal belongings to give them a clue as to what the "pain" referred to.

The vial that had contained the chloroform bore the label of a Hot Springs pharmacy, but when questioned by reporters, a druggist there said they had been out of the drug since August and had they had it in stock would not have sold a sufficient amount to a person to cause death without a prescription from a physician or unless they personally knew the customer.

In addition to her husband and father, Mrs. Adams is survived by one son, John Allen Adams of Arkadelphia; two sisters, Mrs. Gertrude Horton King of Little Rock, and Miss Bessie Horton of Arkadelphia, and two brothers, Rodney Horton of Detroit, and Vernon Horton of Connecticut.

The body was returned to Arkadelphia for funeral services today. The Rev. Robert Pool, pastor of First Methodist Church, will officiate.

The hotel, whose name was thoughtfully omitted from the news article presumably so as not to adversely affect business, was the recently razed Goddard on Central Avenue.

Louise Horton may have appeared to be fifty when she died, but she was only forty three. Her life had not been easy. In 1944 she made her last carnival circuit with the Hennie's Brothers and the Wagner's Shows working as a fortune teller, a "mitt reader," dispensing words of encouragement and hope to her patrons while her own life was faltering to its sad conclusion. Her father who died in the fire at Fairview in 1914 did not survive her as the article states, and the husband whom she consistently praised throughout their marriage had recently separated from her and remained in St. Louis where, if the above article is to be believed, he was working for a newspaper. When they found her body in her room at the Goddard Hotel her beloved John Allen, eight years after his injury, was lying paralyzed forty miles away.

In the boxes of items Joy gave me after John Allen died was a large envelope holding the contents of Louise's purse found in her hotel room when her body was discovered. In the envelope I found a Christmas card addressed to Louise at the Goddard Hotel and signed "John Allen, Bessie, and Al." The envelope is postmarked St. Louis so apparently Al sent the card and signed it for all three; there were Greyhound bus stubs from Chicago, Erie, PA, Jackson and Tupelo, Mississippi, hotel receipts from around the country, an envelope from Mercury Life & Health Co. stamped with a reminder to buy War Bonds, and an out-patient's card from St. Louis University Hospitals signed by Louise Adams. Among all those tattered ends of a poignant life were two things that particularly caught my attention.

The first was a 5 ½" by 8 ½" brown school composition notebook whose ruled pages had been rather crudely sawed off about an inch on the right margin with the front and back covers tucked under, apparently to reduce the width so it could be carried in a purse. This homely book was a testament to Louise's love for her son, a devotional filled with personal messages to John Allen and sentimental rhymes she had run across on her travels around the country, grammatically challenged but heartfelt, meant to be uplifting but tinctured throughout with melancholy, heartbreak and despair.

Samples:

Thoughts of you dear son is [sic] what keeps the world turning round for those that love you, and two of the many that do love you, are your mother and Dad, so keep the world turning. You are the darling of our lives.

Mother

Son:—

I have not money to leave you, but this I can leave you, and it is greater than gold. It's the *"God"* within you. When your days seem lonely and blue, call on your God, which is within all mortles[sic], but there are many who fail to look within; let not yourself be one of the many. For if you call God will answer from within, and will show you all that is good. This I leave you, son of my heart, and I know you will receive courage from God to carry on in this life, so as when your journey is 'oer the world will be a better place by you having lived in it. (Fear not) So here's love to keep you company on your journey through life, and I'll await you on the "Great Divide."

Mother

And this:

I Mary Louise Horton Adams do hereby leave my son, John Allen Adams, 302 Clinton St. Arkadelphia, Ark.

everything that I may have at the time of my passing, in real or personal estate. See that he receives same.

> Mrs. A.F. Adams
> Mary Louise Horton Adams
> Justina Gibbs or
> Madame Justine

It is highly unlikely that John received anything of material value from his mother upon her death and he probably never saw the little brown note-book while she was alive, but he could never doubt her devotion.

The other thing from the purse's content that caught my attention were two 3x5 faded cards, one green and one red with printing on both sides:

Louise had penned in on the green

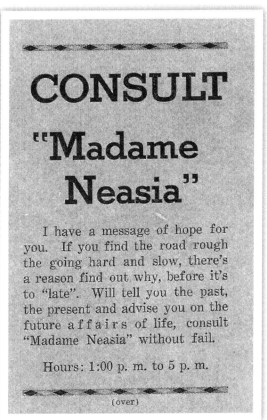

CONSULT

"Madame Neasia"

I have a message of hope for you. If you find the road rough the going hard and slow, there's a reason find out why, before it's to "late". Will tell you the past, the present and advise you on the future affairs of life, consult "Madame Neasia" without fail.

Hours: 1:00 p. m. to 5 p. m.

(over)

card, "Room 111-3rd Flo. Goddard Hotel" and had changed the "5 p.m." to "9 p.m." So apparently she continued to practice her craft in the off season when she could drum up customers.

Since its "magical waters" were first discovered by pre-historic Native Americans, Hot Springs has been a magnet for those seeking a balm for life's afflictions, cures for the physical and spiritual maladies that cannot be assuaged by conventional medicine or divine intervention. Some denizens of the Goddard at that time were no doubt such pilgrims, so perhaps "Madam Neasia" had some success there. But of the various professional names Louise worked under, this was a new one.

Just seven weeks earlier she had stopped in A.R. Smith's nearby print shop at 907 Central Avenue and paid $6 to have a stack of Madame Neasia cards printed. Perhaps with a new name she had hoped to get a new start.

* * *

CHAPTER 3

The Secrets of Madame Justina

See? There's Madame Justina, weaver of dreams
True believer in her own
And half believing those she weaves for pay—
"Cross my palm and the future's yours."
At sixteen she left home where all dreams died
To find a world where dreams led phoenix lives,
And Monday's shining resurrection rose
From Saturday's defeat.
(Mother, Mother,
The years fleshed your body
But never your dreams—
The last one fading
In the chloroform you bought!
"'Round and 'round she goes,
And where she stops nobody knows.")

Mary Louise's first start in life had not been auspicious, in part because her father provided an unsteady foundation for his children. He had been only two years old when his own father rode off to the Civil War in 1861. According to his children, Louis Scott Horton

39

was spoiled by the women at the Fairview Plantation, both black and white, while W.S. Horton, the patriarch of the family, was gone four years to the war. Truth was that Confederate women had to endure such desperate conditions—bringing in crops, tending livestock and feeding and clothing families— that absence of supervision as much as coddling might have bent the twig that was destined to become Louise's father.

When Horton returned from the war in 1865 he set out to restore his estate at Fairview, though his plantation would now be called a farm and his former slaves, sharecroppers. Such were the circumstances throughout much of the agrarian South following the war. But Horton made the most of hard times. He quickly replanted his fields in cotton and established a mercantile business selling dry goods, farm supplies and groceries to his tenants and neighboring farmers while supplementing his income by attaining the position of postmaster for the community and operating the post office from his store.

Through diligence and hard work Horton once more became a relatively prosperous man.

Louis had a sister, Priscilla, older by four years, but he was Horton's only antebellum son and was indulged by his father as he grew up. He became, as a young man, something of a spoiled dandy with a taste for fine clothes and fancy carriages. Louis' second daughter, Gertrude, told me her grandfather was very liberal with Louis who she said was what today would be called a "playboy." The one identified picture of him among the Horton family papers shows a fair haired young man in a high-buttoned coat wearing a bow tie, his wavy hair combed forward, sporting a full moustache and what today we would call a light soul patch. His eyes are his most striking feature.

The sepia tone of the photograph doesn't reveal their color, but it's likely they were blue. They are fixed directly forward, seemingly staring through the lens of the camera into the future, defying the observer to guess the path his life might take.

Louis Scott Horton

Louis Scott Horton and Amy Brown Scales were married in 1886. He was twenty-seven and she was twenty. Her father, John Scales, was also a successful planter who owned slaves before the Civil War, but rather than ride off to battle he remained in Dallas County and supplied leather goods to the Confederate army. Following the war he continued to farm and run a cotton gin, and it was during this period at a yearly picnic at Scales Springs that Louis and Amy met. There Louis carved a heart in an old beech tree with both their initials inside. Vernon said his father liked to show off in those days, riding around in a surrey pulled by four horses. When he first called on Amy, his son said, he "dropped a wad of money on the floor that would choke an ox." But then on the way home in the surrey after their wedding when Amy expected to be kissed, Louis disappointed her by not taking advantage of the opportunity. No doubt Vernon learned these and other stories about his father while growing up at his mother's knee.

Even though Louis may have seemed a prize catch for the young ladies of the county, Vernon told me that both bride and groom married on the rebound. And Amy, who was red head-ed, soon after the wedding overheard her new mother-in-law make a disparaging remark about red-heads. In spite of starting out on a few discordant notes, over the next seventeen years the union produced ten children, Bessie being the first in 1887 and Vernon the last in 1904. Two girls died in childhood.

There is another unidentified picture of a man that, when closely compared with the identified picture, appears to be Louis standing beside a mule-drawn reaper accompanied by two black field hands and a small boy. The boy would be one of his sons, either John William (Pete) or Thad, and the picture would have been taken in the closing years of the nineteenth century. Louis would have been about forty with four children and well beyond his carefree days as a sporting young blade, now pretty much on his own since the Horton plantation at Fairview had deteriorated after his father lost much of his wealth in 1890 defending his eighteen-year-old son, Paul Edward, against murder charges that grew out of a dispute over a fence.

Louis Horton with field hands and son

According to Vernon, Paul Edward had taken a rifle down to the site of the disputed boundary and found their neighbor directing two field hands to move a fence back onto Horton property. He testified that he leaned the rifle against a tree then walked toward the neighbor demanding he not move the fence and a heated argument ensued. When the man started toward him with an axe, he claimed he went back, picked up the rifle and fired. Apparently the jury didn't buy Paul Edward's story so he was convicted of murder and sentenced to hang. It was then Horton hired lawyers to appeal the verdict against his son. The defense convinced the judge to have the body exhumed, and when that was done it was discovered the man had been shot in the chest and not the back as had been claimed at the trial; so the conviction was overturned.

Although Horton was himself an educated man and encouraged his children to further their educations and assisted them in the pursuit, he had no luck with Louis who only made it through the fifth grade, a reasonable attainment for rural Arkansas boys of that period, but far below that of his siblings who all attended college. Horton nevertheless continued to help his son and set him up in a mercantile business shortly after he married Amy in a little community called Pine Grove, but Louis neglected his business and soon his young family was suffering from his dereliction. Horton later provided his son and family a farm plot on the Fairview estate with a comfortable house for his grandchildren, but Louis over the years proved to be as unsuccessful at farming as he had been at business.

W.S. Horton died in 1907 and, with his father no longer there to lend a hand, the situation for Louis and his family in Dallas County grew desperate. By 1910 the quality of their lives had deteriorated to the point where Louis' Aunt, Laura Scott Butler, told Amy she had to get her kids "out of the sticks" and move them to Arkadelphia where they could get in school. Laura was a repository of family history and champion of their cultural aspirations, a person who, along with her daughters Elizabeth and Annie Laurie, would prove to be a powerful positive influence in John Allen's life.

Louise was nine that year when what was left of her grandfather Horton's Fairview Plantation was parceled out and sold and she and her family moved to Arkadelphia. There were four children still living at home, two older brothers, Horace seventeen, Rodney fifteen, and one younger, Vernon, who was six. Bessie and Gertrude had already left and were living in Arkadelphia so the rest of the family joined them there. To make the move the family would have loaded their belongings and provisions into horse or mule-drawn wagons for the twenty-mile journey down the dusty road that is today's State Hwy 7. It was the year Halley's Comet revisited the earth and Mark Twain left it. There's no way to know if the young Louise looked up from the wagon bed at the wandering starry messenger swinging around the sun as they creaked along in the twilight, but she might have.

Wagons had begun to make room for automobiles in Arkadelphia when the Hortons arrived in town. Louise and her family could hear the explosive pops and whines of the first Model T Fords as they went chugging through town; the smell of gasoline and exhaust fumes now mingled with the clop of hoofs and snorts of horses and the aroma of manure up and down Caddo, Clinton and Main streets. One other smell common at the time was the tang of freshly sawn pine. Lumber had become the main source of income in the region by 1910 and the felling of giant virgin timber, a rapacious and exploitative practice which had been a major source of income for Clark County since the first railroads came to the area in the 1870's, was in its final decade. Though the internal combustion engine was making inroads, wagons continued to provide the main means of transporting giant logs from old-growth trees, the likes of which would never be seen again, to the many sawmills of the area. Many smaller trees had been converted to telephone poles which now stood tall up and down both sides of Main Street. Thomas Edison's incandescent invention had started to pose a real threat to the kerosene trade.

After getting his family settled, Louis managed to find a job as a mail carrier but kept it only a year. Out of work he sought comfort in the bottle, a recourse which led to further battles with his wife and troubles for his family. The conflicts between Amy and Louis grew in bitterness exacerbated by his drinking until the marriage ruptured in 1912, the year the Titanic went down and the Horton family foundered. A year later the couple was divorced. To escape the turmoil for which he was largely responsible, Louis left his family in Arkadelphia and headed back to Dallas County, determined once more to scratch out some kind of living in the once productive soil of the old Fairview place.

In the meantime Amy was left with the children at the house on 3rd and Clinton which was thereafter known as the "home place," property presumably purchased with money from the divorce and what was left of the proceeds from the Fairview Plantation. That house would serve for decades as the center of operations, reunion site and battleground for the eight surviving Horton children as they came and went in their various life pursuits. It was the headquarters from which Amy attempted to referee and guide her children while relying heavily on her two eldest daughters, Bessie and Gertrude, to keep order and run the household.

The move to Arkadelphia came too late to help the older children with their educations so they were faced with the problem of finding ways to make a living. John William, "Pete," and Thad stayed with what they knew and became farmers. Thad, who served as a sergeant in World War I, returned from the war to create a successful farm on the old Horton land in Dallas County, a place he also called "Fairview," after his father's plantation. Both sons married and raised families, but it was Thad who continued the tradition of Horton influence at the old plantation site.

Horace, who was fifteen when the family moved to town, like so many young men in Clark County, found work in the timber industry. He got a job with the Eagle Mills Lumber Company and worked in one of their saw mills until the age of nineteen when he broke his back in an accident. He never fully recovered from the injury, and it was in the physically demanding job of nursing him that Bessie got her early training in caring for the disabled. Horace lived twenty-three years as a semi-invalid and died the year John Allen's neck was broken.

Gertrude, next to the oldest child, didn't let age prevent her from getting an education. She entered the ninth grade in her twenties and graduated as valedictorian, winning a scholarship to the University of Arkansas where she graduated with a B.S.E. She began teaching in Arkadelphia in 1916 before moving to other teaching jobs around the state doing most of her teaching in Little Rock; though throughout her life she counted the home place at 3rd and Clinton, where she lived off and on, as the center of her family life.

Howard, who went by his middle name, Rodney, because he was younger readily adapted to his new educational opportunities. He was an outstanding student all the way through high school and entered Ouachita College at the age of sixteen. He became a chemist and after finishing college took a job with the Ford Motor Company in Detroit.

Rodney's baby brother, Vernon, the uncle I first met sitting in Adams Book Store, followed somewhat in his brother's footsteps, graduating from the University of Arkansas then also moving to Detroit to work for the Goodyear Rubber Company. He later earned a masters degree at the University of Ohio, and during World War II worked on the proximity fuse at Johns Hopkins University.

Louis Horton's children, unlike their feckless father, were successful far beyond the norms for the period. When the family moved to Arkadelphia the national stereotype of the rural Southern child, unfair as it might have been, was that of a barefoot, slow-witted, overall-clad, hookworm infested boy. In fact there was at that time a first effort being made to understand and eradicate the scourge which affected families throughout the South. 1910 was the year the Rockefeller Commission for the Eradication of Hookworm began to take action, and Dallas County was one of the first places the Commission started its work. But the national stereotype did not fit the Horton clan who were healthy and for the most part ambitious and hard working.

Louise Horton Adams age 13

Louise, however, was a special case. As is true with many children, her pre-puberty years were relatively serene, at least as far as the family records and accounts reveal, but her teenage years were full of turmoil. Of course she, along with the other children, was jolted periodically with family tragedy and drama. Two years after they were uprooted and moved to Arkadelphia her parents went through their bitter separation and divorce and not long afterward she learned her father had died violently at Fairview, his body consumed in flames. That news was surely traumatic for the thirteen-year-old girl at a vulnerable time in her life. The picture shown here taken around that time, however, gives no hint of that trauma and catches her at the beginning of that brief window of time women enjoy, those too few years when youth's beauty blooms like spring star flowers along the Ouachita. Unfortunately for Louise there would be no smooth sailing ahead, for the sorrows she had just passed through were only the opening gales from a perfect storm that loomed in her future.

After the divorce Louis had gone back to Fairview to the site of the old plantation and was in the process of attempting to reestablish himself as a farmer. He had bought part of his father's property two years earlier and had cleared some land, dug a well and built some out buildings including a chicken house which he was living in while his house was being built near three large post-oak trees. He had in his cramped quarters only the bare essentials, a few utensils, a cot, and a chair which he would place outside when he wanted to escape the stifling heat of the chicken house. He still owned working animals and farm equipment which he had used to put in a crop and was looking desperately for a way to get his life back on some kind of hopeful track.

But Louise's father was now fifty-five years old, and when he looked back on his life he could see little but failure, missed opportunities and wreckage from twenty-eight years of a tumultuous marriage. If, as the Greeks believed, a man's character is his fate, Louis at last had come face to face with his particular destiny. It was a hot August night at the site of the once proud Fairview Plantation when Louis sat alone outside his lowly temporary abode in the shadows of sweet gum, pine and oak, kept company only by the pulsating chorus of tree frogs and the occasional call of a hoot owl or cry of a chuck-wills-widow. Did he know then that the house he had started would never be completed, that the crop he had planted and tended would never be harvested?

The general consensus was that his death had been a suicide. But the circumstances surrounding his death left many unanswered questions. Would a man on the verge of killing himself be sitting outside reading as the baseball team that passed his place that evening had testified? Was the suicide theory credible? What would Louis have been reading and why would he have been so calmly occupied just before taking his own life? Could he have poured kerosene around the chicken house, ignited it, lay back on the cot and shot himself in the head with a rifle as the flames leapt up around him?

Vernon, who was nine years old at the time of his father's death, recalled the scene over seventy years later. The chicken house had burned to the ground and Louis Scott Horton's body, almost totally incinerated, was melted into the springs and fused so tightly that body and springs had to be buried together. But the skeleton was intact and an examination revealed a gaping hole in the back of the skull.

So could Louis have been murdered? His skull had been fractured and two rifles were found beside the cot he had been lying on, one an old Winchester and the other a relic of the Civil War, perhaps the one his father had carried into battle at Poison Spring and Mark's Mills. Crime scene investigations were not very far advanced in rural Arkansas at that time, and since the scene of the crime had been obliterated by the fire there was little chance that, minus an eye-witness account or confession, the mystery would ever be solved.

The hole in the back of the skull could very well support a murder theory since there was no way he could have held the rifle behind him to create such a wound. But what if the hole was an exit wound? Louis could have put the muzzle in his mouth and pulled the trigger. Vernon told me his father had been despondent following the divorce and that in one or more of the family battles he had threatened suicide. It was also likely he had continued to drink heavily after he left the family, so suicide seemed a plausible explanation.

But neither of his two oldest sons could buy the suicide theory. After asking questions around the old Horton neighborhood, they settled upon a prime suspect. As would be expected for that place and time, the suspect was a black man, so little or no evidence would be required to administer a little "Southern justice." Vernon told me that Pete rode off in the night on a horse (some say a mule) and returned hours later with the animal lathered and winded claiming to have chased the culprit out of the county. When the "suspect," no doubt a descendent of one of Horton's sharecroppers, got word that the two Horton boys were after him he disappeared and was never seen again.

The youngest Horton son also told me that shortly thereafter Thad laid claim to the house and property of the fugitive and sold it many years later leaving local citizens wondering how he had gained legal possession of property he had simply confiscated. Vernon also told me there was talk, totally uncorroborated, both within and outside the Horton family that, considering the intensity of feelings among Louis' children, the killing might have been an inside job; he told me

Pete later had second thoughts about the black man and his suspicions began to turn toward his brother, Thad. Why, he must have wondered, would someone committing suicide need to destroy evidence with a fire? In any case the mystery was never solved though suicide has remained the prevailing theory.

Violence is a constant around the world, and just weeks before Louis died, Archduke Ferdinand was assassinated in Sarajevo initiating the string of events that led to World War I. So, if Thad ended up with an innocent man's purloined property there could be a bit of poetic justice in the fact that he was later called to the Army to fight in the war which the Archduke's assassination had precipitated.

In all likelihood Louise knew little or nothing of the Archduke's demise, but she did know she had lost her daddy to a violent death, and for a vulnerable thirteen-year-old, the news was surely devastating. As it turned out, after her father's death her mother turned much of the running of the household at the home place over to her older daughters. Gertrude lived there intermittently between teaching jobs in various towns around Arkansas, but it was straight-backed, iron-willed Bessie, even more than Amy, who directed Horton family operations and tended to the upbringing of Louise and her brother Vernon.

Whether stemming from her own nature or from the stormy recent conflicts in her family, Louise became a troubled and rebellious teenager. Unlike her sister Gertrude and brother Rodney, she cared not at all for school. Too young to work and determined not to be bossed around by a sister who was twice her age, Louise was a problem. There were many stormy days at the house on the corner of 3rd and Clinton.

Outgunned and miserable in her battles with Bessie and her family, Louise found an ally in a boy, Frank Hurt, who lived across the street. He was only a couple of years older than Louise and was himself restless and discontented at home, so the two hatched a plan to escape their troubles by eloping, by running away to get married. It's not clear how they managed to obtain a legal certificate, but they did. They left for neighboring Dallas County, familiar territory for the Hortons, where Frank found a job as Horace had done in the lumber business. They lived in Sparkman for a year while Frank worked his job in a stave mill. But, as could have been expected, things did not go well for the adolescent couple. Frank's meager income and the hardships they confronted inevitably led them to turn on one another, so within a year they had split apart and Louise was back at the home place in Arkadelphia under the thumb of Bessie.

If Louise had had problems with her older sisters before running away to get married, they were nothing compared to the treatment she got after returning in failure and shame. Both her older sisters demonstrated a life-long ability to lay blame and inflict guilt on their siblings, Gertrude was especially talented in that regard, but there's little doubt that Louise, immature and intractable, provoked her family's censure.

Like young girls everywhere Louise discovered a great gulf between her fantasies and the drab reality of her domestic existence. If she could not escape physically from her intolerable home life, she would have to find some release through her imagination. It well may be that this was the time she devised the strategy she would employ throughout her life—papering over ugly reality with pretty pictures and sentimental clichés, a practice that would prove useful in her future career as a mitt reader. But since books and literature had little appeal for Louise, how could she find a way out of her unhappy predicament?

Popular entertainment in Arkadelphia in 1915 was nothing like it would become in succeeding decades, but there were attractions to feed the imaginations of the young. There was on Main Street the Electric Theater which featured "life-size moving pictures," and one block over on Clinton Street just three blocks from her house was the Air Dome Theater which, in addition to showing outdoor moving pictures, also from time to time featured vaudeville acts. Carnivals sometimes made appearances in town and the two colleges offered musical and theatrical performances for the public on occasions. This was the year D.W. Griffith's groundbreaking movie, "Birth of a Nation," first appeared and a new movie house, the Royal Theater, was under construction on Main Street, so there were for Louise some avenues of escape.

Arkadelphia from early on was noted for its interest in higher education and music, and now, with the ragtime era in full swing, a number of local bands were organized to play the new lively music. "Alexander's Ragtime Band" and other jazz-influenced songs were sweeping the nation and the dancers, Irene and Vernon Castle, were wildly popular in this country and abroad. While radio had yet to become a major force in popular music, one of Edison's inventions that surely brightened Louise's life was the phonograph. Sheet music also was readily available so Louise would have had access to the popular music of the day, and her second cousin, Elizabeth Butler, who would later be John Allen's piano teacher, may have provided her some musical diversions as well.

Unfortunately for Louise, however, none of these technological marvels could deliver her from her predicament. There was no way to paper over the troubles she confronted at the home place on 3rd and Clinton where Bessie reigned and no doubt recited Louise's shortcomings and failures to her daily. There is little doubt, however, that Bessie's complaints had merit. Any parent who has coped with a balky child through the stormy teenage years can imagine some of the scenes that took place at the Horton's. But theirs was not the typical family.

From all accounts it appears Bessie was the dominant voice in the family, even though the mother, Amy Scales, was always present. While Amy appears to have been loved and respected by her children, it was her eldest daughter who wielded authority, perhaps because Bessie was the chief provider, the one who dealt with the world and kept things going. Gertrude, who had recently graduated from the University of Arkansas and had taken a temporary teaching job in Arkadelphia, was also living at the home place that year. And it was Gertrude who played a major part in the next chapter of her young sister's life.

Gertrude Horton King

As Louise became more emotional and uncontrollable, the conflicts at the home place escalated. Dealing with her erratic behavior became almost a full time job for Bessie and her mother. The pressing question that confronted the three women was what was to be done with the daughter who had brought nothing but trouble and embarrassment to the family. Both Bessie and Gertrude had a keen sense of family pride, based to a great extent on the memories of their grandfather Horton's distinguished career and respected position in the region and some historically significant ancestors on their Grandmother Horton's side. But now the family name had been tarnished by their parent's divorce, by their father's violent and mysterious death, and most recently by Louise's behavior, her pathetically doomed elopement with Frank Hurt and her recent erratic emotional outbursts. Something had to be done.

If Gertrude was anything, she was decisive. She had, after all, proved her mettle by earning a degree from the University of Arkansas and securing a respected teaching position in town. So she was the one that came forward with a remedy for the problem Louise was afflicting them with. Louise had been acting crazy; she was according to Gertrude emotionally unbalanced, mentally ill, so the solution would be to have her committed to the State Hospital in Little Rock. At that time the institution bore its relatively new name, "Arkansas State Hospital for Nervous Diseases," but only ten years earlier it had gone by the name given it at its establishment in 1873, "The Arkansas Lunatic Asylum."

We can't know the battles, the emotionally fraught scenes that led up to Louise's commitment, but from all available evidence it seems likely that Louise would have vigorously resisted the move and that she would have received sympathy if not support from her mother. But Gertrude prevailed, in all likelihood with Bessie's approval. So the fifteen year-old Mary Louise Horton Hurt was shipped off to Little Rock where she was assigned a bed in one of the twelve buildings that then comprised the State Hospital. Though that facility had been the culmination of the dreams of civic-minded and well-meaning benefactors, it was, as generally were all such institutions at the time, a medieval-like, bleak and unhappy place.

How intense were Louise's fears and how deep was her despair when her family rode away and left her? She was now housed with catatonics, schizophrenics, brain-damaged unfortunates given to bizarre tics and outlandish shrieks. This incarceration for Louise was just the latest in a series of recent traumas, all of which shook the foundations of her sense of self. Perhaps she found sympathetic hearts in other inmates and heard kind words from attendants, but any remaining inner sense of confidence she possessed was surely shattered when the only people in the world she could possibly rely on had shipped her off against her will to a lunatic asylum.

But Louise would not be among those unfortunates for whom commitment to the Arkansas State Hospital for Nervous Diseases was a life sentence. She was determined to find a way out and wrote regularly to her mother pleading for her help while also impressing hospital attendants and doctors with her good behavior. So, six months after Louise was forcibly committed to the State Hospital, Amy relented and went to Little Rock to arrange the release of her daughter.

Amy Scales Horton

What Louise did and how she got along with her sisters at the home place after her release is not known, but records show that by 1918 she was living in Louisville, Kentucky, working in a textile mill. Since, like her brother Horace, she did not care for school, and since Frank Hurt had fled to parts unknown, Louise was forced to find work to support herself. The lumber business may have been suitable for a young man, but a seventeen-year-old girl in Arkadelphia would have to look to other industries in other locations. While the timber industry was booming in Arkansas textile mills were going strong in other parts of the country, so when Louise learned of job opportunities in Kentucky she somehow arranged to make the move.

Work in the textile mill provided Louise an escape from her family and no doubt brought a sense of relief to those she left behind at the home place. It also gave Louise the opportunity to leave behind mistakes of the past and make a fresh start. But the work was tedious, the hours long and the wages low. Lonesome and far from home, from the torments and comforts of her family, from the familiar faces and scenes of her home town, Louise would have looked for diversion as she had done earlier in Arkadelphia, and one of those entertainments she discovered may have been a carnival passing through Louisville.

It was perhaps at that carnival that Louise met a tall and somewhat stylish young traveling man in the entertainment business, Allen Frank Adams, recently returned from military service in World War I. Al, as he preferred to be called, had survived that war and both he and Louise had recently survived the terrible Spanish Flu pandemic that swept the country and the world that year and now chance had brought them together in Louisville. There's no record of how the two met, but it seems reasonable to surmise that the young woman, perhaps visiting the carnival with friends, responded to a friendly overture from Adams and that a romantic relationship ensued. As noted earlier, Louise was at that time a pretty girl, and in spite of the hardships she had suffered, she was yet possessed of a kind of youthful freshness and spirit that would appeal to young men.

Louise had always preferred illusions to unpleasant realities—the vaudeville acts at the Air Dome Theater, the life-sized moving pictures shows at the Electric Theater, the ragtime popular songs of the day, the glamorous pictures she saw in magazines. Escape had been a constant theme in her life, escape from the sticks of Fairview, from her unpleasant home life, from Frank Hurt and her disastrous marriage, from the State Hospital, and now from the "Modern Times" dehumanizing mechanization of the textile mill. What child has never wanted to run away and join the circus or travel with a carnival? And in many ways Louise would forever remain a child, so when Al asked her to marry and come away with him, the decision for her was no decision at all. She would escape once more; she would leave her bleak

Allen Frank Adams

and dead-end job in Louisville and find adventure on the road traveling the wide country with a carnival.

Al may have been a carnival worker but throughout his life he behaved like a gentleman, so before taking Louise's hand in marriage he sought permission from her mother. Amy Brown Scales Horton wrote in response to Al's petition:

My Dear Mr. Adams:

I have received your letter and must admit that it did not find me wholly unprepared for the question you have asked me.

Louise has often spoken of you in her letters to me and always in a very complimentary manner, so it is very natural that I should form a good opinion of you.

I will be frank and tell you that I have no objections whatever to your and Louise's marriage as I think she is old enough and had experience enough to choose her companion for life and it will make me very happy to know that she has someone to love and someone to love and protect her. I have no objections to your age, am really glad that you are a settled man instead of a young boy.

I will close with my congratulations to you and Louise, and hope that you will find in each other all that it takes to make life happy.

> Yours Truly
> Mrs. A.B. Horton

Al and Louise met during the summer carnival season and married following a brief courtship. Vernon told me she was pregnant when they married, but I found no mention of it in any family correspondence. The son she bore the following August would likely have been conceived in November, so it's not certain theirs was a marriage of necessity. If it was, Al, true to character, played the gentleman by asking Amy for her daughter's hand.

Vernon also told me Louise married Al without having divorced Frank Hurt and it's not clear whether she ever told Al about Hurt, how they had married but never divorced. Her mother knew but apparently never brought the subject up with Al. I would guess that was one of the many secrets Louise carried with her. Ever after she lived in fear that she would be exposed and arrested for bigamy, and years later when she heard Hurt had died, she went to the town where he was buried and personally visited his grave to verify that he was in fact dead. And so it was Louise became a keeper of secrets, a skill that would later prove useful to Madame Justina and the other romantic personas Louise used to conceal her true identity.

The following summer Louise traveled with Al on the carnival circuit and returned to Louisville where she gave birth to John Allen at the Jewish hospital there on August 16, 1919, during the closing weeks of the season. Once more she proved to be a keeper of secrets in that she made no mention of her son in her letters home, perhaps from fear her family would learn she was pregnant when she married. Her family did not learn of John Allen's existence for two years, and when they finally got to see him Louise told them he was Al's child by an earlier marriage and that the mother was dead.

Amy and her other children knew that Louise and Al were married, but did they also know that Louise had committed bigamy? Did they ask? There are many questions surrounding Louise's second marriage and the birth of her son—who knew what and when—but for me the most startling revelation came once more from Vernon. He told me in one of our interviews that the family did not learn John Allen was Louise's child until 1944, shortly before her death.

If what Vernon told me was true a number of other questions arise. Did Louise's son know who his mother was? I regret I never questioned him about his background before he died and that I was not a more thorough researcher and note taker over twenty years ago when I first set out to learn about John Allen. I find hard to believe, however, that Louise, who so adored her son and was so proud of him, would never have revealed to him the truth. Did he not learn who his mother was until the rest of the family did only months before her body was discovered in the Goddard Hotel during the closing months of World War II? Or had she told him as a child and sworn him to secrecy? Were the circumstances surrounding Louise's marriage to Al and the birth of their son one of the reasons Martha Greene and W. S. McNutt refused to discuss John Allen's history? If so they had no cause for fear. John Allen's legitimacy needed no validation.

Games of chance are a major attraction on any carnival midway, but what greater risk can a teenage girl adrift in the world take than to marry a transient she scarcely knows? It's true that Al, well-dressed and well-mannered, did not appear to be the stereotypical Carney, the tattooed, low-life grifter looking to make a fast buck in order to buy his next bottle of muscatel. As it turned out marrying Al proved to be one of the few good choices Louise made in her life. Throughout their twenty-five year marriage she never stopped praising her husband, regularly reminding John Allen what a wonderful father he had, and though they went through rough times together there is nothing I have run across to suggest that Al was anything but good to Louise and John Allen and a gentleman in dealing with her family and others.

Al was a versatile handy man on the carnival circuit, a Jack-of-all-trades, an essential qualification for carneys and circus workers throughout the ages. He was no doubt valuable to the owners of the shows and used his influence to find positions for Louise enabling her to pay her way. In one of her early assignments she lived out a long-held fantasy. She and another girl worked out a dance routine which, according to her letters home, was a real crowd pleaser. Her partner took the lead as a male impersonator while the pretty Louise, perhaps imagining herself to be Irene Castle, contributed to an act that was likely more comical than gracious, powered more by youthful energy and high spirits than talent. Her brother, Rodney, working at the Ford Motor Company in Detroit, went to see the show when it came through town and came away with a much different impression of Louise's performance. He later told the family he had been embarrassed to see his sister cavorting around in such a show.

The family evidently had a reunion about this time for there was in the boxes of family materials a photograph of seven of the eight surviving children of Louis and Amy Horton. Perhaps this family get-together was the occasion when Rodney shared his reaction to his sister's dance routine. In the photograph, Louise is the only child missing, perhaps because she was traveling with the carnival. It's fitting, however, that she's absent in the picture because Louise was one who had never fit in, who could never fit in. But there are the rest of them—Pete, Vernon, Rodney, Horace and Thad with their two proper sisters, Gertrude and Bessie, sitting with their brothers in the front row. It is a handsome group, neatly groomed and smartly dressed. Anyone might take them for a family of proper Bostonians rather than brothers and sisters who had grown up in rural Arkansas. Their grandfather Horton would have been proud of that picture seeing in it evidence that the qualities he had tried to instill in his own children—education, diligence, and hard work—had been carried on to the next generation in spite of the failings of his son, their father, Louis.

The Children of Louis Scott and Amy Scales Horton Back: Pete, Vernon Rodney; Front: Gertrude, Horace, Bessie,Thad

While her siblings were pursuing their various goals in life and Louise and Al and their young son were following the carnival circuit, history in the broader world was proceeding apace. The year after John Allen was born women won the right to vote, Warren Harding was elected President and Prohibition began. What followed was the era we now call the Jazz Age, a time of speakeasies, flappers, and the Charleston dance craze. Technology at this time brought new diversions for the public in the form of talking pictures and commercial radio broadcasts. All these developments would have been of keen interest to Louise as she, Al and John Allen traveled from town to town riding in flivvers and other unreliable early motor cars and trucks, hauling concession stands, midway rides, and all the gear and equipment necessary to make a carnival run.

As far as I can tell, Louise never owned a stick of furniture in her life. Al did build them a trailer in the mid-thirties which they pulled behind their car on the carnival circuit a few years, but other than that, except for those times in off seasons when she worked waitress and other menial jobs and lived in rented rooms, she spent her life living out of suitcases and trunks. But while she never accumulated material possessions, she did manage to accumulate weight, so that in a relatively short time she had to abandon her career as a dancer and find other ways to make a contribution. That was the time she fell into her future profession, her life's calling—she would be a fortune teller, a "mitt reader."

Every carnival in those days had a "mitt camp," a tented booth identified by a large sign of a hand, palm out with the crucial lines clearly marked. Who but a dyspeptic skeptic is not attracted to the one who knows all and sees all, who can tell us our heart's desires, of the good fortune waiting for us around the next bend? What does one need to be a fortune teller, to wield such power? A bandana for the head, a deck of Tarot cards, a crystal ball and a gift of gab? Those things are not enough; there is much more to the ancient art.

An old gypsy woman long ago gave the following advice to a young girl looking to join the profession:

> When thou wilt tell a fortune, put all thy heart into finding out what kind of man or woman thou hast to deal with. Look keenly, fix thy glance sharply, especially if it be a girl. When she is half-frightened, she will tell you much without knowing it. When thou shalt have often done this thou wilt be able to twist many a silly girl like twine around thy fingers. Soon thy eyes will look like a snake's and when thou art angry thou wilt look like the old devil. Half the business, my dear, is to know how to please and flatter and allure people.

> When a girl has anything unusual in her face, you must tell her that it signifies extraordinary luck. If she have red or yellow hair, tell her that is a true sign she will have much gold. When her eyebrows meet, that shows she will be united with many rich gentlemen. Tell her always, when you see a mole on her cheek or forehead or anything, that is a sign she will become a great lady....Praising and petting and alluring and crying-up are half of fortunetelling. There is no girl and no man in all the Lord's earth who is not proud and vain about something, and if you can find it out you can get their money. (Gresham, *Monster Midway* chap. 7)

Once in the mid 80's when I first thought to write about John Allen and his family, I happened to pass a fortune teller's little cubby hole on Central Avenue in Hot Springs. A black-haired middle-aged woman in a colorful frock sitting at a small table reading a magazine rose quickly to her feet when I pushed open the door. At first, smiling and eager, she offered me a chair but, when I let her know I had not come for a reading but to ask her some questions about her trade, her aspect changed. Suddenly her eyes were like a snake's and she was glaring at me like the old devil. She dismissed me from the premises with a backward motion of her hand and I found myself once more back on the sidewalk having learned only one thing about fortune tellers, about those like her of the ancient Romany trade.

But Louise did not belong to that tribe. She was a simple country girl trying to make her way in the world and mitt reading offered her that chance; it also provided her an opportunity to use her intuition and love of fantasy to entertain and even help people. She did, of course, learn the tricks of the trade, but there's no doubt she believed throughout her life that she was providing a useful service with her readings. She had seen firsthand in the State Hospital the universal human need for a kind listener, a sympathetic ear. After all she knew something about heartaches and hope, so with her vivid imagination and natural gift of empathy she was well suited for the role of Madam Justina.

Louise Horton Adams

Louise was not the only member of the carnival with a heart. Her correspondence over the years with show owners and other members of the troupes she and Al worked with reveals that the stereotypes often bestowed on them are less than accurate. Members of those traveling shows looked upon themselves as family, offering help to one another in hard times and expressing gratitude for kindnesses received. In 1924 Louise wrote her "Dear Mama" from Philadelphia: "I'm amoung [sic] friends and people I've known for five years. People that if they got fifty cents they will give you 25c of it. That is the kind of friends I've got, not like the two face people there in town that will talk their heads off behind your back like they do me there in Arkadelphia." It's clear the memories of her painful years at the home place never left her.

Louise and her Carney friends were, after all, beneath the grit and the grind of life on the road, a band of adults pursuing childhood fantasies. And if the public was, through sleight of hand and legerdemain, relieved of some of their extra cash, they were getting in return a little excitement in their lives, a colorful break from their dreary routines.

John Allen cut his teeth in carnivals, his earliest lullaby was the stentorian trumpeting of a calliope, he took his first baby steps on a midway and learned the magical power of the human voice listening to the shouts of barkers as they encouraged curious passers-by to step right up and try their games of chance or see their stupendous attractions. The kids of the other carneys were his first playmates, all of whom were collectively looked after by the entire crew, children no doubt blessed with all kinds of entertainment and a great deal of freedom. Of that life he later wrote:

> I see their child, the child I was,
> Curley-headed Carney punk,
> Sure-footed darter through crowds,
> At home on his own turf—
> Those sawdust lots bannered with promises
> Of marvels and rare delights.
> He stops to watch the cotton candy man
> Spinning the pink floss of a sweet world
> And reeling it on paper cones.
> Precociously he learned how it melts
> To nothing on buyers' tongues.

That was the world John Allen awoke to, the one he was born into, but it would not be all—he would find other worlds to explore.

Louise and Al, who at this time were working with the Zeidman and Pollie Shows, visited Arkadelphia whenever their travels brought them near, and it was on such a visit that John Allen first met his mother's family. The young boy liked the town and loved the sense of belonging he felt at the home place with his own real kinfolks. He was very much taken by his Grandmother Amy and his aunts and uncles and they in turn were captivated by the calm and pleasant demeanor of this beautiful boy. They must have marveled that the problem child of their own family, the black sheep, the misfit, could be the mother of such a remarkable son. But then, of course, as Louise had told them, the boy was Al's from an earlier marriage. That would explain it. There was no question about paternity since the resemblance between father and son was readily apparent, so it would have been the birth mother who possessed some of the other appealing qualities so evident in the son.

As fate would have it the two Hortons most proud of their family heritage were destined to be barren. Gertrude had married a young man from Sparkman, Cullen King, who joined the armed forces just before the end of the Great War. They were divorced in 1925 leaving the childless Gertrude with only one advantage—ever after she was able to refer to herself as "Mrs. Gertrude Horton King."

Bessie showed an interest in boys in school but found no suitable prospect before she was in her twenties. Then, when she was still a trim and attractive young woman, she developed an interest in a young man named Shelby Curry.

Vernon told me he once peeped through a keyhole and saw Bessie sitting in Shelby's lap and told Louise who told their mother, Amy, who then barged in on the couple and, in Vernon's words, "read them the riot act." Bessie never again dated and because of that incident developed resentment toward her mother that she never got over. A few years later while still in her twenties she developed menstrual problems which led to a hysterectomy. That operation had a profound impact on Bessie who proclaimed thereafter, "I am neither a man nor a woman; I am an 'it.'"

One of the greatest testaments to the charm of John Allen was the way he quickly vanquished the prejudices of his two aunts. They were embarrassed by Louise and ashamed of her disreputable occupation. They would have been inclined to be cool toward her offspring, for she was not the one best suited to carry the family honor into the next generation. Not only that,

Bessie Horton

but they believed her son had not a drop of Horton blood in him. While blood may be thicker than water, for his two aunts, John Allen's appealing nature proved stronger than blood, and the smiling curly-headed boy quickly became a favorite at the home place.

Over the next several years while Louise, Al and John Allen continued to follow the carnival circuit with the Zeidman and Pollie Shows, Calvin Coolidge became president, and the sensational stories of the Scopes Monkey Trial and the Leopold and Loeb murder case dominated the headlines and the new technological wonder, radio news.

Then in 1923 Elizabeth Scott Horton died, wife of W.S., niece of General Winfield Scott and grandmother to Louise and her siblings. John wrote of Bessie's "beloved grandmother" many years later:

John Allen age 5 with ball and paddle

Grandmother Horton (my great grandmother) was nearly blind in her last years, and her letters are difficult to read. One letter moved me to tears. A postscript wandering across the back of the last page says: "My health is good. Old Father Time seems to have forgotten me while using his reaping hook and has left me standing alone in old age, but am blessed with helping hands always extended ready to help as I need help. For which I am very thankful."

Aunt Bessie had sent her grandmother stationery with heavy black lines to guide her pencil (she probably printed it herself in the printing office where she worked), but as the light failed, even that wasn't enough to keep her pencil in the proper path, and she often apologized. After a life of rectitude (always within the rules), she was troubled by the meandering of her penciled words beyond the bold black lines love drew to guide her failing sight.

Elizabeth Scott Horton

Four years after the death of the Horton matriarch there came both a banner and a fateful year for the nation, for Arkansas and for the Hortons of Arkadelphia. In 1927 Charles Lindberg made history when he flew his Spirit of St. Louis non-stop across the Atlantic, Gene Tunney defeated Jack Dempsey for the world heavyweight title, and the United States suffered one of the greatest natural disasters in its history. The nation was changed forever by the Great Mississippi Flood which saw the river swell to a breadth of sixty miles below Memphis. Plantation owners, cotton farmers and sharecroppers all along its length were forced to load their possessions in wagons and trucks, leave their homes and all the possessions they were unable to carry, and head for higher ground. In Arkansas many fled in the direction of Arkadelphia which had not escaped the water itself since all the tributaries feeding the great river flooded as well, including the Ouachita.

Tragedy struck the Hortons a few months later when Bessie and her siblings lost their sixty-one-year-old mother, Amy Scales Horton, to blood poisoning. Her death that summer brought the children together at the home place for the funeral, and that gathering, perhaps the last time all would be assembled in one place, triggered additional fault lines in the family that would endure to the end.

There was another emotional and noteworthy change in the Adams family in 1927, for that was the year Louise and Al, brought eight-year-old John Allen to Arkadelphia to live with his Aunt Bessie. The decision had not been easy for the parents because their son was their treasure and delight. But he had been showing recently some preference for the stability of the home place and Arkadelphia over the nomadic existence of the carnival, and both Bessie and Gertrude had been stressing to Louise and Al the importance of education for their son. They agreed. Difficult though it was placing John Allen in Bessie's care was clearly the right decision.

John Allen arrives at the Home Place

* * *

CHAPTER 4

Of Time and The Ouachita

Time is but the stream I go a-fishing in.
                                        — Thoreau

*On a summer day just a stone's throw up-stream from the
Caddo street bridge a fat brown moccasin slides silently from
a low hanging willow branch into the current and sinuously
swims downstream angling toward shore until it hits a patch
of slack water where it parts floating willow cotton sending
it tumbling and spreading like smoke before it disappears
into the shadow of a grassy overhang. Three turtles sunning
nearby in single file on a bone-white fallen cottonwood take
no notice of the snake. On a leafless twig at the tip of the tree
now only two feet above the water a dragonfly with multiple
river images in his compound eyes is poised on point while a
squadron of his brothers fly above him, alternately darting
from side to side then holding still in air while below them
a bluegill with orange belly and blue-tipped "ears" hovers
above a platter-sized patch of bright burnished stones on the
river bottom diligently guarding the eggs resting there.*

*Several hundred yards further up stream high atop De Soto
Bluff, oak, sweet gum and hickory stand on tiptoe where*

the river has eaten away at the cliff and exposed their roots to the air and hardened them into elaborate bracings and cage-like scaffolds as they struggle to hold their purchase in the red dirt and so keep from plummeting to the river and joining the trees fallen from earlier seasons. Below them up and down the water's edge other trees stand like soldiers marching into battle, the front rank already lying strewn along the bank, casualties of earlier spring torrents, many in the following tier wounded and headed for the ground in a slow fall while the upright ranks behind stoically wait their turn to contend with the implacable Ouachita.

And so the river runs today as it has for centuries, for millennia, since long before red men or white men followed its course seeking game and fertile spots of ground to plant their seed.

I n the years following John Allen's arrival in Arkadelphia, the Ouachita River, only three blocks from his house, would prove a magnetic attraction for the adventurous boy. He would often be drawn down the hill on Clinton Street to the river to investigate its mysteries. True, it was not the Father of Waters, the mile-wide Mississippi of Tom Sawyer and Huckleberry Finn, but it was a beautiful and ample river whose clear water and shaded paths offered plenty of adventures for John Allen and the local boys of his generation. Standing in privet and poke weed in the shade of beech, cottonwoods and willows, he could look across the water to the thick greenery on the far bank, the current in constant motion beneath his gaze, and ponder the marvels of his world. Living now at the home place he found the nearby river to be an intimate new friend. John Allen would spend many days of his youth swimming and fishing in its waters, exploring its banks, and observing the timeless yet ever-changing life of the Ouachita.

When John Allen came to live in Arkadelphia the Ouachita River had run through his family's history for more than seven decades. His new guardian, Bessie, knew all the Horton stories and shared them with the young boy even though she didn't believe he was of their blood. Bessie was of a type and time imbued with regional and historical prejudices so strong she would never be able to free herself and find other ways of looking at the world. But John Allen did bring down one of her walls—her antipathy toward his origins. What better arrangement can there be for overcoming prejudice than for a person to adopt and come to love a child with an unfavored pedigree? So, even if he were not of her blood, she soon saw in him those qualities she believed distinguished the Horton clan—talent, intelligence, courage, and virtue in the classical sense. Of course her conception of her family's gifts was a romantic one, and selective. She did not look to her immediate family for those admired qualities, though some could surely be found among her siblings, instead she looked back to what for her was a glorious past, to her childhood memories of Fairview, of her grandmother, Elizabeth Scott, and especially of her grandfather, William Saunders Horton. There was a man who to her was a hero, one who had lived a significant part of American history.

John Allen's great grandfather came to the river late—ten-thousand years after the first archaic hunters and gatherers, a thousand years after the Mississippian tribes that farmed the rich alluvial soil of that great river and its tributaries and left their amazing earthen mounds, one of which still stands on the east bank of the Caddo River near Arkadelphia, and three hundred years after the 16th century Spanish explorer Hernando de Soto led his men through the thick forests flanking the Ouachita in his search for gold and a route to the Orient. But Horton, while appearing late in the continent's long history, was one of the early American settlers of Dallas County arriving slightly more than a generation after the first white hunters and trappers came to the area looking for venison, bear grease and animal pelts. He, like all those who preceded him, was drawn to the region because it promised sustenance, for him it was the fertile land and the river which could carry his bales of cotton downstream by steamboat through Camden and Monroe, Louisiana, to the Black River, to the Mississippi and on to the markets of New Orleans.

There is no picture of the patriarch of the Horton clan among the family papers, and perhaps that is just as well since, to his descendents, particularly his grandchildren who remembered him best, he was a hero, attaining in their imaginations an almost mythical stature. Pictures are not always worth a thousand words. How could a photograph of Odysseus, say, do anything but diminish the hero in the mind's eye? Imagination is best. Of course allowances must be made when grandfathers are judged by their grandkids, but there is ample evidence to support the case that Horton was in fact an extraordinary man.

Although Horton died a dozen years before his great grandson was born, John Allen learned many things about him from the stories his Aunt Bessie told, stories so cherished they gave clear evidence that his greatest gift to his family was not so much his name, his exploits and accomplishments, but his love for them. After Bessie died John Allen wrote a beautiful and moving poem about her memories of Fairview and her grandfather, a poem evocative of Whitman's "Out of the Cradle Endlessly Rocking," and his elegy to Abraham Lincoln, "When Lilacs Last in the Dooryard Bloom'd."

In his poem Adams sees his elderly aunt sitting on the porch swing surrounded by heirloom roses, descendents of cuttings from the Fairview Plantation, the only living things that have accompanied her since childhood. Like Whitman, he interweaves birdsong and the perfume of flowers to open the doors of memory.

Star Walk
(For Aunt Bessie)

The night air is heady with fragrance
from the rose-heavy trellis half-shielding
the porch where she sits in the swing;
and these clustering blooms, but a cutting removed
from her youth, have companioned her summers
through lonesoming loss and withdrawing.
The odor, the night and the stars
raise a wavering note from the past,
a fluttering moth of a ghost,
and she pins it down in her mind.

This fragrance is scion to that
which scented her girlhood—the climber
embracing the wellhouse at Fairview
that watered their days. There the butter
pressed from the mould and the cream-covered
milk were suspended in coolness,
sequestered from bee-humming noons.

She remembers that summer when Papa
and she, after dishes were done,
would walk to the wellhouse and stand
watching stars—their star-walk, they called it.
. . . .

In John Allen's imaginative recreation of a scene from
Bessie's childhood, grandfather and granddaughter look
to the skies while he points out and names planets and
constellations, doing that most important thing adults do
for children—putting the proper names on the things of
this world.

Lesson over they turn back to the house.

The mockingbird sang their return,
and the lamplight beckoned them back
to the house with their cargo of stars.

Like Whitman in "Out of the Cradle," the poet here brings
in the familiar and virtuosic singer, the mockingbird, but in
this instance, rather than sing about death, the bird's song
evokes memory, connecting an old woman to the young girl
she once was.

. . . .
Tonight she hears him again,
the mockingbird sings from the cedar tree,
pouring his gospel of joy
down from his nesting place
in the dark spire of branches and shadows.
His message once stirred such conviction,

in the camp-meeting time of her youth,
that she walked down the aisle when he called her,
in those lustrous days when the plum
was a massing of white on the hill,
or, scented and slender, stood
like a taper, alone, a Danae
shower, enveloping earth,
quickened the seed and troubled the stone.

Bessie's grandfather arrived in Dallas County with fifteen slaves and enough money to buy land which he steadily developed until he had seven-hundred acres of the finest farm land in the county. He set to work clearing the land for the new plantation he named Fairview, and soon had it planted in cotton. The year after he arrived he married Elizabeth Scott of Decatur, Alabama, daughter of Major J.D. Scott and niece of General Winfield Scott, hero of the Battle of Vera Cruz in the Mexican War and the first man elevated to the rank of Lieutenant General since George Washington. Elizabeth's uncle was the longest serving general officer in U.S. history, serving in every war from that of 1812 to the Civil War. Horton married well and possessed the personal qualities that would make him one of the most influential and respected citizens of the County, but how did he as a young man acquire the means to go into the farming business in such a bold way?

William Saunders Horton was born in Georgia in 1823 to Thomas and Elizabeth Teasley Horton, the eldest of eleven children. He graduated from the Brownwood Institute in La Grange, Georgia, at the age of twenty one and worked for a while as a salesman for Jones, Phillips & Co. He and his family, who were educated slave owners and apparently people of means, later pulled up stakes and headed for Texas. But when the Hortons reached the vicinity of Shreve's Landing (today Shreveport, Louisiana,) William's father and several slaves came down with cholera and died. Since W.S. was the oldest child and male much responsibility fell on his shoulders following his father's death.

After his father was buried Horton helped establish his mother, Elizabeth, in Harrison County, Texas, near what was called "the Elysian Fields." There they purchased a large tract of land and with their remaining slaves soon had many acres under cultivation. He also helped the family set up a mercantile business. But the year was 1849, and when word reached Horton of the gold strike at Sutter's Mill near Sacramento, he, like tens of thousands of other Americans and people from around the world, could not resist the call. Leaving the farming operation to the care of his mother and older siblings, he outfitted himself with the necessary pack animals, equipment and wagons and started off across the great American plains to seek his fortune in the California gold fields. In doing so he joined the ranks of some of the most celebrated adventurers in American history—he became a "Forty-Niner."

Word of the discovery at Sutter's mill spread rapidly setting off an epidemic of gold fever across the country. Starting from Texas Horton would necessarily take the overland route to California, but many on the east coast who caught the fever were setting out by boat taking a southern route to Panama planning to cross the Isthmus on foot or horseback in hopes of picking up another boat on the Pacific side to take them to San Francisco.

One sober New York merchant of sound business judgment, Franklin Buck, saw the ships along the docks filling with supplies and taking on passengers and could feel the fever:

> When I see business firms—rich men—going into it, men who know how to make money too, and young men of my acquaintance leaving good situations and fitting themselves out with arms and ammunition, tents, provisions and mining implements, there is something about it—the excitement, the crossing the Isthmus, seeing new countries and the prospect of making a fortune in a few years—that takes hold of my imagination, that tells me "Now is your chance. Strike while the iron is hot!" (Brands, *Age of Gold,* p. 71)

Horton was one of those young men who saw his chance and left a good situation in hopes of making a fortune, but he would be going overland. In going through the family papers I ran across the remark that Horton had traveled to California by way of Mexico. Why would he go all the way south to Mexico to get to California, I wondered? When I looked up an early map of the United States I found the answer to my question. Just a year before Horton began his trek to California, all the land west of Texas, including California, was part of Mexico. But thanks in part to the uncle of his future wife, General Winfield Scott, forty percent of Mexico was now about to be annexed by the United States at the conclusion of the war between those two countries, a war considered unjust by many Americans, including Abraham Lincoln, Ralph Waldo Emerson,

Henry David Thoreau, and Ulysses S. Grant who fought in the war.

Grant, who would later play a major role in American history, believed our own Civil War was providential punishment for the sin of taking a large part of Mexico by force in the name of Manifest Destiny. So, shortly before John Allen's great grandfather set out for California, two people who would later be connected to him, one by blood the other by philosophy and spirit, Winfield Scott and Henry Thoreau, were on opposing sides of the burning issue of their day.

There are no records of the route Horton took to California, but he would have gone west toward Santa Fe and possibly picked up The Old Spanish Trail north toward Salt Lake and then west on the California Trail to Sacramento. And no doubt he would have joined other wagons on the way west, for there were many of them and they traveled together for company and security. H.W. Brands tells what the trek across the plains was like:

> . . . . For nine-hundred miles west of the Missouri, every day was essentially like the last. Rise before dawn, cook and eat breakfast, gather the animals, hitch up the wagons, head out, halt around midday, cook and eat dinner, march again to whatever camp the captain or scouts had discovered, undo what was done at dawn with the animals and wagons, cook and eat supper, set guards on the stock, go to sleep under the stars or the canvas. (*Age of Gold*, p. 144)

This was the time when Kit Carson scouted for federal troops out west and the last of the great buffalo herds were being slaughtered presaging the doom of the free-roaming plains Indians. While Americans liked to think of their country as a new Eden, the last bastion of wild nature, they were busily at work wreaking havoc on the natural bounty of their land. On their way to California many Forty-Niners took part in killing the buffalo, partly for food but partly out of boredom, leaving many a carcass to rot in the prairie sun.

Horton spent thirteen months in the California gold fields. Was he panning gravel in streams, digging dirt from the gullies and washing it in sluice boxes, filling sacks with gold dust and nuggets? Did he take his new found riches into San Francisco for some wild nights on the town? Or did he decide to mine that other source of riches—the miners themselves, selling equipment and merchandise to those doing the digging? Considering his education and former business experience, the latter would seem more likely. But we can never know. What we do know is that when news reached him of his mother's death, he headed back for Texas.

When he arrived back at Elysian Fields he once more took charge of the family's mercantile business, sold the estate and divided the proceeds among the nine children. He assumed guardianship of the youngest, his sixteen-year-old sister, Mary, and enrolled her in Van Zandt's College for Women in Marshall, Texas. Afterwards he moved on, ending up in Dallas County, Arkansas, where he bought several hundred acres of virgin soil. With the help of his slaves he managed to clear 200 acres and bring them under cultivation that first year.

Horton married Elizabeth Scott the following year and their first child, Priscilla, was born one year later. These were years of hard work and accomplishment for the young couple as they developed Fairview Plantation raising cotton that was in great demand at the time. Steamboats were now coming all the way from New Orleans to Arkadelphia delivering goods to towns and plantations along the way and returning loaded with bales of cotton and other farm products, steamboats like the beautiful side-wheeler the *Jim Barkman* and the new stern-wheeler *Arkadelphia City*. Boats such as these enabled cotton plantations to flourish up and down the length of the Ouachita.

But the challenges for steamboats on the Ouachita were somewhat different from those described by Mark Twain in *Life on the Mississippi*. True, both rivers confronted pilots with similar dangers, such as submerged obstacles—trees, wrecks, sandbars, as well as treacherous bends and shallows. But the mile-wide Mississippi gave pilots some room to maneuver; it was deeper and there were more boats and more pilots to share intelligence about river conditions and hazards. Steamboating on the Ouachita was a much more "hands on" experience. Anyone who has maneuvered a flat-bottomed boat through the upper reaches of the Ouachita, anywhere from Arkadelphia to Hot Springs, or on the Caddo from Arkadelphia to Caddo Gap, will have some idea of what such a steamboat journey might have been like.

Getting a steamboat up and down the Ouachita required a joint effort between the boat crews and the citizens who lived along the river's edge. Many farmers supplemented their income by selling cordwood from "wood yards" along the banks where steamboats would stop to take on fuel, a process called "wooding." Owners of plantations and farms often built landings where steamboats could swing their stage planks to shore to unload and take on cargo. Mark

Twain describes the transformation the arrival of a steamboat can bring to a small river village, and surely the rural folks of nineteenth century Arkansas were excited when they heard the steam whistle of a paddle boat approaching on the Ouachita.

The steamboat companies hired riparians to work as "snaggers," men who patrolled stretches of the river to remove logs and debris to keep the channels open. On board crewmen had to wield long spars to push away from the banks and fend off various obstacles and obstructions, and at times they found it necessary to use spars and long poles to "walk" the boat over sand banks and gravel bars. And when the water was altogether too low the traffic would stop. One ad that ran in the *Southern Standard* in 1869 seeking business for the "New Light Draught Steamer," the *Bluella* and the "New Orleans, Camden, and Arkadelphia Packet," *Rob Roy* noted at the bottom of the ad that the boats would make regular trips "when the water will permit this entire season." The water had to be right and the key to making successful runs on the Ouachita was vigilance.

For seven years life at Fairview prospered. Horton and his wife, Elizabeth, saw their hard work and diligence pay off and their family grow. When Priscilla was four years old she had to make way for her new brother, Louis. While she could claim status as the first child, Louis was the first son, so both were special in their parent's eyes. We can't look back at that farm and young family and see directly what life was like in mid-nineteenth-century rural Arkansas, but we do know folks of that time could make do. Some idea of what life at Fairview might have been like can be found in Mark Twain's *Autobiography* where he describes his uncle's farm, the model for the Phelps' farm in *Huckleberry Finn*; and though sentimentally filtered through the soft light of memory, his words, a feast of vivid detail, evoke the lost world of nineteenth-century Southern American farm life.

> I can see the farm yet with perfect clearness. I can see all its belongings, all its details: the family room of the house with a "trundle" bed in one corner and a spinning wheel in another, a wheel whose rising and falling wail, heard from a distance, was the mournfulest of all sounds to me and made me homesick and filled my atmosphere with the wandering spirits of the dead; the vast fireplace, piled high on winter nights with flaming hickory logs from whose ends a sugary sap bubbled out but did not go to waste, for we scraped it off and ate it; the lazy cat spread out on the rough hearth-stones; the drowsy dogs braced against the jambs and blinking; my aunt in one chimney corner, knitting; my uncle in the other smoking his corn-cob pipe; the slick and carpetless oak floor faintly mirroring the dancing flame-tongues and freckled with black indentations where fire-coals had popped out and died a leisurely death. . . .

Work—work was what made such transient and idyllic scenes around the hearth possible—men's work, women's work, children's work, and most notably in the antebellum South, slaves' work—work which followed the circadian and seasonal rhythms of the earth. Not only was it necessary to plant, hoe, pick, and gin the cotton each season, but farm folks had to feed themselves by growing and preserving vegetables and fruit, by breeding and raising, poultry and livestock, by milking, slaughtering, butchering and smoking and salting away the meat.

There were many crafts and skills required in the running of a farm or plantation in those days. One I find interesting is mentioned, I believe, in *Huckleberry Finn*, but never explained is the "ash hopper," a wooden box filled with ashes from the wood stove or fireplace sandwiched in between layers of straw. Rainwater or well water would be poured into the hopper and allowed to percolate slowly through the ashes and then drain into buckets or tubs below. The resulting "lye water" would then be boiled with hog fat and poured into pans or moulds to make lye soap which would then be used to wash clothes in big black cast-iron kettles heated over wood fires in the yard. Soap making and laundry were just one small part of a woman's work.

If the burden was heavy for Elizabeth in the early years of her marriage, it would soon become severe, for in the spring of 1861 word reached Fairview that South Carolina rebels had attacked the Union garrison at Fort Sumter. The trouble that had been brewing for some time between the states had at last come to a head. When word of impending secession reached Arkansas many were torn. There were heated debates in Dallas and Clark counties as there were through many parts of the South over the issue; many thought it was a bad idea, but since war fever is the most deadly infectious disease known to man, the secessionists swept away all opposition and soon men in both counties were lining up to join the Confederate forces.

Harris Flanagin, an Arkadelphia lawyer, state senator, and veteran of the Mexican war whose office was located just behind what would later be the site of Adams Book Store, left the state secession convention in the spring of 1861 to accept a commission as captain with Company E, Second Arkansas Mounted Rifles and fought in the battle of Wilson's Creek. After the regimental commander was killed at the battle of Pea Ridge, Flanagin was elected commander without opposition, becoming a colonel in the Confederate Army. While serving in the field with his troops in Tennessee in 1862, Flannigan was elected governor of Arkansas in absentia against the unpopular incumbent, Henry Rector.

Horton, who was in all likelihood personally acquainted with Flannigan before the war, missed the battle at Pea Ridge but served in the Arkansas volunteers for four years and fought with Confederate General Sterling Price's forces in the battles at Poison Spring and Marks' Mills. Whether he crossed the Mississippi and fought in any of the eastern campaigns is not known, but it is known that he was gone from home during most of the war, years when hardship, deprivation, and lawlessness were rampant throughout the state.

When Union General Fredrick Steele's troops approached Little Rock in September 1863, General Price, who commanded the bulk of Confederate troops in Arkansas, withdrew his forces from that city and marched south. He took up positions along the Ouachita River from Clark County to Camden where he established his headquarters. He immediately put his men to work digging trenches, gun emplacements, and redoubts, fortifying the city for the expected attack by General Steele and his Yankee forces. Horton, one of the Confederate soldiers who wintered in 1863-1864 in camps and outposts along the Ouachita River, was now back in his own neck of the woods waiting for spring.

The piney and hardwood hillsides of late winter were spotted with white service berry blossoms on March 23, 1864, when Steele left Little Rock with eighty-five hundred men to join forces with Brigadier General John Thayer near Arkadelphia. As the long lines of cavalry, cannon, caissons, foot soldiers, and mule-drawn wagons passed through Benton and Malvern on the old Military Road that would later become Highway 67, residents of those towns and settlements along the way lined up to sullenly glare at the blue-coated Yankees who had just two months earlier hanged for espionage one of their sons, seventeen-year-old David O. Dodd, who had been caught with diagrams of Union defensive fortifications on his person. The Federals took his young life and gave the state in return a martyr and Confederate hero who would live on in its history.

The plan was for Steele and Thayer to link up with General Nathan Banks, leader of the Red River Expedition that was moving north from Louisiana. When Steele met neither rebel forces nor Thayer's reinforcements in the seventy-mile journey to Arkadelphia, he left a brigade of infantry at nearby Okolona as a rear guard to wait for Thayer, and then led his forces southwest. Learning of the approach of the Union forces, Confederate General Price in Camden sent his two Brigadier Generals, John Marmaduke and Jo Shelby, to harass their advance. Shelby's cavalry discovered the Union rearguard at Okolona and attacked during a fierce spring thunder and hail storm. Shelby's adjutant later described the battle: "Amid the jar of the thunder, the flash of the lightening, and the moaning and sighing of the pines as the pitiless hail-storm tore through them, there was mingled the crash of artillery, the sharp rattle of musketry, and ever and anon as the wind ceased there came the wild blare of bugles and the ring of sabers." (DeBlack, 110)

When Price got word the Union forces had turned south, he concluded their aim was to attack the Confederate state capital which had been moved from Little Rock to Washington, Arkansas, so he gave the order to evacuate Camden and move to protect the new capital. When Steele learned the Confederates had left Camden, however, he immediately moved his forces toward that city for his most pressing need at that time was food and provisions. Our Pilgrim Fathers after first landing in this country had a year they called "the starving time," and for military and civilians, for Union and Confederates alike, 1864 was a starving time in Arkansas. So when Steele's troops entered Camden their first objective was to find food.

John Brown, a city resident, described the experience in his diary. "The awful day of all days—the dread event feared for years. About 6 O clock, an enemy infuriated by combat and hunger came rushing down our main street and diverging into cross streets. . . Northern muskets, swords, and bayonets glittering with the last rays of the setting sun with fierce imprecations and hideous shouts of exultation." The Union soldiers knocked on doors and demanded food; they searched houses and outbuildings for anything to fill their bellies. Brown adds, "I soon handed out all the victuals which were on hand, cooked. After dark they broke into the smoke house & commenced carrying off as they wanted." When Steele, however, became aware of the pillaging, he sent detachments of soldiers to patrol the streets and protect homes from further raids by his troops. (DeBlack, 111)

The food Steele's men were able to garner from the be-sieged town was insufficient to feed the hungry men, let alone the thousands of mules and horses the men depended on, so when supplies failed to arrive from Little Rock and the gen-eral learned there were five-thousand bushels of corn sixteen miles west of town he ordered 198 wagons to move down the Camden-Washington road to secure the corn and any other supplies that could be found. Over six-hundred troops and four cannon from Thayer's recently arrived Frontier Division were assigned the job of escorting the wagon train. Among those troops were 438 officers and men from the First Kansas Colored Infantry Regiment under the command of a white officer, Col. James M. Williams.

When the Arkansans learned that Union forces were on the way they attempted to destroy the corn but succeeded in destroying only half. Steele's men loaded the remainder in the wagons along with all the other booty they could find and started back for Camden the next morning, the 18th of April. Their force was augmented at a place called Cross-Roads when they met a five-hundred man relief column bringing the number of Federal troops protecting the wagon train to more than eleven hundred. But the Confederates had learned about the wagon train and 3,600 cavalry plus Texas and Choctaw brigades backed by twelve cannon lay waiting on the high ground at a place called Poison Spring, fourteen miles from Camden.

When the Federals detected the Confederates they quickly formed an L-shaped defense line around the wagons with the First Kansas Colored in the center and cavalry on both flanks. They succeeded in repelling the first two attacks but the third attack forced the defenders back through the wagon line into a swamp where they broke ranks and began to struggle through dense woods and thickets attempting to escape the cavalry and find their way back to Camden. Their fellow soldiers in the city could hear the sounds of battle from fourteen miles away, but no one rode to the rescue. Thomas DeBlack describes what followed:

> The first Kansas Colored had borne the brunt of the attack, and they were the victims of the action that followed. Out of a force of 400, the regiment lost 117 killed and 65 wounded. (This was an extremely rare occurrence. In Civil War battles the number of wounded almost always greatly exceeded the number killed.) At Poison Spring the Rebels shot wounded black soldiers as they lay helpless on the ground, gunned down others as they tried to surrender, and deliberately drove the captured wagons over the heads of wounded blacks.(112)

One of the First Kansas Colored soldiers who escaped the slaughter by feigning death heard a Confederate cry out, "Where is the First Nigger now?" And the response, "All cut to pieces and gone to hell by bad management!"

There can be no doubt that much of the Southerners' hatred of the black Union soldiers was motivated by fear. In spite of their much vaunted claims to being the slaves' compassionate benefactors, there is ample evidence that slave owners throughout the South harbored deep and imperfectly repressed anxieties regarding their subjugated black servants. Just two days before the Poison Spring battle, there had been a similar massacre of black Union troops at Fort Pillow, Tennessee.

Another aggravating circumstance at Poison Spring was that Rebel soldiers recognized some of the black soldiers as former slaves. A good number of the Kansas Colored were from Arkansas.

One valuable historical document, identified as "The Poison Spring Letter," was written soon after the battle by a Confederate soldier, identified by Mark Christ as "almost certainly" Alfred Hearn from Arkadelphia. It is a long letter addressed to "Dear Sallie." In it the writer describes the long running battle his outfit had with the Federals escorting the wagon train and tells of the aftermath.

> I think there were 10 negroes killed to one white Fed. Just as I had said before, they made the negroes go in front and if the negro was wounded, our men would shoot him dead as they were passed and what negroes were captured have, from the best information I can obtain, since been shot. I have seen enough myself to know it is correct our men is determine [sic] not to take negro prisoners, and if all of the negroes could have seen what occurred that day, they would stay at home(Christ, 100).

The writer tells Sallie to relate what happened at Poison Spring to "Henry and John," presumably family slaves, as a cautionary tale. He even ponders whether Henry and John might have been members of the Kansas Colored Regiment.

Horton was there at the battle, but what part he played in it is not known. There is no reason to believe, however, that his attitude toward the Kansas Colored would have differed in any significant way from that of Alfred Hearn. Did he participate in the massacre? We would like to think not, but we can't know. We do know, however, that otherwise good people whose livelihoods rest on the exploitation of others can be blind to that evil and capable of wicked acts.

The relationships between the two races in the South have always been shot through with irony as chronicled so vividly in the works of William Faulkner. There seems little question that slaves and their owners were not only physically close but emotionally close, that genuine affection often bound them together. Slaves played a significant role in the raising of white children whose playmates were children of slaves. But what happened at Fort Pillow and Poison Spring revealed the fragile nature of those bonds of affection and demonstrated clearly to Americans of African descent the cauldron of potential violence that bubbled beneath the smile of the "benevolent" master.

General Steele got some relief when a ten-day supply of rations came rolling in from Pine Bluff on the twentieth of April. Believing that road now open, he immediately ordered a 240-wagon train to return to Pine Bluff to secure more badly needed supplies. Unfortunately for him and his men General Price, acting on a steady supply of good intelligence, had sent a force of 4,000 men to await the wagon train near a series of grist mills known as Marks' Mills. When the two forces met up the battle that ensued lasted for five hours before the Union commander surrendered. The Rebels took thirteen hundred prisoners and seized all the wagons and equipment, stripped clothes from the wounded and captured, then, as at Poison Spring, they murdered the blacks accompanying the wagon train—some three hundred who were not soldiers but servants and teamsters and others who were only trying to escape from bondage. One of the Federal soldiers remarked later that the battle of Marks' Mill "was one of the most substantial successes gained by the Western Confederates during the war" (DeBlack, 115).

With things now going badly for General Banks and his Union forces in Louisiana and supplies running out in Camden, Steele realized he must evacuate the city, so before daylight on the 26th of April he led his forces across the Ouachita and north toward Little Rock. The path of his march would take his men through Dallas County and by Horton's plantation. So it would have been the 27th or 28th when Federal cavalry rode into Elizabeth's farmyard demanding food and feed for their horses. Elizabeth, who was by all accounts a gentle and loving woman, no doubt expected the soldiers to rob her of food and provisions, but when the Yankees took drawers from her prized mahogany dresser and used them to feed their horses she was horrified; to her that act was a gratuitous insult.

Elizabeth was, as would be expected, an ardent supporter of the Confederate cause. Laura Scott Butler, the mother of John Allen's piano teacher and the future teacher, historian, and Henderson-Brown faculty member, lived at Fairview with her older sister at that time. Many years later she recalled those days in,"A Tribute," to Elizabeth published in *The Confederate Veteran* magazine:

Being her sister, I was often in the home of Mrs. Horton during the first years of the war; and from April 1864, until the close of the war my home was continually in her house. Here I saw her unselfish devotion to her beloved South. Her husband was a

member of Capt. Rubin Reed's company (B), in a regiment of Arkansas volunteers under General Dickery,
Trans Mississippi Department and he served through
the war. Left at home with four small children and
the negroes, with no neighbor within calling distance,
this brave, patriotic woman, only twenty-six years old,
managed the farm and the farm work, besides caring
for every soldier that needed her care. Her negroes
planted and cultivated as much land as when their
master was at home, but cultivated enough cotton to
make clothing for the family, the negroes, and the soldiers. . . . When any of Price's, Shelby's or Marmaduke'
men camped in her neighborhood, Mrs. Horton always
kept her table ready set; and no matter what hour, day
or night, a hungry soldier came, he was taken to the
dining room and a good meal was set before him.

In her tribute Laura goes on to describe in detail how her
older sister worked to feed and clothe and shelter Confederate
soldiers in her home, how after the Union blockade of southern
ports that cut off the import of textiles the women worked
spinning cotton and weaving cloth in a scene reminiscent of
Mark Twain's description of his uncle's farm. The folks sitting
in the glow of the hearth at Fairview, however, were much
more purposeful and intense.

Around the fire at night in the long winter months
Mrs. Horton would knit while she helped her two
older children with their lessons or watched us as we
molded bullets by the thousands to send to our men.
Our only light was the pine fire or the tallow candle

shining from the old candlestick on the mantel. The hum of the wheel and the clack of the loom, and the swish, swish of the winding blades as we hanked the threads to warp for the loom, never ceased during the day and went far into the night. The negro woman who did the weaving was sent to her cabin early, and Mrs. Horton would take her place at the loom.

Laura names and describes soldiers who were housed, clothed, fed and cared for at the Horton plantation, and she names other Confederate neighbor women who contributed to the Southern cause. She concludes describing Elizabeth in her later years as she was when the tribute was written, "Mrs. Horton lives with her daughter and is remarkably strong and active, helping about the housework and doing beautiful fancywork."

Louis, John Allen's grandfather, would have been six years old when the Union soldiers rode onto their place. We can only imagine the fear and fascination he must have felt when he saw the Yankee soldiers riding their lathered horses into their farmyard looking for whatever they could find to sustain them while around the boy the long train of troops, cavalry, cannon and caissons passed through on their way to Little Rock. Certainly Elizabeth, Laura and the girls would have been angry and frightened while the slaves would have been filled with mixed emotions. Many blacks had been following Steele and his Union forces, seeing in them the possibility of deliverance, the hope for a Jubilee. But so far as we know the Horton slaves held fast, awaiting the final resolution of the conflict which would determine their fate.

Elizabeth, however, for the rest of her life would harbor bitterness toward the "Damned Yankee" soldiers who used the drawers of her fine dresser to feed their horses. Bessie, listening to stories at Elizabeth Scott Horton's knee, absorbed Confederate attitudes from her grandmother that she would carry the rest of her life.

Horton was most likely among the Confederates who pursued Steele and his miles-long convoy of troops through the Ouachita bottom lands and on towards Little Rock. After the Union forces passed by the Horton plantation and the town of Sparkman, a brief, intense firefight erupted near Princeton on the 29th of April, close enough to Fairview so the sounds of battle might have been heard there. The fighting broke off but at about 8 a.m. the following morning the pursuers caught up with the rear of the procession once again when it reached the Saline River at a place called Jenkins' Ferry.

Steele had ordered a pontoon bridge put in place there and his forces were hurriedly crossing the river when the Rebels arrived and a fierce battle erupted in the middle of a violent rain storm. The down-hill funnel-like shape of the road prevented the Confederates from bringing all their forces to bear in the battle while the Union forces, slipping and mired in mud, fought furiously to repel the attackers. In the rage of battle at Jenkins' Ferry, soldiers from the Second Kansas Colored Regiment overran a Rebel battery and slew them all, bashing heads and slitting throats of the wounded as payback for the treatment their brothers in the First Kansas Colored received at Poison Spring.

Once all the Federal troops were across the river the pontoon bridge was removed and the tired, hungry, muddy and bedraggled forces of General Fredrick Steele continued wearily on to Little Rock reaching the city on May 3, 1864. So ended the Camden Expedition which, according to Thomas DeBlack, was, ". . . the greatest Federal military disaster of the Civil War in Arkansas. Union forces suffered over twenty-five hundred casualties, lost hundreds of wagons, thousands of livestock, and gained not one inch of ground" (117).

Even though the Confederacy was now being vanquished everywhere east of the Mississippi, Arkansas, which had not played a part in the great battles of the war, did have the satisfaction of delivering three humiliating defeats to the Union forces in the final year of the struggle at Poison Spring, Marks' Mills, and in chasing the retreating Federals across the Saline River at Jenkins' Ferry.

It's hard to think that Horton who was part of all this action would not have found some way to check on his family at Fairview. Surely he and Elizabeth, like Alfred Hearn and Sallie, wrote one another throughout the war, but none of their correspondence survives. There is one unidentified picture of a seated Confederate sergeant in profile which could be him or one of his brothers. Horton survived the war but two of his brothers did not.

When Horton returned to Fairview after the war he found his fortune depleted but his family intact. With the determination and drive characteristic of his clan he set to work to rebuild his estate. His former slaves stayed on to work the land under his supervision and he reopened his mercantile store for the small community that had grown up at Fairview. The end of the war did not bring an end to hard times, however. The price of cotton in those years never made it back to the pre-war level, and the weather added to farmers' problems throughout the state, with alternating floods and droughts.

And, as did all southerners, the Hortons had to deal with the bitter ashes of the Civil war.

Louis was seven now, a handsome child but willful and sometimes difficult. The womenfolk said he was spoiled during the war because he was the only white male on the place. With all her troubles and responsibilities Elizabeth had not been able to give him the kind of firm guidance a young boy needs. Although she had graced the child with the revered name of her fabled uncle there seemed little likelihood that Louis Scott would ever distinguish the family as the famous general had. Priscilla, on the other hand, was the one who, with her intelligence, talents and dedication, seemed certain to bring distinction to the family.

We can never see William Saunders Horton clearly; we can only make out his form dimly through memories of his grandchildren and the veil of years. But one thing I believe can safely be said—like his great-grandson, John Allen, he had a great capacity for love. Evidence for this is found in the adoration of Bessie and Gertrude for their grandfather many years after his death, and in his great tolerance and support for his wayward son, Louis, and in his willingness to expend his wealth in defending his son, Paul Edward, in his murder trial. His success as a father and Elizabeth's as a mother is evidenced by the accomplishments of their children. Horton, like many Southerners of his age, was caught up in the evil of slavery, an institution, as William Faulkner makes clear, that cursed both the white and black races. Yet it is reported that at the conclusion of the Civil War, all his previous slaves chose to stay with him and work the land as sharecroppers.

Horton loved all his children, but his first born, Priscilla, it seems, held a special place in his heart. The love he felt for her was communicated to his descendents as can be seen in the following words from Gertrude's family history:

Elizabeth Priscilla (called Betty) was graduated from a College for Women at Clarksville, Tennessee, in 1876 at the age of twenty-one years. Shortly after returning home from her graduation, she contracted a fever from which she died. She was buried at the back of the garden at Fairview; a lovely white marble monument was placed at her head, and over her grave was built a beautiful lattice house with a square top sloping upwards to a point, out of which rose a spire that seemed always reaching toward heaven. The lattice house was covered with ivy and fresh flowers were kept on the grave when flowers were in season.

In the stately old parlor stood her square top piano that she had loved to play; and on the walls were her diploma and the paintings she had done at college. There were intricate flowers made of hair—framed in a box-like case and also wax flowers of beautiful colors, covered with a dome-shaped glass. On the floor, before the hearth was a hooked rug of red roses, buds and leaves; all made by the skillful hands of the beloved, departed daughter. Departed, yet her gentle spirit was kept ever present in my grandfather's home. Even unto his death in 1907, he cherished her memory and on his death-bed his last words were: "Bury me

by my daughter at the back of the garden and I will
be all happy and right."

Though "Aunt Betty," as we always thought of her,
died long before I was born, she seems more real to
me, and did more in shaping my character than some
of my other aunts—still living. That is why she de-
serves a page in this history.

Priscilla died the year our nation celebrated its first centennial,
the year General George Armstrong Custer wrote his name
indelibly in the annals of American history at the Battle of
the Little Big Horn.

Death was an intimate affair for rural families in Arkansas
in 1876. There were no nearby hospitals, no ICU's, no bevy of
technicians with advanced technology to attend to the ailing
family member; all that could be hoped for was a visit from a
country doctor on horseback with his bag of rude instruments
and generally ineffective nostrums. What rural doctors lacked
in medical cures, however, they in part compensated for with
personal care and concern, often remaining in the home of the
gravely ill giving comfort to the family throughout the illness.
After loved ones died the family themselves often bathed and
prepared the bodies for burial in makeshift plots on their own
land. Some years later ordinances were passed so such burials
were no longer permitted.

When the old Fairview Plantation land was finally divided
and sold the family had the bodies of Horton and Priscilla
exhumed and reburied in Rose Hill Cemetery in Arkadelphia
so the graves could be attended by family. There today father
and daughter still rest side by side.

Priscilla did not get to live out her promise, but her siblings, for the most part, went on to live rewarding lives. Several others pursued higher education at a time when such a thing was a rarity in Arkansas. Gertrude tells about some of them:

Maud Ann Horton, fourth daughter of William S. and Elizabeth S. Horton was educated in Ouachita College Arkadelphia, where she majored in music. After her graduation she thought Aunt Betty's fine old square top piano that had been bought in New Orleans and brought up by steamboat, was not fashionable enough for her so she beset grandpa to buy her a new upright piano. He did and for a time they had two pianos in the parlor. She taught music somewhere in Tennessee for a year or so. There, she met John Milford Williams a teacher who held a masters degree from Vanderbilt University. They were married December 25th, 1899. To them was born one child, a daughter named Horton. Mr. Williams (Uncle John) continued in school work after his marriage. First, he taught in the Clary Training School in Fordyce, Arkansas. From there he went to Henderson Methodist College, Arkadelphia, where he was made dean. From Henderson he went to Galloway College for Women* at Searcy, Arkansas as its president. He remained there twenty-six years, and was held in high esteem by all who knew him.

*(Galloway College opened in 1889 and was at one time said to be the largest school for females in the South. It merged with Hendrix College in 1930.)

Another of the Hortons' daughters married into a prominent medical family:

Ida Belle Horton, the second child of W. S. and Elizabeth Scott Horton was also graduated from the College for Women at Clarksville, Tenn. She then married Dr. O. O. Wozencraft, a physician and surgeon of Dallas Co. They made their home in Holly Springs, Arkansas, and to them were born six children, four sons and two daughters. They were: Hugh (died in early childhood) Louis W. Wozencraft—second son—took the M.D. degree in Louisville, Kentucky and his intern work in the University of Chicago.

Robert Oliver,—third son and uncle of the above mentioned—by the same name——also graduated in medicine taking his M.D. in Louisville, Kentucky, his father's Alma Mater. He then took his intern work in North Western University.

These are all the descendents of Ida Belle Horton Wozencraft who has won a prominent place in Southern Arkansas in her own right.

There are many other successful Hortons in Gertrude's history and she rightfully takes pride in her family's distinctions— teachers, doctors, college presidents, famous generals and distinguished military men, Forty-Niners and Confederate veterans—but of course missing from the Horton pantheon was her father. Her grandfather Horton was the patriarch of the family; her father Louis was the prodigal.

The Hortons would never have settled in Dallas and Clark counties had it not been for the Ouachita River. But the river as they knew it has long since been displaced as the center of Arkadelphia's commercial and recreational activities. While fisherman can sometimes be found along the banks and the sound of an outboard can occasionally be heard on the river, there are few swimmers, and the small attractive parks the city has provided at the end of Main Street and across the Caddo Bridge are seldom used. Other attractions have displaced the river as the focus of interest and recreation for Arkadelphia youth. Almost forty years ago a dam was built west of town on the Caddo River to create DeGray Lake and State Park, and more recently the construction of a city water park have provided citizens with more attractive and convenient sources of recreation and have left the Ouachita to flow quietly on as it has since before memory. Meanwhile technology has provided other enticements to divert our attention from the natural world.

Arkadelphia wouldn't exist if it weren't for the river. Today, however, when townspeople see the Ouachita it is often only for a few seconds as they cross the Caddo Street bridge on Hwy 7 headed for Joan or on south toward Camden, or perhaps they get a glimpse of it near Malvern as they drive down Interstate 30 headed for shopping excursions in Little Rock. But no one anymore gets to know the river the way John Allen and his friends did. For Arkadelphia boys who reached their teens in the decade of the Great Depression the river was their major refuge, replete with mystery and opportunities for exploration, a place to hike and go fishing; and when the weather was hot and unbearable, the Ouachita provided a good selection of delectable swimming holes offering temporary relief from Arkansas' sweltering summers.

* * *

CHAPTER 5

Fallen on Good Ground

———————————▬———————————

A sower went out to sow his seed: and as he sowed, some fell by the way side; and it was trodden down, and the fowls of the air devoured it. And some fell upon a rock; and as soon as it was sprung up, it withered away, because it lacked moisture. And some fell among thorns; and the thorns sprang up with it, and choked it. And others fell on good ground, and sprang up, and bare fruit an hundredfold.

The nation was still reeling from the Great Mississippi Flood in the summer of 1927 when Louise, Al and John Allen, traveling with the Ziedman and Pollie Show in Missouri, got word that her mother had died. The obituary said Amy Scales Horton had died after an illness of ten days. Vernon told me his mother had stepped on a "stob" and the injury became infected culminating in blood poisoning. Leaving her husband and son in Missouri with the show, Louise took a bus to Arkadelphia to attend the funeral of her sixty-one-year-old mother and meet for the last time with the seven other surviving children of Louis Scott Horton.

The meeting did not go well. The weather was unbearably hot and trouble had been brewing for some time in the family, particularly between Horace and Bessie. He had been living with his mother and Bessie at the home place when he began seeing a woman Bessie didn't approve of. According to Vernon Bessie thought of herself as a "blue blood," so when Horace, who was partially disabled from the sawmill accident, married the woman, Bessie threw him out. At the funeral the children learned there was little to the family estate but the home place, and because there was no will, what was left was to be divided eight ways. Furthermore, there was no money to pay for the funeral. Rodney, who was doing very well in Detroit, may have been able to foot the bill, but if he offered there's no record of it. So the children had to borrow money to pay for the funeral. Still, somehow, Gertrude later came up with the money to buy four of the shares of the home place from her siblings.

The Home Place with Al and Louise's car and trailer

When the dealing was done Bessie and Gertrude wound up with the home place, with Gertrude owning the lion's share and Bessie being the caretaker. But the settlement had not come without problems. Horace claimed his mother had told him he would get the house when she died and threatened to sue Bessie for ownership. The conflict went on for some time, but when the other children supported Bessie, Horace finally gave up on his claim.

After the funeral Louise traveled back with Gertrude to her house in Little Rock where she was teaching and spent the night there before returning to Missouri. She later wrote to Bessie telling her that she left Gertrude "feeling blue." Louise's language throughout her life never advanced beyond that of a teenager, picking up on slang and catch phrases from movies, pulp fiction, and Carney talk. She thinks of herself as a "flapper," and promises to send Bessie more money when she gets some "jack."

People in those days like Louise who lived hardscrabble lives didn't have the luxury of attaching fancy names to their emotional conditions, but an analyst today might label such a person bipolar. Louise in her letters swings from states of high excitement about her possibilities to despair over the bleakness of her prospects. At times she dreams of escaping the carnival, going to beauty school as Gertrude had suggested and opening a beauty shop in the room by the porch at the home place. (One can only imagine how Bessie would have felt about such an arrangement.) Other times she laments the hard life on the road and contemplates applying for a job at the State Hospital where she had spent a miserable six months as a fifteen-year-old inmate. She tells Bessie in one of her letters that the hospital pays fifty dollars a month plus room and board and laundry, an arrangement that seemed appealing during some lean times on the carnival circuit.

If Louise had a hard time dealing with her own problems, she was able to dispense cheery and upbeat advice to others in true mitt-reader fashion. In the letter she wrote to Bessie after her mother's funeral she tells her sister to "stand up for yourself," apparently referring to the conflict with Horace, and adds, "If you need any strong arm stuff, just let me know." She tells Bessie that when she feels "blue" to write her. It's not clear how much solace Louise could offer, but her intentions were good, and good intentions were about all she was ever able to come up with.

One good intention, however, she did follow through on. For some time both Bessie and Gertrude had been pleading with Louise to let John Allen come live with Bessie in Arkadelphia so he could get a proper education. Offering to take responsibility for someone else's child's upbringing is a gesture not made lightly, but the truth was that both Bessie and Gertrude had fallen in love with the dark-eyed boy with curly hair and a sunny smile, and both saw in him potential for achievements that could add further distinction to the Horton family story. Never mind that he might not contain a single drop of Horton blood; both sisters had taken him to their hearts and that fact trumped their prejudices.

Their petitions to their younger sister at last bore fruit when, only weeks after her mother's funeral, Louise wrote Bessie and told her that she and Al had agreed that their son could come live in Arkadelphia. This was an unselfish act on the part of both parents for, while the carnival was their living, John Allen was the center of their lives. And so it was the year of the Great Mississippi Flood, the year he lost his grandmother Amy, that John Allen came to live at the home place with his Aunt Bessie, only three blocks from the Ouachita River.

* * *

In the fall of 1971, having recently come from a part of west Texas where there were no rivers and precious few swimming holes, where men were as tall as the mesquite trees, and where the local Dairy Queen was considered an historical site, I soon came to appreciate the natural attractions and fascinating history of Arkadelphia and the surrounding region. Of course in changing climates there are tradeoffs. In place of wide-open spaces, big sky, cactus and sage brush, we now had tall water oaks and pines, rivers, lakes and plentiful greenery. The price we had to pay for rolling hills and beautiful scenery of Arkansas, however, came in the form of humidity, mosquitoes, chiggers and ticks. Like inhabitants of the region since the earliest days, we soon learned not to hike through tall grass and underbrush in the summer, to reserve those activities for winter. Summer was the time to enjoy the rivers and lakes around our new hometown; winter was the time to hike through the woods.

My visits to Adams Book Store helped me learn about the town and some of its people, but it would take me some time to realize that John Allen and the family he came from had lived a significant portion of regional and United States history and that some of the physical evidence of that history was still close by. Not only was Adams Book Store next door to the building that housed a Confederate armory and later the Freedman's Bureau responsible for assisting the newly freed slaves during the Reconstruction era, it was directly across the street from one of the oldest structures in Arkadelphia, a simple shotgun style brick building built in the 1840's that had housed the James K. Benjamin Mercantile business. Just behind the book store was a small house that had been the law office for Harris Flanagin the Civil War governor of Arkansas who had ridden off to war with Bessie's grandfather Horton and the two future owners of the *Southern Standard*, and directly across the street from that little house, which is still a law office and historical site today, is the Clark County Courthouse built in 1899. (The Benjamin building and the Freedman's building in which Joy and her first husband lived have since been torn down, but the others still stand.)

The street on which John's book store was located had been the main thoroughfare of the town since the arrival of the first white settlers early in the 19th century when it was no more than a dirt trail leading to the river. Just four blocks from the book store at the foot of Main Street the Ouachita still flows where a century before, steamboats landed bringing manufactured goods up from Camden and New Orleans to swap for cotton and corn and other produce before making the tricky return downstream. One of those boats brought his great aunt Priscilla's piano all the way from the Crescent City and off-loaded it somewhere in Dallas County for the wagon ride to Fairview. And there on the same river between Main Street and about a hundred yards upstream from the Caddo Street bridge, was one of the favorite swimming holes for young folks and healthy citizens since the earliest settlement, just as it would be in the 1930's for John Allen and his boyhood friends.

* * *

When John Allen came to live in Arkadelphia Bessie was thin as a dried cornstalk, but there were in her dark eyes hints of passion and strength. Her shoulders were somewhat narrow and her chest fallen, but her pelvis was wide and she appeared as though she could have borne children well. But that was not to be. She was now forty years old, and though there had been young men twenty years earlier, things had not worked out. Later came the problems that led to her operation, so now, as she told her brother, she was not a she and was not a he. She was an "it." So there was about Bessie a look of faded beauty and lost promise. But the fire in her had not been extinguished; it still glowed warmly, banked deep beneath the ashes. And now with the arrival of her eight-year-old nephew her life was given new purpose and she was ready for the challenge.

Bessie was accustomed to responsibility. As the eldest she had cared for her brothers and sisters for years. She had changed their diapers, tended them in their illnesses, had cared for them during the stormy eruptions between their parents which left the children frightened and confused. And when Horace, that very same brother who was now making trouble with claims against her rights to the home place, broke his back working in the lumber mill, it was Bessie who nursed him and fed him and lifted him from bed so he could go to the bathroom. After the death of her mother she even took some responsibility for the baby of the family, Paul Vernon, who lacked a year finishing his degree in chemistry at the University of Arkansas. Now she was taking on one more family responsibility—the care of her wayward sister's eight-year-old son.

But there could hardly be a starker contrast than that between the rebellious teenager Louise had been and her son John Allen. Ten years earlier Bessie had all kinds of trouble with Louise who didn't like books, hated school and fought with her mother and sisters. John Allen, on the other hand, from the beginning loved school and was a favorite of his Aunt Bessie and all her siblings. Of course he loved his parents and life on the carnival circuit had been fun, but Louise had earlier written Bessie and told her John Allen was getting tired of life on the road.

As young as he was John Allen recognized that carnival life was not for him. He had gotten to know and love his family in Arkadelphia and saw in them and their town a different path, other possibilities. The ambition and accomplishments of the Hortons did not escape his notice, and the town had allurements beyond the Ouachita River. He immediately hit it off with the children he met there and learned from them about the good schools they attended. Arkadelphia was small but it prided itself on education. It further possessed deeply held cultural aspirations evident on the masthead of the *Southern Standard* where Bessie worked which boasted the town was: *"The Athens of Arkansas,"* not without some justification. When he came to live in Arkadelphia, as in Jesus' parable of the sower and the seeds, John Allen fell on good ground.

That ground had been prepared by men like W.S. Horton and others who worked in the fields from dawn to dusk while setting their sights higher than the furrows their mules were pulling them down, and women like his wife, Elizabeth, who recognized there were values beyond feeding and clothing her family. For them Priscilla's piano was much more than a musical instrument; it represented to rural folks of the nineteenth century cultivation and culture. Horton had learned the importance of education from his own family as Elizabeth had from the Scotts—her father and famous uncle.

Arkadelphia was particularly blessed with visionary and aspiring people who promoted education. As early as 1851, when the town had only 250 residents, a Baptist minister, Samuel Stevenson, with the help of a relative opened the Arkadelphia Institute. In 1859 a blind Baptist minister named Haucke succeeded in getting legislative support to open the Arkansas Institute for the Blind which was moved to Little Rock nine years later. Like everything else, education in Arkadelphia suffered throughout the Civil War while so many men were gone and so many other citizens were working to provide arms and supplies for the Confederate cause. After the war ended public education arrived and provided instruction through the graded levels, but there were no institutions of higher learning.

That changed in 1886 when Ouachita Baptist College was established under the leadership of Dr. J.W. Conger. Four years later Arkadelphia Methodist College opened, a school that would undergo several incarnations, both private and public, before becoming today's Henderson State University. From the beginning both colleges stressed the liberal arts and teacher education generating a sense of pedagogical inquiry and enthusiasm that exerted a strong influence in the area's public schools.

John Allen attended his first year of school in Ft. Smith where his parents wintered in 1926, but Arkadelphia was the place he would put down roots. When he came to live with his Aunt Bessie the following year the ground had been prepared, both culturally and intellectually, to receive him. For a town its size Arkadelphia provided a wide range of social, cultural, and educational opportunities for young people. John Allen found in his new hometown a family and school system that valued achievement, a community that could provide the care, love, and resources required to nurture and guide the gifts of intellect and character he so clearly possessed.

The separation was not easy for the parents, however. Louise wrote Bessie in September:

> I guess you are right about J.A. And I don't want him to ever be on the road, but I want you to tell him the facts of life and how to control his self [sic] as he is big enough to know . . . tell him if he ever has anything to happen to him he can't understand to come to you . . . I want you to explain things to him. That is my only worry, for I never knew anything when I was growing up. . . .

John Allen wrote a letter to Santa in December letting him know he was now living in Arkadelphia. (If he still believed in Santa it probably could be attributed to his mother's love of fantasy.) The following summer of 1928 he took his last carnival tour with his parents. Louise wrote Bessie in July telling her that if anyone wanted to know where they were not to tell them. They had bought a car on credit and were a month behind on payments. She says she will make the payment "next week" and then "everything will be Jake." She went on to say she'd be home in the next eight weeks, that she was just waiting to make some "jack" before coming back."

It was clear by that time that the life Louise and Al were living was not for John Allen, that he now considered the house on 3rd and Clinton his home. Louise wrote in August, 1928, from Holyoke, Colorado, (a name which must have jarred her memory, for she asks Bessie how the hollyhock she planted was doing) and tells Bessie that her son has just had his 9th birthday on the 16th, and adds, "He sure wants to get back to see you. He said he wanted to stay there next year with you, that he is tired of the road." John Allen would often write a note to his aunts at the bottom of his mother's letters, such as the following from Springfield, Missouri: "Dear Aunt Bessie and Aunt Gertrude wish I could see you all. Am comming [sic] home soon. Loving J.A.A [accompanied with arrow-pierced hearts and circled X's for kisses].

But John Allen did not make it back in time for the opening of school. Louise wrote from Missouri on the 25th of October that they hoped to make it home the first week in November. As in almost all her letters she expressed great concern for her sister, no doubt from genuine love but also from her awareness of how much she depended on her, on how much Bessie had done and would continue to do for her. She says to Bessie, "Honey please don't stay up so late again—for you can't stand it, working like you do."

There's no doubt Bessie sacrificed for her family and little doubt that she took some pleasure in being recognized for her sacrifice. But caring for John Allen was a pleasure not a burden; she was looking forward to the return of her nephew who wrote at the bottom of the letter: "Dear Aunt Bessie. I am keeping up with my school work. I have all the third grade books. With love, John Allen." [circled X's].

John was late getting started in school that year but that was no problem for him, just as any schooling he had missed before coming to Arkadelphia had been no problem. With his quick mind and eager attitude he closed any educational gap between himself and his fellow students and soon found himself among the top students of his class, and the qualities that had won over the Horton sisters at the home place were equally effective with his schoolmates so he was quickly surrounded by new friends. The extra time on the road that summer had given him the opportunity, as he told Aunt Bessie on one of the letters, to go swimming six times thereby applying some of the skills he had learned on the Ouachita River.

Louise spent the winter of '28-'29 working in the dining room of the Dermott Hotel in Dermott, Arkansas, while Al wintered in El Paso, Texas. She wrote often to Bessie and John Allen, worried about her boy and solicitous of her sister:

Feb, 1929
My Only Son:

Mother sure is lonesome without you, but Aunt Bess will have to take my place for a while & I know she will be good to you. It isn't like leaving you with someone that will be mean to my darling, so honey boy don't forget your onlyest mother for I love you so much and will forever and always so write me often and study hard and I know you will always be a good boy and say your prayers every night for God will hear them and take care of my darling. Don't let Aunt Bessie do the washing. You go down and ask Mag to come and get them but don't go near the river for dear I don't want anything to happen to my boy. And always be careful crossing the street so you won't get run over.

Louise goes on to tell her son to write to his "fat mother," though she says she's lost some weight, a "very few" pounds. She tells him to study hard and "when school is out you can spend a week or so with your flapper mother. . . I'm strutting my stuff in the dining room."

In the envelope with the letter to her son was one to her sister containing a single refrain, "Don't do that washing!" She repeats the plea over and over, "Don't do it, you have got to save yourself to take care of J.A. if not for me. So honey please don't do it. I'll try and send 50c more and you have it done do you hear?" Louise, fearing Bessie will kill herself with overwork, repeats the same warning for an entire page.

There's no question that Bessie was a hard worker and that she sacrificed for her family, but it's difficult not to get the sense that she knew how to play the martyr. Louise was right, however, in assuring her son that his Aunt Bessie would take good care of him.

John Allen by now had found his place with new friends in the Arkadelphia school system and Bessie was finding fulfillment in her new mission. She had always been the cata-lyst, the facilitator, the one to provide support for her family members in their life pursuits while forgoing her own aspira-tions. To help her see after her nephew while she worked at the newspaper office she called upon her friend and neighbor Alberta Culbertson who had a daughter about John Allen's age. We get a glimpse of John Allen as a ten-year-old in a letter Alberta wrote to Louise in the summer of 1929:

> . . . John Allen is fine and happy; he is a sweet good child. No one can help but love him. He and Helen play checkers and different games. They hardly ever disagree on anything. . . .

Well the kids have come from the library. They read the biggest part of their time and it helps them pass the time away. We have a skating rink here now. Bessie and I and the kids have gone twice. The kids had a good time skating. . . .

Now don't you or Mr. Adams worry over John Allen for I know every minute where they are, and they never go anywhere without asking me, when Bessie is not here. I love them both dearly and would do so much more for them if I only had this worry off me. Any way we will all be fine.

Love from all—Alberta

The worry Mrs. Culbertson refers to is one the Hortons were familiar with, one that rocked the home place next door fifteen years earlier—marital strife. Elsewhere in the letter she says, "Louise, I can't tell you how I'm worrying but there's no one can help me, only the one who has higher power over all. I just can't see my way out right now, but surely he can't have my baby—all that I have." She also testifies to Bessie's dedication: "Bessie works so hard she's too tired to write anyone after her work is over."

In her letters to Bessie, Louise continues to inquire about the state of the Culbertson's marriage. Apparently things didn't work out for Mrs. Culbertson whose husband had accused her of infidelity, for Louise writes the following summer from Iowa, "It sure is bad about Alberta, isn't it. Did he get Helen?" Of course Louise and Al had problems of their own as could be expected, but there is never in her letters any indication of conflict or anger. She complains several times that Al seems to be losing his spirit or nerve and says she may need to strike out on her own. But those moods pass and they go on with their lives together. At times they spend the winters apart because they find work in different places but they are back together when the carnival gets ready to roll.

Louise herself was no doubt a challenge for Al. As she acknowledged to her son, she had gotten fat. Vernon told me his sister was a heavy smoker, a habit she picked up from other carneys reinforced by her self-image as a "flapper;" he also told me she had a problem with drugs beginning with the anti-diarrheal paregoric, a tincture of opium, which perhaps then led to other opiates. Also, because of her experience in the State Hospital at Little Rock, Louise feared for her sanity and throughout her life sought reassurance from various medical practitioners that she was not crazy. She was also haunted by guilt over committing bigamy and fear of Frank Hurt, fear that he might have designs on her son. He certainly knew the neighborhood since he had lived across the street from where John Allen was living then. She wrote Bessie from Illinois while on the summer circuit in 1929,

Dear Bessie:–

I've just wrote J.A. and you know who I'm talking about. Frank H. I dreamed about that S.B. the other night, and don't you let him get his hands on J.A. if he should come to life and show up there, for you know if anything should happen I would just go bugs, so I'm depending on you to look out for him until I'm on my feet, so honey don't fail me. With love to you & J.A. Lovingly, Lou

Being apart from her son for long periods led to other worries. When two dogs in her show came down with rabies she wrote Bessie and told her to get rid of John Allen's dog, even if it had to be shot. When John Allen wanted to play the horn in band, Louise instructed her sister to get him a nickel plated one because she thought brass could harm his lungs. Realizing how dependent she was on her sister, she was also concerned about Bessie's health, warning her and John Allen at one time not to eat melons because she believed they caused chills and fever. She said people up north where she was never ate melons. Another time Louise reported that she had had a boil on her breast she thought was cancer, but after she took some of the patent medicine, 666, the sore disappeared. She then recommended that both Bessie and John Allen try the healthful elixir.

Whatever problems Louise and Al had, the pattern of their lives—summer, carnivals, winter, menial jobs—established the year John Allen was born lasted for twenty-five years, right up to the time Louise's body was discovered in her room at the Goddard Hotel. It's worth noting that in the investigation following her death no druggist could be found who sold her the chloroform, a fact that suggests she may have brought it with her to Hot Springs. Is chloroform a drug that would appeal to a drug abuser, or had she been planning all along to kill herself? She had been for some time telling Bessie in her letters that she felt she could not live much longer, she carried with her a last letter to her son, and in the little brown notebook in her purse she had written her last will and testament. But sixteen years earlier while working in the Dermott Hotel Louise did not feel the end was near. Back then she could hold in her mind a bright picture of her beloved boy headed toward a promising future under her sister Bessie's guidance.

It didn't take long for John Allen's latent abilities to sprout in the fertile soil of his new home town. Not only was he making new friends and doing well in school, he was exhibiting a precocious intellectual curiosity which would lead him to a wide range of interests. He kept up with his parents on their summer tours and collected the picture postcards they sent him from around the country. That interest led to a scrap book and a stamp collection. He put a map of the United States on his wall and tracked the routes of the carnival and learned something about each of the towns they stopped in. Louise wrote to him about his love of collections and suggested he start one of butterflies since she had just seen a particularly beautiful one. There's no record of whether or not he added a butterfly collection to his many hobbies, but it's interesting to consider here John Allen and his relationship with his parents, particularly his mother.

Almost all children go through an "orphan stage," a time in adolescence when they want to distance themselves from their parents. They may be embarrassed to be seen with them, or even ashamed of perfectly respectable parents. Doctors, lawyers, teachers, or barnstorming airplane pilots might be cut some slack, but having a mother who is a carnival fortune teller carries little prestige in youthful circles. Carney parents who spend their summers on the sawdust circuit may have some appeal for the kindergarten set, but beyond that level they would not be a subject the child would want to talk about. It's widely recognized that children can be cruel toward their peers over any anomaly in name, appearance or family background. There is no indication, however, that John

Allen ever attempted to distance himself from his parents or that he was ever taunted or discriminated against by friends who came from stable and respected families in town. His acceptance by his classmates can perhaps be partially attributed to Bessie and Gertrude's solid reputations in Arkadelphia, but the major reason must have been John Allen himself, his open and friendly demeanor, his obvious intelligence and his natural dignity.

His rapid intellectual development is evident in the letters he writes to his parents. Louise throughout her life had problems with grammar and spelling and worked with a limited vocabulary marked by slang expressions from popular culture. Her son's language, on the other hand, as evidenced by the letters to his parents shows soon after his arrival in Arkadelphia unusual maturity and awareness of the rules of grammar and punctuation. He loved to read, was alert to his surroundings and discriminating in his interests.

For one of his talents John Allen found a mentor in a local music teacher, his third cousin, Elizabeth Scott Butler. Her mother, Laura Scott Butler, the much younger sister of his great grandmother Horton, had told Amy Horton twenty years earlier that she must get her children out of the sticks at Fairview so they could get proper educations. Laura Butler a widely respected teacher, writer, and student of history who taught in various rural schools around the area, concluded her career on the faculty at Henderson Brown College; her two unmarried daughters also carried the popular family given names, Elizabeth Scott Butler the piano teacher and her sister Annie Laurie Scott Butler who together operated a flower shop on Caddo Street where John Allen worked from time to time. The two sisters were close throughout their lives and when the Elizabeth died at the age of sixty-six in 1943, Annie Laurie, seven years her junior, suffered a stroke the day after Elizabeth's funeral and two months later followed her sister in death.

Elizabeth Scott Butler

Though Arkadelphia was a small town it provided great advantages for its youth, and John Allen was ideally located— three blocks from the river in one direction, four blocks from town and the library in the other, school within easy walking distance, two college campuses nearby and friends all around. It was in Arkadelphia schools that John Allen formed strong bonds which would endure for the rest of his life with boys like Billy Vestal, Chuck Meador, Billy Gill East, W. S. McNutt, Jack Arnold and many others. One, William F. "Buddy" Whitten, would be his closest friend throughout his school years.

All parents are concerned that their children choose good associates in school, and as it happened John Allen's friends could not have been a more promising group, all destined, like W.S. McNutt, to be successful later in life. In classes of students as in crops, there are good years and not so good years. John Allen benefited from and contributed to one of the most outstanding groups of students ever to pass through the Arkadelphia school system. The boys and girls in his class were part of that larger group that would one day be called the "Greatest Generation.

* * *

CHAPTER 6

When He Ran Through
A Supple-limbed World

*April 19, 1935 **Camden First, Arkadelphia Second***
in Dist. Track Meet

*In the junior division, Vestal, Mitchell, East and **Adams***
showed well. . . .

*440 Yard Dash—**Adams** (Arkadelphia); Burton*
(Norphlet); Barker (Standard Umsted); Cathey (Camden).
Time 59.9 sec. . . .

*Javelin—Gillespie (Camden); Kennedy (Norphlet); **Adams***
(Arkadelphia); Taylor (Camden). Distance, 124 feet 10
inches.

After the Stock market crashed in 1929 men may have been leaping from building ledges in New York City but in Arkadelphia things didn't change all that suddenly. Bessie continued walking each day to her job at the *Southern Standard* while John Allen walked to school often surrounded by his friends. A more pressing problem for Arkansans was the drought that had begun seriously affecting crops. Uncle Thad who would occasionally stop by for dinner at the home place was more concerned with his cotton crop at Fairview than with high finance in the big city, though eventually economic conditions there would affect him as well.

Like small town America everywhere, events in the broader world had little immediate impact on life in Arkadelphia. Of course Bessie kept up with national and international news by virtue of her job as a Linotype operator in the newspaper office and brought home each day the latest in world news and local doings. The headlines that grabbed the most attention were the lurid ones like the St. Valentine's Day Massacre the previous February when Al Capone ordered a hit on his rival Bugs Moran. His goons missed Bugs but lined seven of his associates against the wall in a Chicago garage and blasted them with Tommy guns and shotguns leaving one slumped on a chair and the other six strewn in puddles of blood on the floor.

Not all headlines were grim. Over the next several years there was some positive news. In 1931 the Empire State Building was completed and "The Star Spangled Banner" was adopted as the National Anthem. In November of 1932 Franklin Delano Roosevelt was elected president bringing some hope to a nation in distress with his economic program that would be called the New Deal. That year Amelia Earhart became the first woman to fly solo across the Atlantic giving Americans something to think about besides soup lines and hobo jungles. But that same year the nation's heart was broken by news of the kidnapping of Charles Lindberg's baby, son of the hero who had been the first man to fly solo across that ocean just five years earlier, the year John Allen came to live with Aunt Bessie. That sensational story and the long investigation and trial which followed gripped the nation's attention for months. But whether the news was good or bad Arkansans continued to suffer from the regional drought and the worsening economy in these early years of a decade that would come to be known as the Great Depression.

During those hard times many in Arkadelphia and elsewhere had to fall back on pioneer skills like those practiced by Bessie's grandparents at Fairview—growing their own vegetables and fruit, raising their own poultry and livestock, and sewing, quilting, and knitting for the family. Many, in fact, had never let go of those crafts and skills. Backyards and empty lots around town became sites for vegetable gardens and poultry pens. The eerie whine of the spinning wheel of Mark Twain's memory may have grown quiet, but folks were finding new ways to clothe and provide for their families. Many houses around town had a room with a quilting frame suspended from the ceiling where up to four women would sit and quilt while they gossiped and told funny stories. Quilting had not disappeared as the spinning wheel had, in part because of its social value, but hard economic times once more demonstrated its utility. Another domestic sound that could be heard in many houses was the hum of sewing machines where mothers' feet pumped the treadles as they sewed school clothes for their children. In some families during the hardest times, clothes were made of flour sacks. Nothing could be wasted.

Mr. Singer's invention proved to be a great contribution to domestic life, and there were other technological advances as well in the 1930's. Rather than relying on smoke houses and root cellars, most people in town now kept their perishable foods in iceboxes. When that modern amenity came to

Arkadelphia there came with it a new profession—the ice man. This familiar neighborhood figure would load his truck each morning at the ice house on Pine Street in huge blocks frozen with seams so he could with his ice pick divide it into 50 pound, 25 pound, and even 12 ½ pound blocks to fit in the iceboxes of his customers. After loading his truck he would cover the ice with a heavy canvas tarp and set out on his route. His tools were an ice pick, a pair of large tongs for wielding the big blocks of ice, and a thick leather pad he wore on his back to protect himself when he slung the block over his shoulder to carry into the house.

Children, and John Allen was likely among them, would often follow the ice man on hot summer days and snatch up the chips of ice left on the back of the truck when he separated the blocks with his pick. Kind-hearted ice men would sometimes make an extra effort to see that some larger slivers were left for the kids. A common practice for the lucky recipient was to take his prize, go sit on a sidewalk and alternately suck on the ice then set it on the hot concrete and watch tiny vertical air tunnels and white lines form in his dissolving, refreshing treasure. What the ice man didn't understand in those years was that an underlying process was at work, one still going full steam today: technology which makes our lives easier steals jobs. The appearance in town of a new appliance around that time, the "Frigidaire," spelled the ultimate doom for his profession which would, like the kid's chunk of ice on the sidewalk, slowly melt away.

John Allen was happy to be off the road and settled down in his new home in Arkadelphia. Since times were hard he had especial reasons to be grateful for Aunt Bessie's generosity, her sacrifices, her providing him a good home and loving guidance. But she profited equally from the arrangement, not only from the boy's bright company but from the many ways he helped her around the house. He took pride in the home place willingly doing yard work and performing all sorts of family chores. The greatest thing for him was that he now had his own room. No more living out of suitcases and packing up to move every week or two.

Seeing how efficiently John Allen had ordered the desk where he worked and his book store on Main Street, it's not difficult to imagine the pride he must have taken in arranging his room at the home place. For sure there would have been books, and perhaps boys' magazines, such as *The Open Road for Boys, Boy's Life*, and some of the fairly new comic books that were becoming popular. There would have been his scrap books and collections reflecting his various hobbies and interests and the usual implements of boys of that generation—marbles, tops, yo-yo's, pocket knives and perhaps a bb gun. There was now an airport in an open field across the Ouachita and airplanes, particularly since the feats of Charles Lindberg and Amelia Earhart, had so taken the imaginations of many young boys, perhaps there could have been model planes in John Allen's room.

Arkadelphia now offered more attractions for young people than it had when Louise lived at the home place. Since John Allen loved books the public library close by proved a valuable resource to stoke his imagination. There he would have found rich sources of entertainment from authors such as Mark Twain, Jack London, Booth Tarkington, Jules Verne, Robert Louis Stevenson and many others who could grab the attention of a young man and pull him into exciting stories and expand his world in the process. And movies had advanced since Louise sought to escape her troubles at the Electric Theater.

The Royal Theater had now been moved to its final location on Main Street where it offered double features on Saturdays with stars like Johnny Weissmuller in *Tarzan of the Apes*, and Johnny Mack Brown, Bob Steele, Gene Autry in many exciting westerns. John Allen would have taken advantage of all these educational and entertainment resources, for he demonstrated throughout his life a questing nature, one seeking not only adventure, but knowledge and understanding.

Once he wrote his parents that he had gone to hear a well known speaker named Halliburton who had passed through town. Louise wrote back,

> Honey Boy you just cram all the knowledge you can in your head while you have the chance, as Aunt B. is giving you something every road boy doesn't get. The more I see of the kids on the shows the more thankful I am that you don't have to tramp around. So be sure and make good use of this chance, for if you get it in your head there is no one that can steal it from you. Therefore you will always be able to make money . . . So study hard and don't ever think of going on the road for it will just make a bum of you and I know you were borned [sic] to better things than to be a bum.

It was through the influence of his school friends and because of the reputation of his high school principal, Mr. V.L. Huddleston, that John Allen became part of an organization that helped satisfy his hunger for knowledge and adventure.

As soon as he was old enough John Allen joined the Boy Scouts and became an active member of Mr. Huddleston's Troop 23. The spirit and ethic of that organization had a strong appeal for him and many of his friends and schoolmates like Billy Vestal, Dan Grant, Jack Arnold, W.S McNutt, Bill Newberry, Charles Moores, Brown DeLamar, Charles Clark, and Buddy, all of whom were fortunate to come under the guidance of a remarkable leader of young men. Their Scoutmaster, a square-built, tobacco-chewing, cigar-smoking outdoorsman in his mid-forties, physically a Teddy Roosevelt type who still carried vivid memories of his own youth, was a man who could look through his round gold-rimmed glasses into a boy's eyes and discern his innermost aspirations and concerns and quickly win his respect and confidence.

V.L. Huddleston

No one can capture V. L. Huddleston's essence better than those who knew him first hand. John Allen years later wrote a poem about his Scoutmaster in the section of his book of poems titles "Lineaments of Love":

Only the Lover
(for Vere L. Huddleston)

A hillsman born, deep rooted as the pine
Drawing its nourishment from the Ozark hills
(these rocky holdings stubborn courage fills),
He loved this land that bore his hardy line.
The seasons wove his homespun soul's design:
Here redbud dyed and shot with mating calls;
There withered leafage of his youthful falls
Blent strands of scalybark and muscadine.

He harried quail and scouted rabbit runs,
He conned the spoor of deer; but as his aim
Improved, he stalked the leaping and the flight:
When heart grew weary with the weight of guns,
He sauntered empty handed, after game
Only the lover gauges in his sight.

John sent this poem and one he had written for his friend W.S McNutt to his former Scouting buddy, then a professor at Tufts University in Boston. Here is McNutt's response to the poem:

Man, was I glad to be in the same class with Mr. Huddleston! [Referring to John's poems about the two men] There was a man! That title, too; it really hit me. You said it. With him you knew he loved you. There was a magic about him. He could squeeze out more juice from life than seemed to be there in the first place. He really cared for people and what they had on their minds. And there weren't any limits, so if you were afraid to talk to your parents you talked to him about your masturbation without his being shocked. You came out feeling less a freak. That's important to a boy, and it meant a hell of a lot more then.

He knew how to stay a boy and still grow older. That was his magic. What do you think made him tick?

I think he had a strong attraction to people (it was probably even sexual) that he used for their improvement, and his reason for doing it was because he loved them. Having been brought up the way he was, he probably thought he was terrible feeling for people the way he did, but he couldn't help it. So he turned out to be a lot more admirable than other men could be. That's the way I figure it. He really loved us. And it turned out great. He probably thought we were beautiful right down to our balls. We never discussed it, but I'm willing to bet. What else could have made him so much like a poet? What do you say?

Here we see the wit, humanity and penetrating intelligence of W.S McNutt. The reference to masturbation is pertinent because in the 1930's and 40's there were ominous warnings in the Scout's *Handbook for Boys* concerning the horrible consequences of "self abuse." These hypocritical warnings pictured dire conditions which could follow such a practice—pimples, stunted growth, stooped shoulders, high-pitched voices— and offered as defenses against such urges physical exercise and cold showers. As it was the greatest dangers the boys faced were psychological, needless worries precipitated by such horror stories from adults who had survived the scourge themselves with no apparent lasting scars.

As far as McNutt's Freudian speculations concerning Huddleston's motivations, I will let that go. But in light of the many recent abuses by mentors against their charges—teachers/students, Priests/parishioners, and adult leaders of youth in many fields—it is worth noting that human beauty blooms in youth, and adults, including mentors, are not blind to that beauty. Recognizing beauty in all its forms is both healthy and normal. But we all understand where the boundaries are and should note that while there have been too many instances of adults violating the trust given them by parents and community, the overwhelming majority of leaders of youth view that trust as sacred and devote themselves to protecting and bringing out the best in the young folks entrusted to them. V.L. Huddleston was clearly such a man.

Adolescents have a strong inclination to bond with others of their age group; they are ripe for initiations, tribal mysteries and esoteric secrets of nature. The Boy Scouts of America has always provided graduated challenges and awards for its members, adventures designed for and especially appealing to boys, a fact which accounts for its longevity and success in channeling youthful energies into constructive and socializing activities. The organization has proved adaptable and has changed to keep pace with the times from its beginning up to the present digital age of the Internet. But it can never again have the same kind of appeal it had for boys in Arkansas growing up during the Great Depression.

In those days boys had fewer technological allurements and were closer to the country's pioneering past. Troop 23 met once a week and the enthusiasm generated at those meetings spilled over to many outdoor activities. Mr. Huddleston's boys were living on the exact spot where Caddo Indian villages sat two and a half centuries earlier and he made them keenly aware of that fact. He took them on frequent hikes through the woods and along the rivers and streams around Arkadelphia teaching local history and woodsman lore, teaching them the ways of regional wild creatures and the distinguishing characteristics of native plants, and sharing with them as well his enthusiasm for Native American culture.

During winter months Mr. Huddleston would take his Scouts across the river where they could stand and look over the plowed cotton fields and see down the rows the gentle rises that marked places where the thatched houses of the Caddo Indians once stood, where children had played and generations of people had lived and worked, raising beans and squash and corn in plots around the village where their hunters, men and boys, brought home birds, rabbits, squirrel, deer and occasionally bear and buffalo meat from the hunt, where the whole village swam and fished in the nearby Ouachita and gathered mussels from its rocky shallows. As the boys walked down the rows toward the former settlement the Scoutmaster would explain how the growing number of flint chips exposed by recent rains told them they were nearing their destination and would be pleased every time he heard one of his boys shout out in excitement that he had found an arrowhead, spear point or hand-decorated pottery shard.

Mr. Huddleston led the boys on many hikes along both sides of the Ouachita and along the Caddo pointing out historical sites like the old cistern which once was used by a stage coach station near the Indian mound at Caddo Valley, a mound around which early settlers raced their horses. The mound was built from earth carried in woven baskets, thousands of baskets over a long period of time, for what purpose we cannot be sure. The Scoutmaster's enthusiasm for the natural world and for history infected the boys and inspired John Allen and his friends to do a great deal of exploring the river and its surrounding woods on their own.

Some of John Allen's most enthusiastic letters to his parents centered on his Scouting activities. During Boy Scout week, he told them, the boys wore their uniforms every day. He wrote his dad in June of 1933 that he was preparing to go to camp, and the following May he wrote to both parents telling them, "Troop 23 . . . went to the rally at Hot Springs last Saturday and won second place. Malvern won first. We wanted to win first

John Allen and Buddy Whitten at Camp Bonanza

because we had won it the last two years." In 1984 I interviewed Jack Arnold, one of John Allen's friends and fellow Scouts, about the Scouting jamborees they attended. He told me they were great fun, that there were all kinds of competitions at Camp Bonanza in Hot Springs—fire by friction, fire by flint and steel, wall scaling, knot tying, signaling, semaphore, Morse code and bugling contests. He said their Troop went on many hikes, some at night, both at the Jamborees and around Arkadelphia. They worked hard, building bridges, towers, and even helped build the log cabin that still stands in Arkadelphia's City Park.

But they were boys after all and at times stepped over the line. Arnold said some of them got in trouble at the Jamboree in Hot Springs when they were caught by the camp director playing "put and take," a gambling game popular at that time played with small hexagonal tops with "P's" and "T's" inscribed on the flat sides along with a number. Players would spin the top by spinning a little post on the top of the top between thumb and forefinger; if the top stopped and fell over with a "P" up, the spinner would put in the pot the number pennies called for. If the letter was "T," he would take the designated number of pennies from the pot.

Indian crafts and lore have been an integral part of Scouting since it first came to America; images of Native Americans appeared often in the Scouting literature, such as a picture of Scouts around a campfire at night with the faces of Indians appearing in the smoke rising above their heads. So when Troop 23 went camping along the Caddo River near the Indian mound, or along the Ouachita near the places where Indian villages once stood, there is no doubt the boys felt the presence of the former inhabitants. Mr. Huddleston would have made sure of that.

I have no doubt that John Allen, considering his love of nature and literature, was familiar with Henry Wadsworth Longfellow's poem, "Song of Hiawatha." The most famous poet of his day is rarely read today, but he was well known to school boys in the 1930's and the tom-tom beat of that poem could work magic for them.

> By the shores of Gitche Gumee
> By the shining Big-Sea-Water,
> Stood the wigwam of Nokomis,
> Daughter of the Moon, Nokomis.
> Dark behind it rose the forest,
> Rose the black and gloomy pine-trees,
> Rose the firs with cones upon them;
> Bright before it beat the water,
> Beat the clear and sunny water,
> Beat the shining Big-Sea-Water.

Never mind that Hiawatha was a total figment, one of the many misrepresentations by white men of the Native American as the romantic Noble Savage, as was James Fennimore Cooper's Uncas and Chingachgook in *The Leather Stocking Tales,* all stock literary types that endured all the way to the Lone Ranger's sidekick, Tonto. And never mind that the tom-tom beat and the trochaic repetitions of the poem tend to wear on the reader after a while. Still, for a Depression era Boy Scout who sat gazing into the dancing flames of a campfire surrounded by black and gloomy pine trees in woods where the Caddo people once walked, it was the images of Hiawatha and other fictional Noble Savages that floated in the smoke above the flames, not the actual people who had created the artifacts Troop 23 found in the fallow cotton fields across the river. Those people and all their brethren, the actual Native Americans, were viewed much differently by the white Europeans who took their land. Those Indians were never romanticized until after they were got rid of.

Just as W.S. Horton on his way to California with the Forty-Niners and other citizens of the 19th century took pride in America as a New Eden, an unspoiled continent rich in nature's bounty while mindlessly slaughtering the passenger pigeons and buffalo, razing the forests, and stripping the mineral wealth from the ground leaving toxic slag heaps for future generations, so their attitudes toward the native inhabitants of the land were equally conflicted and at odds. We all know how the story of the treatment of Native Americans goes, from the "purchase" of the Island of Manhattan to the tragic "battle" at Wounded Knee; we know how, broken treaty after broken treaty, the land was taken from the Indians. The irony for the compassionate John Allen Adams, strongly anti-war and pro-environment, was that his celebrated kinsman, General Winfield Scott who led the decisive battle at Vera Cruz in 1847 which deprived Mexico of a large part of its territory, a decade earlier had played a role in the removal of the Indians from the Southeastern United States, an operation that led to the tragedy that came to be known as "The Trail of Tears."

On orders from President Andrew Jackson, Scott delivered the bad news to the Cherokees in 1838, attempting to cloak the cruelest ultimatum in benevolent language. The following paragraph from Scotts' "Address to the Cherokee Nation" illustrates:

Chiefs, head-men and warriors! Will you then, by resistance, compel us to resort to arms? God forbid! Or will you, by flight, seek to hide yourselves in mountains and forests, and thus oblige us to hunt you down? Remember that, in pursuit, it may be impossible to avoid conflicts. The blood of the white man or the blood of the red man may be spilt, and, if spilt, however accidentally, it may be impossible for the discreet and humane among you, or among us, to prevent a general war and carnage. Think of this, my Cherokee brethren! I am an old warrior, and have been present at many a scene of slaughter, but spare me, I beseech you, the horror of witnessing the destruction of the Cherokees.

From 1830 to 1840, 60,000 Indians along with their African slaves and some white spouses passed through Arkansas, some going up the Arkansas River by steamboat and others on foot, horseback, and in wagon caravans across the state by various routes. That decade brought some of the coldest winters and driest summers in memory. Over 4,000 of the 15,000 Cherokees who set out for Oklahoma Territory died from starvation and exposure in the bitter cold weather. In addition to the Cherokee, there were Choctaw, Chickasaw, Seminole, and others from smaller tribes who made that heartbreaking journey.

Of course the suffering of the Indians was history, and most young folks are neither knowledgeable about nor concerned that much with history. Many are like Huck Finn who got interested in Miss. Watson's Bible stories until she let it slip that Moses had been dead a long time. At that point

Huck lost interest remarking, "I don't take no stock in dead people." Of course Bessie knew about Winfield Scott and was proud of her kinsman and his role in American history, and justifiably so. We must take care not to judge our forebears by the standards of our own time. Who among them could escape such judgment, from George Washington and Thomas Jefferson to W.S. Horton?

But there have always been a few people like Henry David Thoreau who morally and ethically stood above and apart from their times. In *Civil Disobedience* he explained how he went to jail rather than pay taxes to a government that tolerated slavery and financed the Mexican War. He was strongly opposed to the military seeing how that instrument was so often used for unjust purposes.

It became clear to me in 1984, as I interviewed townspeople and talked to life-long friends of John Allen, that it was not just the extraordinary courage and spirit he revealed in facing his devastating injury that explained the universal admiration he evoked. From the beginning, from the time Louise and Al brought the curly-haired eight-year-old from Ft. Smith to live with his Aunt Bessie, he had impressed everyone who met him. Alberta Culbertson's letter to Louise expressed a widely held view of John Allen: "No one can help but love him."

In weighing the question of nature vs. nurture, it's clear that the young John Allen possessed extraordinary potential; but if he had remained a "road boy" on the carnival circuit, if he had not been transplanted to the home place under the guidance of Aunt Bessie and gained access to the good schools of Arkadelphia and the quality friends he made there, that potential could never have blossomed as it did. The qualities he possessed, nurtured in his new environment, quickly erased any handicaps that might have resulted from his early life on the road. Certainly his classmates and teachers recognized those qualities and regarded him highly as he advanced through school. An honor student, he was elected President of his class every year from seventh grade on.

In high school his class voted on the characteristics of their fellow classmates; there can be little doubt how John Allen was viewed by his peers:

Class votes:

Smartest	*John Allen*	*Mary Sue*
Best Athlete	*Billy Gill*	*Dorothy*
Prettiest Girl	*Aletha*	
Best Looking Boy	*John Allen*	
Laziest	*Howard*	*Frances Jane*
Most Popular	*Billy Gill*	*Aletha*
Best Dressed	*John Allen*	*Carolyn Jane*
Sissy Boy	*Edward Huggs*	
Tom Boy Girl	*Dorothy*	
Best All round	*Billy Gill*	*Mary Sue*
Healthiest	*John Allen*	*Susie Jane*
Most Polite	*John Allen*	*Mary Sue*
Biggest Tease	*Billy Gill*	*Susie Jane*
Biggest Baby	*Edwin Smith*	*Susie Jane*
Best Acrobat	*Jimmie Green*	*Carolyn Jane*
Most Common Sense	*John Allen*	*Mary Sue*
Best Natured	*Billy Brown*	*Clara Lou*

Of the eleven positive categories for boys, with competition from a class of outstanding young men, John Allen got the top votes in six.

Not many boys are celebrated in their home towns while still boys, but John Allen was. My two colleagues in the English Department at Henderson State who had been classmates of his in high school were eager to provide testimonials concerning his character and accomplishments. Clarice Freeman and Bennie Jean Bledsoe said many of the girls at Arkadelphia High had crushes on John Allen and told me how he was highly regarded by all his classmates and teachers as well. They also told me a story that I heard from several others about an incident well known around town.

One summer day while John Allen and his friends were swimming and wading in the river near De Soto Bluff one of the boys stepped on a piece of glass or sharp metal in the stream and cut a severe gash in his foot. The boys were a long way from help and the injured boy was bleeding profusely, so John Allen grabbed him up in his arms, somehow got him past the bluff to the pecan bottoms where, according to all accounts, he ran with the boy across the fields to 8th Street and then all the way into town to a doctor's office, a distance of a mile and a half, most of it up hill. Now, hearing of such a feat of strength and endurance surely tests one's credulity. Whether he was able to run all the way, whether he had to stop at times to rest, whether he was assisted by some of the other boys, we can only conjecture. But what is certain is that all those who told the story gave the same account. And it is certain as well that he got the boy to a doctor. What the story reveals beyond doubt is John Allen's concern for others and the pride the community took in him.

For a brief nine years John Allen watched the seasons turn in Arkadelphia. Walking the three blocks to the river he discovered the first signs of spring in the star-flowers, henbit and dead nettle blooming along Clinton Street soon to be joined by dandelions, wild onions, clover and a myriad of humble but remarkable botanical specimens. Dogwoods and azaleas brightened the neighborhoods in April, and by May honeysuckle and privet perfumed the streets of Arkadelphia and the paths John Allen followed along the banks of the Ouachita. The white parasols of Queen Anne's lace made their appearance in June and remained till the coming of the first frost. Such seasonal changes are not the focus of a boy's attention as he goes about his pursuits, but from the periphery of his awareness they imprint his nature with an indelible sense of identity and place, a sense of belonging that a road boy could never know.

Though the country was in the depths of the Depression all the years John Allen was in school in Arkadelphia, children, as they always do, accepted the world as they found it, and their world was not without its attractions. In those days people had not yet closed themselves off in air-conditioned boxes with television and other electronic diversions; they lived more among their neighbors, in the real world not in virtual worlds. During the long hot dog-days of summer when yards around town were festooned with crepe myrtle and the ventriloquial chirr of cicadas swelled and collapsed and swelled from giant water oaks, people sought relief with funeral parlor fans and iced drinks on shady porches while the hum of the new oscillating Hunter electric fans could be heard in more and more houses. To escape the heat some people slept unafraid on screened-in porches or even on beds set up in their yards.

Before community recreational centers, city parks and public swimming pools, John Allen and Buddy Whitten and their friends found their entertainment largely outdoors. Boys played marbles and mumbly peg, spun tops, walked on stilts, flew home-made kites and played baseball in the streets. In the evenings neighborhood children would gather to play hide and seek and Red Rover; at night they would sometimes roam freely through town and hear voices floating through open windows and see families around radios listening to shows like *Amos and Andy, Lum and Abner* or *The Shadow,* families illuminated by circles of light from bare incandescent bulbs suspended from wires on the ceiling. Walking through the dark children would see lightening bugs winking among shrubbery and high in the trees and catch the lemon scent of magnolia blossoms and the sensual perfume of gardenias. For the most part boys spent their summers barefoot and shirtless, relying on nature, their friends in town, and their own imaginations and ingenuity to fill long summer days and, when the heat became unbearable, seeking relief in the shaded swimming holes of the Ouachita.

John Allen arrived in Arkadelphia two and a half decades after his nine-year-old mother made the wagon ride from Fairview with her parents the year of Halley's Comet. Then there were many horses, mules and wagons in the streets and only a few Model T's. Now there were few horses and wagons to be seen and more and better cars were parked up and down the streets, some as yet unpaved. Since Amy Horton first bought the home place in 1910 blacksmith shops had given way to filling stations and livery stables to garages, though farmers still brought their produce to town in wagons, some announcing their produce loudly, "Watermelons! Watermelons! Get your red ripe watermelons!"

On hot summer afternoons during those years John Allen and his friends, Buddy Whitten, Billy Gill East, Billy Vestal, W.S McNutt and other high school friends and members of Mr. Huddleston's Boy Scout troop, could often be heard whooping and hollering as they splashed and chased each other in the swimming hole at the bottom of Caddo Street.

On weekends when not working at the Linotype machine in the office of the *Southern Standard*, Bessie could sometimes be seen sitting on a blanket on the high bank of the river watching the boys swim below. Her straight form and stolid exterior gave no hint of the pride and vicarious pleasure she took in watching John Allen and his healthy limbed young friends sporting in the water.

Bessie was ever conscientious in watching over her prized nephew and ward. Now, in her mid-forties and having long since given up on the possibility of carrying on the Horton legacy through her own issue, she had channeled all her hopes for future family glory in the handsome, talented, affectionate and totally unaffected son of the most unlikely mother, her wayward sister, Louise. Her highest hopes for her nephew lay in the musical talent he demonstrated as a student of her cousin Elizabeth Scott Butler. Everyone who had attended her recitals had been impressed by John Allen's musical abilities and Bessie harbored in her heart the dream that he would someday bring recognition to her family as a distinguished classical pianist. She worried about his exuberant physical activities, his swimming and sports, particularly his football. She was afraid he might injure his hands and damage his prospects as a musician. So she kept a close eye on his activities.

Aunt Bessie continued to bring home news from her job at the *Southern Standard*. In 1933 while Louise and Al were traveling the country with the Barker Shows, President Roosevelt launched his New Deal and the Chicago World Fair opened with great fanfare. That same year brought news of the repeal of Prohibition, a blow to the business interest of Al Capone and countless other mobsters and bootleggers; there also appeared a short report of a fire in the German Reichstag in Berlin.

John Allen was always modest and matter-of-fact in writing to his parents about his ambitions and achievements, but it is clear that he very much enjoyed his life in Arkadelphia and that he took pleasure in facing challenges and testing himself. He wrote in May 1934 telling them, "I have been swimming about three times and the water sure is fine." The river may have been a little cool at that time but he was an avid swimmer and would be voted by his classmates the healthiest among them. He thanked his parents in the same letter for the stamps they had sent him for his stamp collection and told them he had been working on the yard for the past week and that he and Bessie had been plastering the room they had been using for a kitchen converting it into a bedroom for his Uncle Vernon and Aunt Frances. That same month the *Southern Standard* reported that less than two hundred miles due south of Arkadelphia, the notorious outlaws Bonnie and Clyde, after stopping for take-out sandwiches at a café in Gibsland, Louisiana, were waylaid eight miles out of town by a sheriff's posse that pumped 130 rifle bullets through their 1934 cream-colored Ford sedan.

The following November John Allen told his parents in a letter that he now wore a size 11 shoe.

In March of 1935 he wrote:

Buddy Whitten and I are going out for junior track. We don't expect to win any races, but it's fun and good exercise. After I run around the track once or twice and get limbered up I can bend over and put my whole hands on the ground. I'm still taking my exercises and have only three more months to go before I can get the merit badge for "Physical Development."

In the same letter he tells them he and Buddy are thinking about applying for admission to the Naval Academy at Annapolis. He says there he could get a free college education and if he discovered he didn't like the Navy he could get out after a few years. He acknowledges that getting accepted would not be easy and approaches the topic with characteristic modesty, but for those with benefit of hindsight it's clear that an honor student, Eagle Scout, class president for four years, two sport letterman, with the highest recommendations from everyone who knew him, that John Allen would have been a prime candidate for admission to the U.S. Naval Academy.

The following September John Allen wrote his parents:

I'm going out for football. We've been practicing for the last two weeks and our first game is tomorrow night at Smackover. I am playing end but don't expect to get in any games since this is my first year. We have a poor team and a hard schedule so we will be doing good if we win two or three games of the nine. It's fun going out every day for about three hours and then coming in and taking a shower. I lost a few pounds the first day but have gained it back. I weigh about 140 pounds now.

I think I'm going to like all my classes except Latin. . . .

He also told his parents the Gold Medal Carnival Shows had come through Arkadelphia and that it was well equipped with new trucks. He said it was the best show to come to Arkadelphia in a long time. Though he had happily given up his life as a road boy, he shows in this letter that he had not totally forsaken his interest in his parents' occupation and the sawdust circuit.

Thoreau says in *Walden* that hunting is good for young

Allen Frank and John Allen Adams

boys for it gets them out in the woods, but he believed as boys grow older they should seek bigger game, just as V.L. Huddleston had done when he left his guns behind and ". . . sauntered empty handed, after game/ Only the lover gauges in his sight." At fifteen John Allen felt the old calling to go in search of game and wrote his dad about the gun he owned. "What kind of gun do you have? Is it a 12 gauge, 16 gauge, or 410? I would like to have it if you don't need it."

Apparently Al gave John Allen the gun, perhaps for Christmas, for two months later, in January 1935, he wrote his parents, "I went hunting again last Saturday with Buddy Whitten. We didn't get anything. We jumped two coveys of quail but they scared me so that I forgot to pull the hammer back."

He went on in the same letter to say, "I am learning to dance pretty good. I went to a dance Friday night at Aletha Sloan's, Mr. Sloan's girl, the man Dad met at the drugstore." (The drugstore was "Sloan's Drugstore," and the girl was Aletha Sloan, the one voted "prettiest" and "most popular" in their class.) Clearly John Allen was developing social skills along with his other talents. I didn't know about Aletha when I spent time in Adams Book Store so consequently never spoke to him of her, but I wonder about his teenage relationships. Clarice Freeman told me that Mary Sue Allen, another pretty girl who was class secretary every year John Allen was president, was his sweetheart, but there were a number of his classmates who would have been proud to have had that distinction.

Years later John Allen wrote a poem which begins:

I Held Her Once

I held her once within my arms,
I felt her swift surprise of lips,

and knew that richer radius
can draw when love
encircles them.

Is this poem about Aletha, Mary Sue, or someone else?

Even though the country was in the grip of the Great Depression, for nine years John Allen led an idyllic life for a growing boy. Though he found himself in the care of a contentious and combative family, there was no ill will ever directed toward him. All members of the family loved him and, in spite of what Louise had told them about his origins, they were all proud to claim him as family. He had many friends, attended good schools with good teachers, was active in an outstanding Boy Scout Troop, pursued many hobbies, excelled academically and athletically, and was a promising piano student as well, a talent which filled Aunt Bessie with hope for his future.

Throughout these years Bessie continued entering news into the Linotype machine at the *Southern Standard*, where daily news of world events continued to cross her desk—Hitler's growing power in Germany, the Spanish Civil War, the ongoing Great Depression, ravages of the Dust Bowl, and the implementations of various New Deal programs—but on summer Saturdays she could escape the troubles of the world by accompanying John three blocks to the river, blanket in hand, where she would find a shady vantage point from which to watch her treasured ward. Bessie looked upon her part in these outings, not so much as a break from her duties, but more as an exercise of responsibility toward her sister's son. If she was to see that John Allen was properly educated and socially accomplished, she could not let him drown. Of course she could not have jumped in and saved him if he had gone under, but she could direct his strapping friends in the rescue.

But she need not have worried about him drowning. In 1936 he sent her a postcard from Scout camp in Hot Springs saying, "I am getting along fine. I got senior life saving last week. I may get a chance to be a life guard at a girl's camp, but I doubt it." John Allen could take care of himself.

Just a couple of weeks earlier Bessie had written Vernon's wife, Frances, and told her about the Centennial activities in Arkadelphia:

My Dear Frances:

. . . For the past several weeks it seems very nearly everyone in the city and county had some part in the Centennial celebration of Arkadelphia and Clark County's 100th birthday on May 15th which proved a great success. For the most part the program was planned, written and directed by Amy Jean Greene, an Arkadelphia girl, and she has been asked to present some of the best features of the pageant at the State's Centennial celebration in Little Rock in June when Roosevelt comes to speak. It has also kept John Allen busy practicing for all these things and trying to keep up with all his other school work . . .

Tomorrow is to be a big day here for all the Boy Scouts of this (Ouachita) area, and for the past few days John Allen and some of the other boys of his troop have been working on some of the contests which they have entered and are trying for first place. . . .

Bessie goes on to give the news of "two sad deaths, that of Virginia Sloan, aged 20, just finishing Henderson College this term, whose family has always been like a near relative, and that of Uncle John Butler, father of Elizabeth and Annie Laurie." She notes that Butler's death was not unexpected since he was ninety years old. But the death of the young Virginia, (the older sister of Aletha?) was indeed sad.

The highlight of John Allen's Scout experiences came the following month at the Boy Scout Jamboree when, now an Eagle Scout and one of the senior officers of Mr. Huddleston's Troop 23, he and his fellow Scouts demonstrated the skills they had been practicing and saw and heard President Franklin Roosevelt who had arrived in Hot Springs by train with his wife, Eleanor, the morning of June 10th to speak at the Arkansas Centennial celebration.

Scouting was an important part of John Allen's life growing up in Arkadelphia, but it was only one of his many interests. At that time he was an honor student who had served as president of his class for four years, editor of his class's newspaper the *Badger*, had won letters in both football and track, was recognized for his talent as a pianist, and was known and admired by the citizens of his home town. He would have one more year of high school after this one and was already making plans for his future education, seriously considering applying to the United States Naval Academy at Annapolis.

John Allen enjoyed two more months of summer vacation in Arkadelphia before school started. Then on Sunday, September 27, 1936, he wrote the following letter to his parents. It would be the last hand-written letter they would receive from him:

Dear Mother and Dad,

> School starts tomorrow morning. I am taking algebra,
> chemistry, English, and social civics. I have joined the
> glee club and am going out for football too.

> Mother, the new flour mill opens in Oct. They will
> employ twenty or thirty women to make sacks. Aunt
> Bessie thought maybe you would like to try to get a
> job. They will [pay] one cent a sack but you may have
> to get a special machine.

> Uncle Thad hopes to finish his new house [at
> Fairview] soon. It has two stories and will be a nice
> one when finished.

> I'm going to stop football at the end of this week.
> Aunt Bessie wrote you a letter last week about the
> flour mill job. Did you get it?

> We are both well and hope you are the same.

Love
John Allen

Although completely devoted to his life in Arkadelphia with Aunt
Bessie, John Allen through the years always missed his parents
and wanted them close by. This letter reveals that desire and also
shows how hard times were during the Depression. ("one cent a
sack!" And you may have to furnish your own machine!)

The letter also shows that Aunt Bessie, fearing her nephew might injure his hands, had finally persuaded him to drop football. John Allen had informed Coach George Emory of his decision, but, with a small team of only fifteen players, the coach wanted him to help the team one more time in the upcoming game against one of their toughest opponents, Malvern.

The Friday after John Allen wrote the above letter the young coach and math teacher gave a pep talk to his Badger football team outside the five-year-old high school building on 12th and Haddock (today Central Elementary) but, like the year before, Arkadelphia faced a tough schedule and the Malvern team would be one of the toughest they would face. Youthful spirits were high, however, as the team boarded the bus.

Coach Emory had made the final decision. When Arkadelphia High took the field the starting lineup would be: Dodson, Left Tackle; Donald Meador, Left Guard; Harlan Sloan, Center; Jessie Franklin, Right Guard; Woodrow Ligon, Right Tackle; John Allen Adams, Right End; Charles Moores, Quarterback; William Winburn, Left Halfback; Johnny Hall, Right Halfback; Weldon Lookadoo, Fullback.

Professor Alford's all-male band and the Badger yell leaders would accompany the team to give support. The Pep Squad girls, Carolyn Jane Carpenter and Ann Clark wore white calf-length dresses emblazoned with "A.H.S. Badgers" in red on the front, and the boys, Dick McFarland, Roy Mitchell, and John Allen's best friend Floyd "Buddy" Whitten, wore white pants and shoes and red shirts with white ties.

And there were many other supporters. Aletha Sloan, Mary Sue Allen, Billy Vestal, Billy Gill East, W.S McNutt, and a host of John Allen's friends and Arkadelphia High fans, some in sweaters decorated with big red "A's," piled into busses and automobiles and joined the procession up Highway 67 to Malvern in high spirits, following the Old Military Road route General Fredrick Steele and his Union forces marched down in the spring of 1864 when John Allen's great grandfather and thousands of other Confederate soldiers under the command of General Price were bivouacked and dug in up and down the Ouachita River waiting for the Yankees to make their appearance.

* * *

CHAPTER 7

Broken Promise

—————————◾️—————————

Southern Standard, Thursday October 8, 1936

A Popular Boy Is Badly Injured
John Allen Adams Had His Neck Broken
In football Game at Malvern

*Our entire city has been concerned this week as to the out-
come of injuries sustained by John Allen Adams in a high
school football game at Malvern on last Friday night. He
was taken to the Baptist Hospital in Memphis on Saturday
morning and an operation was performed on him on Monday
afternoon but no positive assurance has been received here as
to the beneficial results of the operation.*

*John Allen, a 17-year-old student of the Arkadelphia High
School was playing end for his team against the Malvern
High School team. Running interference, he was knocked
down when a number of players from each team came together. While he retained his mental faculties he was unable
to move a limb and was brought to the Ross Hospital in this
city, by the Harris ambulance, and it was found that he
was totally paralyzed from the neck down. An x-ray exam*

163

at Memphis showed that the sixth vertebra of his spine was dislocated. The sixth vertebra is located about even with a man's collar button. Had the fracture been just a little higher it would have been instant death.

John Allen was taken to Memphis in the ambulance by Alva Harris, and was accompanied by his aunt, Miss Bessie Horton; his coach George Emory, and Mr. Harris' son, Robert. The Big Brothers organization of this city has assumed responsibility for the treatment of John Allen, and everything possible will be done to save his life and restore him to usefulness. He is one of the most deservedly popular students of the high school and has always carried his end of the school activities. He is an Eagle Scout. For the past several years he has been making his home with his aunt, Miss Bessie Horton. His father, Mr. Adams and Mrs. Adams were in Mississippi when the accident happened, and arrived here after the boy had been taken to Memphis; they went there to be with him.

The football team took the field with their pep squad cheering them on with some new yells and routines they had coordinated with the Arkadelphia High School Band. But their supporters, as is always the case in an out-of-town game, were outnumbered by those cheering for the home team, and the Badger players, with only three substitutes, faced a grueling challenge from the larger and more powerful Malvern team.

At some point in the one-sided game the quarterback, Charles Moores, called a running play around right end. When the physically dominating defense stopped the play at the line, boys from both teams cascaded together into a pileup where John Allen, who had been running interference, found himself on the ground in a sitting position when a player, charging from behind, landed on his back snapping his head forward and leaving him lying unmoving on the ground. The blow had forced the sixth cervical vertebra violently forward severing forever the communication between John Allen's head and his body leaving the seventeen-year-old crumpled on the ground like a marionette with its controlling strings cut.

When such a calamity strikes there is always a delay, a lag of time before the minds of the witnesses can begin to comprehend the seriousness of what has happened. John Allen himself would have been the most surprised of all lying there on the ground helpless, struggling to breathe, seeing and hearing Coach Emory and his teammates gathered round, bending over talking to him, having lost all feeling in his body as though someone had flipped a switch.

His coach and those adults in attendance were not prepared for such a catastrophic accident, and in the confusion and uncertainty of the situation John Allen was loaded into an ambulance and taken back to the hospital at Arkadelphia rather than on to Little Rock or Memphis where there were better facilities for treating spinal cord injuries. Presumably there were those present who knew the first aid procedures John Allen learned in the Scouts, the importance in such cases of keeping the head and spine immobile while transporting the injured.

By the next morning in Arkadelphia the magnitude of the situation had taken hold and word of John Allen's injury began to spread throughout the town. Al and Louise Adams had been contacted in Mississippi where they were traveling with a carnival and were now headed for Arkansas to be with their son. All other family members were notified as well.

Aunt Bessie's worst fears had become a nightmare. It seemed her nephew had lost not just the use of his hands, but of his whole body; there also appeared the real possibility that the young man recently voted healthiest by his classmates would not survive his injury. Arkadelphia doctors determined that the hospital at Memphis offered the best facilities for treating John Allen, so Saturday morning he was once more placed aboard an ambulance, this time for the two hundred mile journey to Memphis; he would be accompanied this time by his Aunt Bessie and Coach Emory.

The days and weeks following John Allen's injury were the darkest and most turbulent in the history of the Hortons at the home place. The battle lines between the three sisters formed during the conflict and breakup of their parents' marriage over twenty years earlier had become habitual, and now with the tragedy that had befallen John Allen, the one common object of all their love, the old rivalries came to life with a new passion.

To be sure all three would have presented a grateful and respectable front to the many townspeople who generously came forward to offer support for John Allen—his teachers, schoolmates, the churches, the Boy Scouts, the Big Brothers—virtually the whole town. But the pain the sisters felt required release, an outlet, so, in keeping with their long-standing love/hate relationships, they fell back on their default response—they blamed one another for the tragedy.

Louise as always was at a disadvantage in dealing with her strong-willed older sisters, yet ironically she was the one who had provided not only herself but her two sisters the one best thing in their lives—John Allen. Now he lay broken in a Memphis hospital where the question quickly changed from "will he regain movement in his body?" to "will he live?" There's no way to know what desperate consultations and emotional clashes took place in Memphis and back at the home place those two winters Louise and Bessie were together struggling to keep John Allen alive. But that arrangement between the two sisters was doomed as can be seen in the following letter Gertrude wrote to Louise:

Dear Louise:

I cannot sleep for worrying about the condition there. The friction between you and Bess is crucifying John Allen.

You claim him and she claims him and each of you are [sic] green with jealousy. One of you will have to give up. Let's suppose she gives up and says, "he is yours, take him." What could you do for him? Nothing.

Let's suppose you give up and say, "he is yours, take him." What can she do for him? Everything.

Then show your love for him by giving up.

Real love is self-sacrificing, and you will gladly sacrifice yourself for him if you love him.

If you two could get along smoothly, it is best for you to be there, but if you are going to be fighting all the time, it is better you separate. If it comes to a showdown, give up to her and go away. Tell John Allen you have found a job and feel you ought to go to work and make some money to help him. He will understand and love you all the more for it.

Louise, do help to give him peace these last days of his life, I beg you.

G-

P.S. I will lend you $10.00 if you decide to go.

Louise would have been justified to feel a bit suspicious of this advice coming from the sister who had been instrumental in having her committed to a lunatic asylum when she was fifteen, even though the letter concluded with the generous offer of a ten dollar "loan."

Years later two notes were written on the back of the above letter. The first reads: "Louise carried this in her hand bag from the time she received it until she died. All this time I shared every penny we could spare until her demands became too great. B.H." (This note apparently written by Bessie)

The second note reads: "This is a falsehood and you know it. I know neither of us ever thought of such a thing. What you were trying to do was to make Mr. Adams and Louise take John Allen away from her [Bessie] and so you stirred up one of your great jealousy schemes." (These remarks likely written for Gertrude by Vernon.)

Three years earlier, during the depths of the Depression, Gertrude had written to Bessie complaining of Louise and the financial hard times:

Louise came in on me again March 2 and like a fool I gave her every cent of cash I had. She hit me for $15.00 but I only had ten and gave it to her. She came in boo hooing saying Al, that man she lives with, was sick and would die if I did not give her some money and I think it was all a gag but I let her have my last cent anyway and now I have no money for gasoline or lunches or anything. . . .I will have to do without lunches and walk to school until I can get some money. I hate Louise. What has she ever done for me? What will she ever do for me? Nothing but try to drag me down and cause me all the misery she can.

Recriminations from the two older Horton sisters proved to be a life-long enterprise. In 1954 Bessie wrote to Gertrude about the cruel letter she had written to Louise eighteen years earlier:

This poison letter of yours explains why Louise treated me as she did after John Allen's injury. It is enough to make anyone insane under such prevailing conditions. You are the one who made her leave home, the one who would not let me get the store and filling station* in operation again so they could stay here and help care for John Allen and with making a living and being independent. It was you who told her I was the cause of John Allen's injury, and it was all I could do to keep her from committing suicide when we came home from Memphis that horrible night. It all came to light the last winter she spent here, so I told her the boy you hired to dig the dirt on the west side of the house was totally paralyzed from sunstroke after he left here that evening and died—and that is what you wanted to make John Allen do to earn his keep—so you said, and got angry because I did not want him to do it. I knew it would kill him. That clay was like flint. It made sparks when those fellows struck it with a pick, and that 1936 sun was terrific. When those fellows stopped for a minute of rest you brought them ice water and put them to work again. This is what the other man told me when he came over to ask about John Allen and what we were doing about caring for bed sores.

Bess

*(When I first arrived in Arkadelphia there was an old-fashioned filling station, long abandoned, alongside the home place on 3rd Street. That was the one referred to above.)

The problems John Allen faced in learning to live with paralysis were made much more difficult because of the ongoing conflicts between the Horton sisters. In November 1943, after six years of living in the middle family wars, the twenty-three-year-old nephew wrote his uncle Vernon about troubles at the home place. Vernon, who at that time was working at the Johns Hopkins University Laboratory of Applied Physics on the top-secret program that produced the proximity fuse, wrote back thanking John Allen for his "very excellent letter" which he said he "enjoyed greatly," and tells him, "you are making good headway in understanding (Bessie and Gertrude) yourself." Then he goes on to explain,

The basic trouble with our family is that our mother and father were never happy together because of the things they said and did to each other in the first part of their marriage. The children were brought into the world by them and they were not emotionally well adjusted to provide the feeling of emotional security for the production of normal happy children. The troubles you are witnessing now are but the inherited continuation of the emotional discords of our parents when we were children in our impressionable years. Our little souls were warped by the discord existing between our parents.

While I can understand the agony you must be faced with at times, my advice to you is to seek to rise above emotional involvement by assuming an attitude of sympathetic interest in the . . . causes of their unhappiness. Face the situation as a physician does a patient. You will learn much of the deeper motives of human nature and at the same time make both your life and theirs happier.

Vernon goes on in some detail in the letter recommending a number of books on psychology and psychiatry from such authors as Karl Menninger, Will Durant, and Sigmund Freud.

He concludes his letter with the comment, "Someday the work we are doing here (at Johns Hopkins) will make history." (The proximity fuse he was working on enabled bombs to detonate above ground or when approaching or passing a target rather than on impact thus converting near misses to hits and wreaking much greater damage. It was a major weapons development of World War II.)

In early 1954 when Bessie was mistakenly diagnosed with tuberculosis and told she must go to the sanatorium at Boonville she wrote the following note at the bottom of Vernon's letter:

Dear Vernon:

It is being my painful task to destroy the old letters before going to Boonville because I don't know whether I will ever come back and I don't want to leave them for those of so much curiosity to read. A few of interest I am saving. I am saving this one of yours to John Allen and I am glad you wrote to him because it is just as I have tried to explain to him but you did it so much better and gave him so much reference.— This is a fine letter and I think it would help him to read it again sometime. Thank you. Bess

As the days and weeks passed after that tragic football game it came as a surprise to many that John Allen did not die, and during the time he was struggling to survive the response from the citizens of Arkadelphia was remarkable. The Big Brothers organization under the leadership of a life-long friend and supporter, B.W. McCormick, assumed responsibility for all medical expenses by having one hundred members pledge one dollar a month for his care, and the churches and his teachers and fellow students surrounded John Allen with love and support. The financial commitment of Arkadelphia to the injured football player was such that his Aunt Bessie was able to leave her job at the *Southern Standard* and devote her full time to caring for her nephew.

Before the 1930's the life expectancy for quadriplegics was less than three years. It was not uncommon for those unfortunates to be dumped in warehouse-like wards where they would quickly succumb to bedsores, internal infections, and respiratory failure. Such a fate could easily have befallen John Allen had it not been for Aunt Bessie's strength and determination, her absolute commitment to his care. John Allen survived because of Bessie's indomitable love for him.

Louise heeded Gertrude's cruel injunction and showed her love for John Allen by leaving Arkadelphia after that second winter and rejoining Al on the road. In March, still fearing he might die at any time, she mailed Bessie an identification card with John Allen's burial policy on it and followed that with a series of letters to her son pouring out her maternal love and offering her heartbreakingly cheerful Madam Justina advice:

May 1938, Clinton, IL

You have brought so much happiness to us and everyone else and I want to tell you I'm thankful to God just to have you to call son. You know you say "mother" so grand you make me feel air [sic] to all of life's riches. . . .

July 1938, Bridgeport,
IL

My Darling Boy:—

Just the thought of you and knowing you are coming over the hill makes life worth the living for me. You bring me all the joys of life to know you love me and I'm loving you. Tho miles may part us in our hearts we will never be parted. So keep your chin up and remember we love you with all our hearts. . . .People can't be kind enough to one another so let's be kind and tolerant as we go through life. And tho the way looks dark at times, just keep in mind that there is never a cloud so dark but it has a silver lining, and the silver will come through soon for us all if we just wait. So let's march on with a smile looking for good and it will come to us. Keep that thought in mind, and I'll be seeing you this fall. So I'm loving you always with love hugs & kisses, to our darling.

Mother and Daddy

December 1938, Pine Bluff, AR

. . .I'm loving you with all my heart, so keep your chin up. Hope this finds you and Bessie well. . . .

February 1939, Natchez, MS

Hope this finds you and all O.K. Just keep pulling, never give up, there's hope, hope and faith is what makes life worth living. . .

Do you know I've got a hunch that this year is going to be good to the Adams family. You are going to improve greatly and with that I'll be happy, and we are going to look for the breaks so you keep your chin up and come on up the hill o' health for you can do it. . . .Let's play our hunch and pull together so here's love to you and Aunt Bessie.

Mother and Daddy

Many people shared Louise and Al's grief. One of the more touching expressions came from John Allen's third cousin and piano teacher, Elizabeth Scott Butler, who wrote him three months after the accident:

January 21, 1937
Dear John:

. . . As I talk to you—to myself—and think about you so much maybe you might have some curiosity to hear about it. It runs something like this:

"Good morning John."

The response I get is the famous grin accompanied by, "Good morning Cousin Elizabeth."

I like to go over that little greeting you and I have enacted innumerable times when you came to your lessons. You didn't suspect you had given so much pleasure did you?

To me some of the most beautiful things in life are those little things; they keep coming back to cheer me and when I sum them up I find they amount to a contentment and a gaiety in my heart that is my most precious possession.

We can't tell many people these deep down little secrets in our hearts because they wouldn't understand—I think you will because I think you have this same thing too.

When you are as old as I am it will make up for your youth that has passed. . . .

Less than two months after he was injured Aunt Gertrude wrote from Little Rock where she was teaching:

I thought of you all night and wondered if you were getting a good rest. I know how terrible it is to be bunged up and all my sympathy goes out to you. I pray all the time that you will soon be up again. But while you are convalescing, I want you to remember that Aunt Gertrude loves you and is pulling for you and will do anything she can do to help you.

She included a check with the letter and signed, "Lots of Love, Aunt Gertrude." When I interviewed the ninety-six-year-old Gertrude Horton King in 1984 after John Allen's death, she told me he had called her every day to tell her he loved her.

In the days, weeks and months following John Allen's injury, Bessie became an expert in quadriplegic care. She had had some experience in caring for the disabled when she tended to Horace after his back was broken while working at Eagle Mills Lumber Company, but he was left with movement in much of his body and his condition improved over time enabling him to walk on crutches. John Allen, on the other hand, retained only very slight movement in his shoulders and arms while the rest of his body was completely paralyzed, and it became increasingly clear as time went by that he would not be regaining any control or feeling in his body.

Handling a completely paralyzed person is the most difficult challenge for a caregiver since there is no way the patient can assist physically in his own care. When the mind is clear, however, as it was in John Allen's case, when the patient is alert and intelligent and does not succumb to depression and despair, he can contribute a great deal to his own care by learning everything about his condition and providing verbal guidance to those attending him. That was the case with John Allen throughout his life as I learned in his book store when he would sometimes ask me to perform small tasks for him. He had such a calm and pleasant way about him he could make you feel privileged to be of some assistance.

Of course Bessie and others who attended to John Allen had to quickly get past any sense of modesty or squeamishness in taking care of his physical needs. Since his bowels and bladder as well as his limbs were paralyzed it was necessary to replace those lost functions with enemas and catheters. He had to be bathed carefully and repositioned frequently to prevent bed sores. Lifting and moving him before there were any mechanical assists would have been a strenuous challenge and

Bessie would have required strong arms to help. Fortunately there were always friends around, and John Allen's remarkably calm disposition and his careful attention to detail would have been a great help in all such operations. Still, more than anyone he understood what he had lost, and he looked at his condition squarely as he did everything in life, and without a trace of self pity:

Paralyzed

When they turn him on his side
and his cheek is pressed to the pillow
life's low throbbing still sounds
in his ear—the blood jetting out
and the valve slamming shut.
And still—warm in its shell,
like a crab sconced in its whelk—
his brain, surveying a battlefield
stinking of sweat and urine
and the drainage of sores,
sends orders to outposts now fallen.

Where has it gone, all the motion and ease,
when he ran through a supple-limbed world?
He tires of the wallpaper's pattern
and the door's varnished grain
peeled from the fir's lopped trunk;
he closes his eyes to remember
the watery weaving of trees
when they weightlessly danced
under fathomless seas.

So far as I can tell John Allen, after the accident, spent little time reflecting on what could have been, on what his life might have been like had he not been injured; but others may speculate. The one time he had shared future possibilities with his parents was when he wrote telling them he and Buddy Whitten were thinking of applying for admission to the U.S. Naval Academy, not because he had a strong desire for a military career, but because it would be a way to get a free college education. Clearly at that time, however, he had no anti-military feelings. It was, after all, peacetime and the Great War his father Al and his uncle Thad had served in was "the war to end all wars."

If he had not been injured and had applied to Annapolis in all likelihood with his outstanding record he would have been accepted. If he had entered in 1938 he would have been a senior at the Naval Academy when the Japanese bombed Pearl Harbor and would have heard President Roosevelt, who had spoken at the Arkansas Centennial in Hot Springs five years earlier, denounce over the radio that attack, famously calling Sunday, December 7, 1941, "a date that will live in infamy." He would have been commissioned shortly after the outbreak of World War II and joined his many classmates who fought the Axis powers doing their part to save the world from fascist tyranny. All of the physically able boys he had gone to school with, who served with him in Mr. Huddleston's Boy Scout Troop 23, boys he hiked with and swam with in the great swimming holes of the Ouachita River, heeded the call.

Ever since his injury John Allen's classmates had continued to come by and see him including those now in the armed services. He wrote his mother March 23, 1943:

. . .Buddy Whitten and his wife came to see me last week. He was home on leave from maneuvers in northern Louisiana. I also saw Billy Gill. He has gone to Fort Bennings, Georgia for three months' training.

So far the rationing hasn't hurt us at all. We don't eat much meat, so I think the meat, butter and fats ration will be plenty for us too.

On May 5th he wrote:

. . . I have been sitting in the yard every afternoon until dark. The chinaberry tree in the corner of the front yard is blooming now and is very pretty.

Buddy will be home next week, and Mary Sue [Allen] will be here the last of this week. So I guess I'll get to see them both in a few days.

Mary Sue, according to Clarice Freeman, was John Allen's sweetheart when he was injured, and now eight years later she and his best friend Buddy Whitten are coming to visit. She was now married to Lt. John Riggins, a graduate of Henderson College where she also attended before transferring to the University of Arkansas. It is characteristic of John Allen that he was able to channel and transform the emotions of their youthful romance into a deep and lasting platonic friendship while releasing Mary Sue from any feelings of obligation she might have had.

It is also a mark of the caliber of John Allen's friends that so many of them served as officers in that conflict. Some of those closest to him fought in major campaigns of the war. Three of them—Johnny Hall, the right halfback for Arkadelphia High the night John Allen was injured; Billy Gill East, voted best athlete and most popular; and Buddy Whitten, member of the Arkadelphia High Pep Squad and John Allen's closest friend—took part in the greatest military operation in the history of warfare—the Normandy invasion on D-Day, the 6th of June 1944. All three became casualties of that battle within eight days of one another. 1st Lieutenant Billy Gill East was wounded on the 26th of June; Captain William "Buddy" Whitten who landed at Utah Beach was wounded on the 3rd of July; and 2nd Lieutenant John Hall was killed in action the following day, Independence Day.

In his twenty-eight days of combat Buddy Whitten saw a lot. He wrote home:

Yesterday I borrowed a tin wash tub from a French dame, put some water in it and took it out in a big grassy field and had a bath, the first one since June 4. While I was bathing a German Me-109 came over me so low I could have reached up and hit him with a fishing pole. He didn't shoot as there were two of our beautiful P 51's on his tail giving him just a little bit of hell.

John Allen's former hunting buddy wrote his wife Manie Louise on the 27th of June:

I don't believe I'll go hunting any more. I've heard all the guns I want to hear. When Tommy asks me to take him down to the beach on the Fourth of July to watch firecrackers, I'll just tell him to run along by himself, as Daddy has seen all the fireworks before. I've also camped out all I want to.

He tells of the terrors of the German flat-trajectory rifled cannons: . . . the "bloomin' 88's are the things that scare everybody. They don't give a guy any warning whatever, just Wham!" Then Whitten adds:

The planes, though, are worse. Thank God they don't have many of them. One of them strafed and bombed us one night just at dark and honestly it sounded like the world was coming to an end. I may live to be 100 but I'll never forget the helpless feeling when we heard him start his dive. A hole doesn't seem to help much when they are coming straight down.

War isn't all like that, though. For a few days things will be hot as a firecracker and then there are a few days of not doing anything much. . . .

The terrible part of the war is the waste of life and property. I probably won't be writing you any more letters telling you what war is like. I just don't like to talk about it. After I get home I'll tell you all I

know, if you want. Anybody else can come over here
and see for themselves if they're curious.

I don't want to forget all about war when this is over.
If I did forget I wouldn't have gained a thing by being here.

Buddy Whitten didn't get many more chances to write home;
four days after he wrote the above words he was wounded in
the battle for Cherbourg.

By this time John Allen and Bessie were thoroughly
settled into their daily routine. While he had been totally
bed-bound for a long time after his injury, he was now able
to sit in a wheelchair and spend some time in good weather
sitting outside at the home place. The two of them, as did
everyone in Arkadelphia, kept up with the news of the war
by reading the *Southern Standard,* the *Daily Siftings* and the
Arkansas Gazette, and listening to reporters like Gabriel
Heatter, Eric Sevareid, and Edward R. Murrow on the radio.
Mrs. East, Billy Gill's mother, told John in August that her
son's wounded arm was healing well in England and that he
was now in the Army Air Force.

If John Allen had not been injured he almost certainly
would have served in the war as an officer, whether Navy or
not. Considering the character traits he exhibited throughout
his life it's safe to say that he would have been an able and
courageous leader of men. He would certainly have been
cool under fire for he demonstrated that ability as the calm
center of many Horton family storms. As it was, rather than
commanding forces in the field, he employed his tactical and
strategic skills in mediating family battles and guiding Aunt

Bessie and others who attended him in the care of his non-functioning body.

I am reminded of Ralph Waldo Emerson's tribute to Henry David Thoreau. In his essay and eulogy he laments his friend's unrealized potential. He says that Thoreau with his talent "seemed born for great enterprise and for command; and I so much regret the loss of his rare powers of action, that I cannot help counting it a fault in him that he had no ambition. Wanting this, instead of engineering for all America, he was the captain of a huckleberry-party."

What limited John Allen's potential was not a lack of ambition, but an accident. And when that accident closed off many possibilities for him, drawing upon another of Emerson's ideas explored in his essay, "Compensation," John Allen compensated for that loss by tapping deep reservoirs of spiritual strength, grace and talent, resources which enabled him to live a remarkably creative and useful life in spite of his handicap.

While the Allied forces were pushing toward Hitler's citadel in Berlin, Louise Adams was making her last carnival tour as a mitt reader, a tour which would come to its sad end at the Goddard Hotel in Hot Springs. She and Al had separated by this time but remained on friendly terms. In Arkadelphia John Allen, though still restricted to bed and wheelchair at the home place, had made considerable progress both in expanding his intellectual horizons and finding ways to provide for himself financially.

That progress was made with the help of family and many friends. Visiting shut-ins is not high on the list of favorite pastimes, even though we know how important it is. But in John Allen's case it was different. He seemed always surrounded by friends and well-wishers. People loved to visit him, to be welcomed by his warm smile and enjoy his peaceful and thoughtful conversation. In those days it was easy to see how he had been voted best-looking boy by his classmates. Even from his wheelchair he radiated such warmth that the eight-year-old Amy Thompson dreamed of marrying John Allen when she grew up so she could take care of him.

But for the rest of her life Aunt Bessie would be the one to take care of John Allen, with daily liftings, turnings, catheters, enemas, baths, positioning in his chair, getting him out of and into bed. After his injury and after the last hope for any recovery of movement died, what did she see when she looked at him lying in bed? She saw broken promise. She saw her beautiful young man, every muscle, sinew and bone in place, lying perfectly still, a strapping handsome marionette with cut strings.

For John Allen, what was it like to sleep so still, so straight, never able to turn in bed? Perhaps his aunt sometimes studied him in his sleep; perhaps she noticed the rapid movement of his eyes under his lids. What were his dreams? Did he, in the flickering images of night, become once more the supple-limbed youth running down the hill on Caddo Street with his friends to the Ouachita, did he again swim with Buddy Whitten, Billy Gill East, W.S. McNutt below De Soto Bluff, did he sit around campfires in the shade of dark and gloomy pine trees with his fellow scouts from Troop 23 transfixed by the stories of Mr. Huddleston? How painful it must have been to awaken from such dreams.

185

John Allen on the porch of the Home Place
with reading material

* * *

CHAPTER 8

Finding His Way in a Changed World

———————■———————

From the moment the seventeen-year-old John Allen found himself lying on the ground struggling to breathe, looking up into the concerned faces of Coach Emory, Charles Moores, Johnny Hall and his other teammates bending over him, his world was forever changed. He was aware that hands were lifting him, placing him on a stretcher and carrying him to the ambulance because he could see the ground drop away and move under him, but he could not feel the hands that lifted him and could not even feel the weight of his own body lying on the stretcher. He discovered then that the most desperate feeling in the world is to have no feeling at all.

He would still have been struggling to understand what had happened to him the following day during the long ambulance ride to Memphis with Coach Emory and Aunt Bessie and during the consultations with the doctors there. Louise, Al, Bessie, Gertrude and all family and friends gathered round would have clung to the hope that John Allen could be fixed, that somehow surgeons could repair the damage and return their healthy and beautiful young man to them. But the surgeons surely had no such illusions knowing well the prognoses for spinal cord injuries.

John Allen of necessity had become a passive observer of the activities that surrounded him, but he was a perceptive observer. The concerned but smiling faces and cheerful voices family and friends presented to him at the hospital could not completely conceal the anguish expressed in the waiting room and hallway conferences and exchanges that took place away from his hearing before they entered his room. But he needed their encouraging words. He very much needed to believe he would regain feeling in his body—that he would be able to walk again. So when he was rolled into the operating room he too had hope.

Days, weeks and months were to pass in a swirl of faces and voices—family, friends, doctors, nurses—before resignation set in. Finally, however, all had to accept the bitter truth—John Allen was a quadriplegic. Feeling and movement would not be returning to his body. Hope springs eternal but it dies hard.

At least John Allen didn't die. But what a choice—death or a lifetime of paralysis! We all have heard someone say and perhaps have felt ourselves that death would be preferable to a life of total paralysis, of complete dependence on others. Of course such decisions are easily made when we are not the injured. For many who suffered severe spinal cord injuries in the 1930's, however, the question was moot because there were no options; once the damage was done in most cases death soon followed.

Such a fate would likely have befallen John Allen had it not been for one person, his Aunt Bessie. She refused to let him die. She was not willing to let go of the dreams she had for him. He would not be a classical pianist, but he was still the possessor of what she perceived to be the Horton family virtues. In the troubled history of her family there had been only one other man she had loved without reservation—W.S. Horton, the patriarch who had taught her the names of the planets and constellations, the Forty-Niner, the Confederate hero, the Lord of Fairview Plantation which for the young Bessie and her sister Gertrude had been their childhood paradise. Her grandfather was gone, but Bessie was determined to hold on to John Allen.

None of this is to say that John Allen's parents weren't equally committed to caring for their son. Louise remained in Arkadelphia for two winters to be near John Allen and help care for him, but Gertrude's letter to her, though brutal, gives some idea of how that arrangement went. All three sisters when separated by some distance could at times be civil to one another and considerate and even loving, but when they found themselves in close proximity for any length of time the old fault lines quickly reappeared and battles from twenty years earlier picked up where they left off. As it turned out Louise was neither constitutionally nor financially able to be of much help, so, from necessity, the responsibility for caring for John Allen fell upon the willing shoulders of her sister Bessie.

John Allen's father who clearly loved his son was devastated by the tragedy, but he proved once more on this occasion to be a kindly though ineffectual presence. Vernon told me Al was a warm and likeable, gentlemanly fellow who never discovered the knack for making money so he was unable to offer much material support to Aunt Bessie. He did, however, write a heart-felt letter to the Arkadelphia newspaper thanking the Big Brothers organization and all the citizens who had been so supportive and helpful to his son.

By the spring of 1938, with Al and Louise back on the road, Bessie's dedicated care for her nephew had greatly improved his chances for survival. So with the possibility that John Allen might now have a future the question became what kind of future would be possible. Fortunately the accident that had taken away command of his body below the sixth cervical vertebrae had left his mind and character intact.

The adjustment to his new condition was of course neither quick nor easy. But as hope for recovery faded, John Allen surveyed his circumstances and began to consider his possibilities. The drive to explore his surroundings and develop the abilities that he had demonstrated over the past nine years had not been extinguished by the accident, but now the scope of his activities were cruelly restricted. He would no longer be able to write his parents with news of his physical milestones—his swimming and lifesaving skills, his football workouts, his development as a runner, his ability to stand flat footed and place both palms on the ground. In fact, though he was less than two years away from graduation, he would no longer be able to attend school at all. Fortunately, however, he was the beneficiary of the solid education he had so far received from the Arkadelphia school system, and the network of friends and mentors he had developed through the years would provide him a strong base of support for the challenges he now faced.

So far as I can tell John Allen was never afflicted greatly with depression. But it's impossible to imagine how anyone suffering such a devastating injury would not undergo a period of bleak despondency. Vernon told me that after his nephew was injured he attempted to console him by reminding him that his most remarkable asset, his mind—his character and creative intelligence—had survived the accident. Surely John Allen would have heard similar words of consolation and encouragement from many others at that time, words he would have acknowledged in his now weakened voice and with a nod of his head.

If he did go through a period of despondency it was not permitted to last. Surrounded by family and friends, former classmates and teachers, the atmosphere around his bed was most often warm and cheerful. The team quarterback, William Winburn and his older sister, Martha, and all his other football teammates came by to visit. Other close friends, such as Billy Gill East, Billy Vestal, Aletha Sloan, Mary Sue Allen, W.S McNutt, were frequent visitors, as well as his best friend Buddy Whitten. A student leader throughout his school years, John Allen would have been eager to keep up with the news from his classmates and teachers, just as they would have been eager to keep him informed. Furthermore, his teachers were determined to see that his education did not stop at the beginning of his junior year. One of those most dedicated to that end was his history teacher, Amy Jean Greene.

I became aware of Miss Greene shortly after arriving in Arkadelphia around the time I first met John Allen, but I had no idea then of their connection or any knowledge of her history. One day a colleague called my attention to an impressive older lady as she made her way toward Arkansas Hall on the Henderson campus and identified her as Amy Jean Greene. The erect and stately woman attracted attention in her long dress and broad-brimmed hat as she promenaded down the walk wielding with authority her long cane, an accessory which seemed to serve as much for style as for support. She appeared somewhat theatrical in her dress and demeanor as might be expected from someone who had written over one hundred plays and sketches for various occasions over the past four decades. It was she who had written the dramatic program for Arkadelphia's Centennial, the one presented at the state ceremonies in Little Rock thirty-five years earlier when John Allen made Eagle Scout and President Roosevelt visited and spoke in Hot Springs.

By the time I first saw her Amy Jean Greene was something of a celebrity on the Henderson campus. She had been a student there in 1927 when John Allen arrived in Arkadelphia and one year later she was one of several student leaders, including the future distinguished historian, C. Vann Woodward, who spoke out against the autocratic policies of President Clifford Hornaday and managed to bring about positive changes on campus. In one of his letters Vernon tells John Allen that he had been a classmate of Amy Jean and that for a while he had a secret crush on her.

Following graduation in 1929 Miss Greene began teaching at Arkadelphia High School where she taught up to the end of World War II. In 1944 she received her Master's in education from the University of Arkansas and because of her solid reputation in the Arkadelphia school system, Henderson added her to its faculty in 1945. She continued pursuing graduate studies during the summers—American University in Washington D.C., 1949, University of Florida, 1950, and the University of Arkansas, 1953. Over the years she held many high offices in both state and national educational and professional associations and was selected Arkansas Woman of the year in 1963. She taught at Henderson up to the time she retired as associate professor of education in 1971. At that time the Henderson "Alumni Association established a $10,000 endowment scholarship in her honor, the largest in the institution's history" (Hall, 159).

Whether or not future generations will realize it, Amy Jean Greene is now a permanent part of the Henderson State tradition by virtue of serving as a founding advisor to "Heart and Key," the service society of the school and by inaugurating the "Pine Tree Speech," still a key element of Freshman Orientation at Henderson. She was in her teaching days on campus widely recognized as "the spirit of Henderson State College."

Miss Greene along with her cousin Martha Greene were frequent visitors to the young stricken John Allen bringing gifts of food, flowers, and books. Once he became able to sit he was provided a wheelchair with a platform for reading material, and since he was left with some movement in his arms and hands he soon learned to turn the pages and thus occupy his time doing one of the things he had always enjoyed—reading.

Other teachers also came visiting and brought lessons and learning materials and spent time talking to John Allen about subjects of mutual interest. Mr. Huddleston was a frequent visitor as was coach and math teacher Mr. Emory. In addition there were Mrs. Thomas, English and Dramatics teacher, and Mrs. Clark, also an English teacher, all willing and eager to help. Family members as well, Uncle Vernon and Aunt Gertrude in particular, contributed to John Allen's education, but principally it was the ever-present Aunt Bessie who, though having missed her own opportunity for a college education, was certainly articulate and well-read even though mightily opinionated. She was the day-to-day facilitator of John Allen's home place curriculum.

All of these people and more were helpful in providing John Allen with good books and showing him the way to various portals of knowledge, but from his still place he would open the gates himself and find his own way to some of life's great questions. But what most immediately drove him to read and explore was his desire to understand as best he could the world and his place in it and to discover, even with his now restricted abilities, those things that he still could do and should do with his life.

He says in the "Afterword" of *I Walk Toward the Sound of My Days*,

> When my neck was broken, I was provided a new perspective, several nagging questions, and an uncommon amount of leisure. Through some compulsion I kept beating my head against these questions, and while I am unable to report any progress toward answers, I have learned to live with the questions. They stand there, solid, landmarks in my life. In some strange way, my long engagement with these questions has been enriching and has produced some of the poems.

One of the first questions that must have arisen in John Allen's mind was why such a terrible thing had happened to him. We have all heard and perhaps thought ourselves when we have seen victims of genetic tangles or unfortunate accidents,

"There but for the grace of God . . ." without really considering the afflicted person, without reflecting on what divine
comfort he can find to ease his suffering. Why would God's
grace smile on me and not that poor victim of misfortune?
How could John Allen reconcile what had happened to him
with such a facile and false idea knowing that, like Job, he was
himself a good person? Why good people suffer is a question older than Job and one for which there has never been a
satisfactory theological answer.

And there were other eternal and unanswerable questions
that occupied the young John Allen—the related question
of evil, for example. If God is omnipotent and good, how
can evil exist? John Milton wrote a beautiful and powerful
Christian epic in an attempt "to justify god's ways to man,"
but while *Paradise Lost* is edifying and entertaining, unless we
are willing to accept a competing evil power that God cannot
or will not destroy, it leaves the question of evil unanswered.
And where did that evil power come from?

Another theological paradox is the problem of God's fore-
knowledge and man's free will. If God is omniscient he must
know the future, and if the future is known or knowable,
the future is fixed leaving no room for man's free will. This
straightforward logical proposition in part led the Calvinists
to the idea of predestination and the Elect. God must have
known everything and willed everything from the beginning,
therefore at the creation He chose those who would be saved.
Everything that will ever happen was preordained at the beginning including the "accident" that broke John Allen's neck.

Such questions have occupied men for centuries. Shelves
in libraries are full of books purporting to answer the

questions—but the questions, solid landmarks in John Allen's life, still stand unyielding.

Early on John Allen sought answers to some of the questions by reading the Bible all the way through. And while he found much to admire in the scriptures—the poetry of Ecclesiastes, the stories of Joseph and his Brothers, Naomi and Ruth, the Beatitudes of Jesus—he could not bring himself to accept the bloody and vengeful tribal god of the Old Testament. In 1968 he wrote his friend Mike Vogler:

> In my twenties I read a good deal in comparative religion and free thought literature, and I read the Bible through. I never quite recovered from the Bible reading—couldn't swallow the God-commanded slaughters in the Old Testament and a few other items. There is much that is beautiful in the Bible, and for some time I have felt a need to re-read parts of it. There are many priceless things in the scriptures of the world.

Another friend with whom he shared his theological questionings was his former schoolmate W.S McNutt who wrote in 1954 from Caltech where he was pursuing graduate studies in biochemistry:

> What you have to say to the discredit of the fundamentalist position is true enough, of course, but I very much doubt whether it is anymore necessary. Religion is in much more serious difficulty than they are prepared to admit. Matters of mere scientific certitude or doubt regarding peripheral aspects of

religion somehow miss the point. What I would like
to know is whether there is anything left over after the
error has been removed which has value and is true
and has significance for our time. This is the question thinking men discover for themselves and with
some pain, if, like myself, they grew up in a strong
religious tradition. For there is so much beauty in
literature, music, and art associated with it; it is as
though we were to see the burning of the library at
Alexandria all over again. The problem is that it isn't
something that can be added to or modified and made
again as great a force in our lives as it was in the days
of Chaucer, or Luther, or John Locke—intelligent men
with a zest for life and the whole truth. But we are
the in-between generations with a little more of the
truth than they had but not enough to lose ourselves
in it—but just enough to be thoroughly miserable with
what we have.

What are you going to invent to save us?

Sincerely, Dub"

John Allen admittedly had more time to consider these questions than did most of his family and friends, and no doubt his
injury gave him some special insights not available to others,
but he was never able to "invent" any satisfactory answers to
the big questions.

His great grandfather Horton was a Methodist, a relaxed
denomination that today advertises itself as a church with
"open hearts, open minds, and open doors." His Aunt Bessie

somehow over the years made a transition to the Presbyterian Church, one whose Puritan roots may have had more appeal for John's iron-willed guardian. But for the most part folks in Arkadelphia, like those everywhere, simply accepted the faiths of their fathers. It requires much time and trouble to sift through all the evidence to come up with one's own answers to the ultimate questions and most people aren't that motivated; it's much easier to join an established church and adopt its creed.

Religion, after all, addresses one of the most basic yearnings of human consciousness. As one of Bessie's Presbyterian brethren expressed it, "We long to know both that our personal lives will not vanish without a trace into the void and that somewhere, somehow swords will be permanently beaten into ploughshares and the lion will indeed lie down with the lamb." Nothing that we know of the empirical universe, however, supports this hope, but its power goes a long way toward explaining the wide-spread appeal of religions.

Adopting an existing creed, however, would not work for John Allen. He liked to do his own thinking. He was a great admirer of Ralph Waldo Emerson who admonished, "Whoso would be a man must be a nonconformist." As for signing up with an established denomination, Emerson said, "If I know your sect I anticipate your argument." Members who join these religious groups, he said, are like hired lawyers unable to reason freely and speak openly and objectively for themselves; instead they must present and defend only the doctrines of their sect. Emerson started his own career as a Unitarian minister but soon found even their liberal doctrine too confining.

In addition to the Bible, John Allen filled his "uncommon amount of leisure" time reading many other books, some provided by his history teacher, Miss Greene. From her he would have learned about the 18th century Enlightenment, about the Deism of our Founding Fathers and its influence on the birth of our nation, those thinkers who looked for evidence of the creator, not in Holy Scripture, but rather to the creation, to what they thought of as the natural laws of the universe.

As for scriptures which are held to be divine revelation, Emerson asks the question, why would God speak to man two thousand years ago and not today? John Allen's thinking was further influenced by the Revolutionary War hero, Thomas Paine, who explains in his book *The Age of Reason* that the word "revelation" means God speaking directly to an individual. If the recipient of the divine message writes it down or tells a second person what God told him it is not revelation to that second person or to anyone reading the transcription. Paine rightly explains that such second-hand messages from God are hearsay, not revelation. So in one fell swoop he cuts the ground from under all religions which claim their doctrines are based on scriptures which are divine revelations from God, leaving standing only those charismatic sects whose members claim ongoing and personal revelations from the deity.

Regarding so-called sacred texts John Allen wrote: "All the various scriptures have a great deal of beauty, insight, and value; but—if I may judge from my limited knowledge—they all contain large amounts of nonsense that can lead to fanaticism when . . . taken as fact and God-given Truth."

Whatever ideas and books came his way John Allen's intellectual pursuits through the years demonstrate that reading and thinking are subversive activities. He was as spiritual as any person I have known, but in pursuing his own answers to the big questions he parted company with many of his family and friends. To Mike Vogler he wrote:

. . . I seem to be prejudiced against organized-institutionalized religion. That one man could solemnly utter words to sunder another man from God; and that a man would feel shattered by the ritual–that seems ridiculous to me [referring to an act of excommunication]. Panoply and traditional ritual do not move me–and yet I might be willing to create my own ritual. I sometimes wonder how we could stir children to a reverence for life, to a feeling of love and responsibility for our earth, and it occurs to me that ritual might play some part–though the deeper need is for us to labor in love and to permeate our entire society with this reverence. And can an industrialized society attain this? Is love compatible with science and technology, with the profit system, with Madison Avenue? Perhaps science and technology could be pursued in the spirit of Schweitzer's "reverence for life," but they would be greatly changed, wouldn't they?

So I contain a normal number of contradictions. I am a nominal member of the Presbyterian Church; make a small annual contribution–and never attend. (I have a good excuse; but if I thought it worthwhile to make the effort, I could go occasionally in the summer.) My inclination is to withdraw from the church–though

there are many good people there who have been kind
to me; and I have sympathy with some of their aims.
I sometimes say that I wouldn't want to upset my
aunt; but the truth is, very likely, simply that I don't
have the courage.

It was no doubt important to Bessie to have John Allen on
the membership roster of her church since church membership
was a community expectation and since her congregation had
done much to help her and her nephew. So, in spite of his
reservations, he continued his membership in the Presbyterian
Church in order not to disappoint those church goers who
had supported him or to upset his caregiver, Bessie. But he
adopted no creed and looked to no religion for explanations
of the natural world.

About his own injury John Allen said, "It may be illogical,
but 'accidents'—such as my own—do not disturb me. What
we call 'accidents' are natural laws in action; place excessive
strain on a neck and it will break; drive a car into a wall and
natural law takes over. When life inadvertently transgresses
natural law, it must suffer the consequences."

He found it much more comforting to see his injury and
all the natural misfortunes that befall mankind as the simple
consequence of readily understood physical laws rather than
as part of some divine operation of fate.

The laws of nature may be totally indifferent to man's
suffering, but at least man's suffering is not the consequence
of some vengeful god out to get him. A meteorite sixty-five
million years ago may have led to the destruction of the di-
nosaurs and much life on earth, a tsunami in 2004 took the
lives of a quarter million people, and the recent earthquake

in Haiti has claimed an untold number of lives, but terrible though those disasters were they were not personal.

Recently when a televangelist was rightfully disdained for claiming God used the Holocaust to remove the Jews from Europe and bring about the creation of Israel, he defended himself by protesting that he would never do anything so awful as to defend the Holocaust. God ordained that tragedy. God was the one responsible.

But of course God was not responsible for that evil; it was the Nazi regime of Adolph Hitler. Not God, not nature, but man is the only willful creator of suffering. Only humans can be malevolent, can delight in inflicting pain on other humans, and the social instrument of that willful evil is war—and war is as old as man. Later in his life John Allen would focus a great deal of his energy and attention in confronting that evil.

* * *

For years John Allen was dismayed by the quality of television fare that Bessie and other family members seemed addicted to. In 1968 he wrote Mike Vogler: "With many interruptions and distractions, my life seems disconnected. There is no escape from TV, though I work a little through the evening racket and sometimes stop to watch a show. A sane person would take his TV set out in the backyard in the dark of the moon and burn it."

But in 1980 he was particularly moved by Carl Sagan's thirteen-part series, *Cosmos*. A spiritual rationalist, John Allen looked to science, literature and philosophy as well as scripture for inspiration and understanding, coming to believe what seems incontrovertible, that we are creations of the universe and we are its witnesses; or, as Sagan expressed it, "we are a way for the cosmos to know itself."

Being restricted to his bed and wheelchair in a very small space for years set him apart from his friends, family and former schoolmates who were free to move about, but in watching Sagan's series on the universe he came to understand more clearly how we all are confined in a very small space between earth and sky, all of us floating together on our "pale blue dot" in the immensity of the cosmos, as Sagan says, "like a mote of dust in the morning sky."

Revisiting that series nearly thirty years later a viewer will be amazed at how well the production has stood the test of time. The music of Vangelis is haunting and the knowledge and impassioned scientific meditation of Carl Sagan remains powerfully moving.

Long before *Cosmos*, however, John Allen had marveled at man's peculiar and awe-inspiring position in the universe. He admired and recommended to friends a humorous poem by Conrad Aiken that captures man's place on his small tilting planet lost in a vast and dizzying universe. Aiken's character, Senlin, is aware of our remarkable cosmic predicament, but with a kind of "heroic nonchalance," John Allen says, he performs his daily routine.

From: **Morning Song of Senlin**

. . . .

It is morning. I stand by the mirror
And tie my tie once more.
While waves far off in a pale rose twilight
Crash on a white sand shore.

I stand by a mirror and comb my hair:
How small and white my face! —
The green earth tilts through a sphere of air
And bathes in a flame of space.

There are houses hanging above the stars
And stars hung under a sea ...
And a sun far off in a shell of silence
Dapples my walls for me ...

. . . .

Vine leaves tap my window,
The snail-track shines on the stones,
Dew-drops flash from the chinaberry tree
Repeating two clear tones.

. . . .

The earth revolves with me, yet makes no motion,
The stars pale silently in a coral sky.
In a whistling void I stand before my mirror,
Unconcerned, and tie my tie.

. . . .

Unlike Senlin, most of us go through our daily routines without giving any thought to our jaw-dropping position in the cosmos. Like the man on the high wire, perhaps it is safer to keep our eyes on our feet and the wire and not look down. Still, how sad to go through life without ever imaginatively escaping our comforting confinements. In a poem "Split-Level" John Allen reflects on how we spend our lives in houses and offers a bit of advice: "a man/ has to give shape to his life, /but he'd better raise the roof sometimes /and take a fix on the stars." Is it possible there are people who have never, on a clear moonless night,

204

looked up at the stars of our galaxy, our own Milky Way, in awe of where it is we live?

Though John Allen's body was confined to his bed and strapped to his wheelchair his imagination was free to soar. Our space program and the Soviet cosmonauts inspired him to write his own poem regarding the new perspective man had acquired of his home planet:

From a Space Capsule

See the earth as it turns
Against the bright blade of the sun
Scything down days and dropping sheaves
In swaths of darkness

See the earth as it turns—
No crazy patchwork of thine and mine
But clothed in the seamless garment
Of its being

See the earth as it turns—
And when its old simplicities of weight
Draw us back to rock and frond
We walk as men

The first stanza of the poem captures space-age images of our blue planet; the second echoes Emerson's poem, "Hamatreya," which treats man's vain belief that he can divide the earth into parcels and claim ownership; and the third calls our attention to the earth beneath our feet, to the simple force of gravity that holds us close, and to wonders such as Thoreau seemed always to find close by in his rambles around Concord and his little cabin at Walden Pond.

Bessie left Gertrude right with John Allen
and friend and Children

* * *

Even with the abundance of leisure time his injury had provided him, however, John Allen found that the search for the answers to cosmic questions reaches a point of diminishing returns, that it is best at some point to turn one's attention to more practical matters. About those big "nagging questions" he wrestled with he says, "I don't believe we can ever attain certainty regarding these ultimate questions. . . . They are interesting . . . and it is well for us to give some thought to them; but I doubt any healthy person becomes obsessed and anguished by his incertitude."

One of the practical questions he faced was how to find a way to contribute to his own upkeep. Here Mr. Huddleston came to the rescue by helping establish John Allen in a magazine subscription service, a business that could be followed from home and that required only the use of head and hands. Of course townspeople gladly bought their subscriptions from John Allen to help him out, but it was not charity. His customers got fair value for their investments, and he in turn took his business responsibilities seriously keeping careful records of his customers and their purchases and adding his own personal touch to all transactions.

John Allen was determined to do whatever he could to be productive, and it was his magazine subscription service that began what would eventually become a world-wide web of friendships and influence, a network that would make a positive difference in the lives of many people. There's no doubt that his story moved people to use his subscription service, but there's also no doubt that the personal touch he added to every subscription induced customers to return and to tell family and friends about the rewards of doing business with him. So as his business grew so did his circle of friends.

But in those early years he was very much constrained being limited to bed and wheelchair and dependent on Bessie to lift him and perform the laborious duties of caring for his paralyzed body. So, in spite of John Allen's admiration of Emerson and Thoreau who saw technology as "improved means to unimproved ends," in this one case he ignored that view and eagerly sought mechanical aids to restore some of his lost physical functions. Such technology was largely unavailable in the 1930's and 40's.

But in 1949 he read about and began communicating with a young man, a quadriplegic in Oshkosh, Wisconsin, who had devised a self-operated mechanical lift that could move a paralyzed person from bed to chair. Coincidentally, around that same time Aunt Bessie hurt her back. The result of the two young men being in communication proved fortuitous.

W.W. Halliburton told the story in the April 13, 1950, *Southern Standard*.

Oshkosh Youths come 1,000 Miles to Befriend An Arkadelphia Boy

Being a quadriplegic is not so bad if one has a great many friends, as John Allen Adams of this city has, and some who are willing to come a thousand miles to set up a hydraulic lift in ones bedroom-office, so a fellow almost totally paralyzed can move himself about not depending on an attendant to pick him up bodily and deposit him in his wheelchair.

. . . . From far away Oshkosh, Wis., last week came Ted Hoyer, himself a quadriplegic and two friends, bringing the bed lift on, and in, their automobile. Saturday the two able-bodied youths installed the 200-pound mechanism in the Arkadelphia youth's room, at the home of his aunt, Miss Bessie Horton. Ted Hoyer sat in on the procedure, giving expert advice on the adjustments and coaching Adams on its operation.

The article goes on to explain how the lift invented by Hoyer would enable John Allen to move from bed to wheelchair by himself thus saving Aunt Bessie's back and giving her nephew more control of his daily routine. The two young men were both the same age and ironically had been injured less than a month apart, one while playing in a football game, the other in a car wreck on the way to a football game. The Big Brothers organization again played a major part in financing the mechanical lift for John Allen, and Hoyer, after providing his first customer with the lift in Arkadelphia, went on to establish a company to manufacture the lift and other mechanical aids for the handicapped.

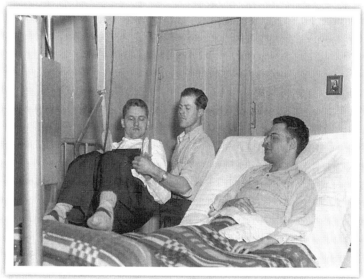
Ted Hoyer demonstrating lift to John Allen

Not long after the lift was installed in his bedroom, there was a push to get a motorized chair for John Allen, and again Big Brothers and the community pitched in. Uncle Vernon enthusiastically mailed a check for $100 to help make the purchase and soon his nephew was provided a measure of mobility not known to him for the past fifteen years.

Throughout all those years the paralyzed young man had lived amidst the battles of the two elder Horton sisters. Gertrude owned the major share of the home place but Bessie was its permanent resident and caretaker. Much of the time Gertrude lived in Little Rock where she taught school, but when she came to Arkadelphia during the summers the old conflicts would flare. The *Casus Belli* for these internecine struggles ranged from who was responsible for sugar ants getting in the house to alleged patricide. Recriminations continued to fly back and forth over who was responsible for John Allen's injury and that argument echoed one that had been going on for decades. Each of the sisters had been accusing the other through the years of being responsible for their father's suicide, even though no one knew whether Louis' death was in fact a suicide, and certainly if it had been it could not be blamed on his children. No doubt the reluctance of Martha Greene and others to speak of his family situation and the letters that his friend W.S McNutt determined to destroy rather than share had to do in part with what John Allen had to endure at the mercy of his two aunts.

Conflicts at the home place became so heated the two sisters armed themselves with domestic implements and separated themselves by elevation, with Gertrude living upstairs and Bessie downstairs. At times their income was supplemented by renting out rooms of the large house, and even the roomers were pulled into the conflicts and encouraged to take sides. Gertrude, when in Little Rock, wrote angry letters to Bessie and John Allen complaining of certain roomers and protesting that it was made clear to her that she was not welcome in her own home. At one point she wrote John Allen and told him she was giving him the house and suggested how he could use it to provide income.

It would require many pages to chronicle the drama that played itself out between the two Horton sisters at the home place, and through it all, either lying in his bed or sitting in his wheelchair, John Allen found himself at the center of a storm that would not end. It would be reasonable to conclude that the strength, patience and forbearance he always showed during those times were formed in the crucible of that family conflict, but such a conclusion would be wrong. The elements of his character predated his injury and were in fact evident upon his first arrival in Arkadelphia.

Both Gertrude and Bessie unburdened their grievances to him and sought his sympathy and support in their battles and no doubt John Allen listened with understanding, but his understanding would have taken into account, not the rightness of either side, but the conflicted family history that had brought the two sisters to that condition. He would have put into practice the advice his uncle Vernon had given him about viewing his aunts with some detachment and through the perspective of family history. His great contribution to the Horton clan during his years at the home place was that he served as the calm center of family storms, that he always played the role of peacemaker between the warring sisters. It was not simply because he was physically unable to raise his voice; it was because he had the strength not to be pulled into the maelstrom.

Mediating the battles between the Horton sisters was a chronic challenge, but in 1954 John Allen faced his greatest trial. That year Aunt Bessie's doctor told her she was suffering from tuberculosis and had her admitted to the Arkansas State Sanatorium leaving her nephew without the life support he had relied on since his injury. For all her fierce passions and bitter enmities, her devotion to John Allen never wavered. It was Bessie's daily labors in caring for his physical needs—the daily enemas, baths, frequent turnings and cushionings to prevent bedsores, getting him into and out of his chair, cooking and attention to diet, and many other responsibilities—that enabled him to enjoy a life of the mind and the warm social relationships with his many friends. Bessie was, in a way, like the man at the air pump in the early days of deep sea diving; if something happened to him the diver whose life depended on a constant flow of air was literally in deep trouble. And that was the way John Allen felt when his aunt was sent off to the sanatorium.

There were, of course, many friends around willing to step up and help through the crisis; and in all likelihood others would have been found to assume the duties Bessie had performed for the last eighteen years, but they would not have been family, and no one could have matched his aunt's dedication and devotion. So when she went away John Allen felt desperation unlike any he had experienced since he discovered he could not feel the weight of his own body on the stretcher as they carried him off the football field.

Years later he recalled this period of his life to one of his intimate friends and correspondents, Elizabeth Thomas, an Egyptologist and student of Eastern religions who lived in Trenton, New Jersey. After describing to her a mystical and emotionally powerful dream he had had the night before, he goes on to say:

The only comparable experience I have had occurred twelve or thirteen years ago when I took 70 aspirin tablets in an effort to cure the massive headache my life had become. Later I read that not much is known about the effect of overdoses of salicylic acid, but 150 grains was thought to be fatal. 70 five-grain tablets is 350 grains. An overdose produces aural and visual hallucinations. I "saw" some weird things—some frightening, some merely strange and interesting. Once I seemed to be looking into a whirlpool—the source of all things—out of which came a tumultuous gush of creativity: human forms, trees, houses, chairs, –hundreds of things swirled out.

There's no need of going into details (many of which I've forgotten, happily), but the situation reached a crisis when some fool doctor had Bessie sent to a TB sanatorium (after four or five weeks they decided she didn't have TB). Her suffering on top of mine was too much. It was while she was gone that I took the tablets, and she never knew what had happened—just that I had been sick. In fact, I don't think anyone knew except the doctor and a friend who stayed with me several days until the effects wore off. I was half deaf for several days and profoundly depressed for a week or two.

John Allen called Bessie while she was in the hospital and wrote cheerful letters reassuring her that all would be well, characteristically keeping his own suffering to himself. He felt much better after learning she did not have tuberculosis, but still she was afflicted with some kind of debilitating illness and suffering with her back. He wrote:

February 25, 1954
Dear Aunt Bessie:

It was good to talk with you last night. I forgot to ask if there was anything you wanted us to send you—but I guess you would let us know if there was. . . .

I'm glad you have your bed arranged a little more comfortably and that your back is somewhat better. Just rest as well as you can and try not to worry— you'll be home before long. . . .

You'll be surprised to find our room freshly painted when you return. I think you will like it, it looks so clean and cheerful. The ceiling and the east wall (the one I face from bed) are a soft green; the other three walls are a color almost peach, though has more tan than pink in it. The Van Gogh prints look pretty on the green wall. We also painted your bed. Truman Lollar had one of his workmen paint the room and he wouldn't let me pay him. Jack Brown painted the bed. . . .

Tuesday I was on the chair around 11 o'clock and stayed up about ten hours. I may sit up as long today. I'm trying to catch up with subscription work, and I want to write Uncle Vernon and Dad and tell them what has happened.

I'm glad you thought to take your radio with you. We are doing all right, so don't worry and just concentrate getting to feel as well as you can. Martha, Amy Jean, the McCormicks and many others have been very good to us and they all want you home as soon as possible.

Love,
John Allen

In all his letters to her he describes the kindnesses of their friends and neighbors, and there were always many around willing and eager to help. But this crisis revealed how emotionally essential Aunt Bessie was to John Allen. Sure, there were others who could assume the duties Bessie had performed over the years; professional help could be hired to do the job and churches and community organizations would contribute to his care. But such a thought was devastating to John Allen, devastating because none of these people were family.

Deep inside John Allen carried vivid memories of his first meeting with Grandmother Amy Horton and his aunts and uncles at the home place, and he recalled clearly the great sense of relief and joy he felt when later he was granted his wish to come live with Aunt Bessie and attend school in Arkadelphia. He loved his parents and they adored him, but while he cut his teeth in carnivals and had as a child enjoyed the excitement and fun of the midway, early on he knew he could not live his life as a road boy. So when Al and Louise brought the eight-year-old from Fort Smith to Arkadelphia in 1927, the year of the Great Mississippi Flood, John Allen knew he had found his home. Embraced by an extended family and living under the guidance of his stalwart Aunt Bessie his future seemed assured.

Over the next nine years John Allen's progress and development exceeded even the great expectations of Aunt Bessie, fulfilling her hopes for future Horton family distinctions. All those hopes, however, were dashed that October evening on the Malvern High School football field in the accident that would prove fateful for John Allen and require of his aunt a lifetime commitment. Now, instead of having him for only a few more years until he graduated from college and departed with his classmates to serve in World War II, Bessie would have John Allen to care for the rest of her life. She would not have to share him with a wife and children, but she would pay for that privilege with years of devoted labor. As he said to his friend, Mike Vogler, the relationship between the two was symbiotic, each dependent on the other. Bessie tended to the needs of her nephew's non-functioning body and was rewarded by finding a worthy life purpose, by having him and his many friends near and seeing the talents and gifts of a most remarkable man continue to unfold.

With Bessie now in the sanatorium, however, the symbiotic bond had been sundered; John Allen had lost his life support and was suffering. Though not given to depression, without his aunt he could not see a clear way ahead. The deepest fears of quadriplegics must have to do with being abandoned in their helpless state, being left alone unable to move, a nightmare we all have experienced—caught in a terrifying predicament knowing we must flee but finding ourselves unable to move. Such bad dreams for the rest of us are reality for quadriplegics. So John Allen, feeling trapped and unable to run, looked for another way to escape.

Those familiar with Horton family history might see a pattern in John Allen's response. His grandfather, Louis Horton, having played out all his cards after his last battle with his wife Amy and his kids, sat outside the improvised chicken-house cabin at Fairview that hot summer evening listening to the calls of the chuck-wills-widows as lightening bugs winked overhead in the dark and gloomy pine trees. What would he have been thinking while reading his book as the country baseball team walked by? All we can know is that his body was found the next morning in the charred ruins of his makeshift cabin, his bones fused with the springs of the cot he had last rested on, a gaping hole in the back of his skull and two burnt-out rifles lying beside his skeleton.

And John Allen's forty-three-year-old mother Louise, having completed her final tour of the sawdust circuit and now separated from Al, the husband and father she had always loved and praised, found herself alone in Hot Springs handing out recently printed advertisement cards in her last mitt reader incarnation as Madame Neasia:

> I have a message of hope for
> you. If you find the road rough
> the going hard and slow, there's
> a reason find out why, before it's
> to {sic} "late". Will tell you the past,
> the present and advise you on the
> future affairs of life, consult
> "Madame Neasia" without fail.

But for Madame Neasia the road had become too rough and the going too hard, and though she had been offering messages of hope to others for years, she now could see no hope in her own future. So, after conversing pleasantly with other guests in the lobby of the Goddard Hotel, Louise retired to her room where, after carefully placing a suicide note beside the bed telling the world she could no longer take the pain, she either inhaled or swallowed the deadly dose of chloroform. The newspaper report does not explain.

Like John Allen, both Louis and Louise came to a point in their lives where they felt trapped and unable to run. Louis apparently solved his problems with a rifle while his daughter Louise escaped hers with chloroform, but John Allen, having no access to such effective means of escape, reached for the aspirin bottle. Three generations of Hortons seemed to have arrived at the same dead end.

Someone reflecting on Horton family history might assume this third generation attempt at suicide suggested an inter-generational defect in the descendents of W.S. and Elizabeth Scott Horton, perhaps traceable to their prodigal son, Louis. All of his siblings had profited from their solid upbringing, gone to college, led successful lives and made their parents proud, but in spite of his father's best efforts Louis was never able to find his own way in life. Though he did succeed in fathering eight surviving children, most of whom were successful, his marriage to Amy Scales ended in bitterness and ashes.

If, as the Greeks believed, a person's character is his fate, then the ends for Louis and his daughter seem to follow some kind of fatal logic. Both seemed to carry within themselves character traits that would lead to their own sad ends. Louis, the young dandy who loved to put on a show in his fine clothes and four-horse surrey tossing around big rolls of bills that his father's years of diligence and hard work had provided was himself unwilling or unable to apply similar diligence and hard work to care for his own family, so throughout his life he saw a widening disparity between his material needs and aspirations and his ability to provide them. That failure, in part, created discord in his family, led Louis to drink, and ultimately led to his sad end in the ashes of the old Fairview Plantation.

Louise's problem from early on was the great gulf between her fantasy world and the gritty reality in which she lived. She sought to escape the battles with Bessie and Gertrude at the home place by attending the moving picture shows at the Electric Theater, listening to ragtime music and reading pulp fiction stories papering over her unhappy home life with romantic fantasies. When those diversions proved inadequate, she eloped with Frank Hurt. When that ill-starred union failed she found herself even more deeply in conflict with her older sisters leading finally to her commitment to the State Hospital in Little Rock. It was not until she escaped to Louisville and met Al Adams that she found her calling as a mitt reader, a profession that would enable her to put her love of fantasy to practical use. But twenty-five years on the carnival circuit selling dreams for pennies is a hard way to go. And with the one good thing she had produced in her life lying paralyzed a few miles away, her dreams and fantasies could no longer sustain her. She could no longer peddle illusions she no longer believed in. So, after bidding her fellow guests in the Goddard Hotel lobby a pleasant good evening, she retired to her room and made her final escape.

But John Allen was not marked by any family curse. Unlike his mother and grandfather he possessed no personal trait that would foreshadow a sad end. On the contrary, his affectionate nature, keen intellect and love of challenges seemed to promise for him a bright future, and his years as a student in the Arkadelphia school system bore witness to that promise. His despair when Bessie was sent away for an indefinite period could not be attributed to any innate fatalistic tendency but was rather the consequence of circumstances beyond his control, most specifically his paralysis. Perhaps he shouldn't have felt so dependent on Bessie, but it's not difficult to see how, after eighteen years of following a faithful daily regimen with the help of a trusted relative, a quadriplegic could feel a sense of hopelessness when that trusted support was taken away.

Fortunately John Allen survived the aspirin overdose and Bessie returned from the sanatorium with her back improved and free of tuberculosis, so the two were able to resume their regular life at the home place. Equipped with the hydraulic lift on his bed and the motorized wheelchair, John Allen and Aunt Bessie now were able to look to the future with some optimism.

There were of course still the ongoing conflicts between the sisters at the home place, but Aunt Bessie's cunning and ingenuity would come up with a solution that would remove John Allen from the battlefield and allow him to experience his best and most productive years as a quadriplegic.

* * *

CHAPTER 9

Touching People

———————————

Since John Allen's body no longer responded to his will it became clear to him that the principal territories left for him to explore would be intellectual, that whatever he would be able to do with the rest of his life would depend on the resources he could find within himself. So, each day after his arduous daily routine of guiding and assisting Aunt Bessie in caring for his unresponsive body and when friends and family were not around and his magazine subscription business was taken care of, John Allen spent much of his time reading and thinking. He had not lost his drive to take advantage of whatever opportunities came his way, but now his possibilities had been drastically restricted and he was faced with a new and daunting set of challenges. No longer the energetic, active teenager in motion, he was now a still John Allen—but he was still John Allen, so he would find ways to make the most of his new and unwelcome leisure time.

In good weather, once he was able to sit in a wheelchair, he would have Aunt Bessie roll him out onto the porch of the home place where he could look down Clinton Street toward the Ouachita only three blocks away. Though he could no longer make his way down the hill, he could remember the pleasures the river had provided him, the times he and Buddy Whitten, Billy Vestal, Billy Gill East, W. S. McNutt and his many friends from high school and Troop 23 journeyed to its banks to cool off in its swimming holes and explore the river up beyond De Soto Bluff, sometimes all the way to the next little town of Friendship. He remembered vividly the hikes with Mr. Huddleston and his friends from Troop 23, the camp-outs, the hunt for arrowheads and pottery, the smells of hickory smoke, crushed grass, pine needles and fresh dug earth, the challenges he faced in qualifying for merit badges on his way to becoming an Eagle Scout, the pleasures of sweat and physical exertion in his football practices and track workouts.

And there were many other happy memories from his school years in Arkadelphia—the activities, social events, his four years as class president and his work with his classmates as editor of the school paper. While John Allen had many close friends in his Boy Scout and athletic activities, many of his friends were admiring girls, and the admiration was mutual. Well before that last football game he had shown his interest in the opposite sex when he attended dances at the home of the girl voted "prettiest," Aletha Sloan. In addition to his good looks and youthful achievements, other qualities that would have added to his appeal was his good humor, social ease, and the natural and respectful way he treated others, boys and girls alike. So when his female fellow high school students visited their stricken friend and stood by his bed and looked at him and he looked at them, all must have had bittersweet thoughts about what might have been.

It's unlikely any lasting romantic bonds had taken hold in John Allen's life when he was injured only two months past his seventeenth birthday. Having been left at that age with no sensation below his shoulders he would never be able to experience the full range of emotional and sensual pleasures loving a woman gives a man, and he was surely aware of what he was missing. John left no written thoughts about that loss though he may have shared his feelings with his good friend, W.S McNutt.

Other quadriplegics, however, have described what it is like to be unable to experience sexual pleasure. One paralyzed for thirty years, a man named Graham, said that for him desire "had neither disappeared nor found an outlet." He tells Jonathan Cole, "'I've been forced to get used to it. It does not mean that I don't miss it; I think about it and ogle every attractive woman who's around. But there is absolutely nothing I can do about it. I have not found anything. The mental imagining remains important, because I cannot feel anything. I don't get an orgasm anyway.'" He adds, "'Part of it is not sex itself, but feeling that you are a man. That's a major part of it'" (Cole, 30).

John Allen was far too courteous and tactful to ogle pretty women, but there's no doubt he enjoyed looking at them for he was a lover of all kinds of beauty, including the female form. Some years later he sent a poem about that subject to one of his friends, Boulware Ohls, who was ailing at the time:

Dear Boulware:

To spread sunshine and cheer up the shut in, I'm sending you the only cheerful poem I ever wrote. There isn't likely to be another, since the muse seems to have departed. Incidentally it's the only one Amy Jean has seen. When I intimated that she might consider the few other ones uncheerful she evinced no further interest. She is so depressingly cheerful on the outside and so depressingly the reverse on the inside that it troubles me. I wish she could mix the two elements; an alloy is less rigid.

The first two verses of my poem came many years ago in a flash of inspiration; and the fact that the lines have stuck in my memory so long without keeping a copy of them is proof, I think, of their deeply poetic quality. Perhaps I never kept a copy because I subconsciously felt that, even though the lines were poetic, it was a serious breach of decorum to perpetrate so close a parody of Mr. Emerson (his Rhodora). I've felt much better about is since adding the last four lines last summer.

Philosophical Reflections On A Pin-up Girl

Sweet damsel, if the sages ask thee why
These charms are visible to every eye,
Tell them, dear, that if eyes were made for seeing
Then nudity's its own excuse for being.

Why thou wert bare, O fair as Gypsy Rose!
I never thought to ask, I never knew,
But in my simple ignorance suppose
The selfsame power that made me stare moved you.

Apologia

May Concord's sage forgive this gross
Perversion of his lines; It's bold,
I know, unchaste, untranscendental;
But ours is an era over-sold
On sex and undermental.

John Allen's wit is evident in both the letter and the poem. Of course he is being ironic when he speaks of the "deeply poetic qualities" of his parody, and the cleverness in his "Apologia" should not go unnoticed. He was a genuine admirer of Emerson and Thoreau, but he had to have a little fun with Emerson's concept of the "Oversoul,"—the spirit that pervades each of us and the entire creation—with his play on the word in the penultimate line of the poem. It's also interesting to note his perceptive comment about his life-long friend and mentor, Amy Jean Greene.

She, as did many other close friends, continued to stand by John Allen through the years. He may have felt abandoned when Bessie was sent off to the sanatorium, but he was attended by many friends and neighbors during her absence, including the mother of his high school buddy and wounded World War II veteran, Billy Gill East. Mrs. East sent reassuring letters to Bessie in the hospital detailing all the help her nephew was getting and encouraging her to rest and get well.

Bessie may have been involved in fierce battles at the home place, but she had friends around town, many of them unaware of the Horton sibling rivalries. One of those friends who knew well the story of the battling sisters was

Vernon's wife, Frances. She and Bessie exchanged warm letters for decades even after her divorce from Vernon and remarriage to a widower and father of several children, Dan Whelchel.

From the day the curly-headed eight-year-old arrived in Arkadelphia he began to accumulate friends. Throughout his school years, because of his athletic and scouting activities, his closest companions were boys, but he always had female friends as well. As my colleagues at HSU, Bennie Jean Bledsoe and Clarice Freeman told me, many of his girl classmates had crushes on John Allen. His natural social skills, his intelligence, empathy, and the fact that he was a good listener explain why he was always surrounded by admirers even after his injury. As many of his male friends departed, however, first to serve in World War II and then to marriages and jobs in other locations, those closest to him came to be increasingly female.

Always nearby were Aunts Bessie and Gertrude, and Amy Jean Greene and her cousin Martha continued to be faithful visitors and friends. And there is evidence in John Allen's correspondence that other female friends, like the eight-year-old Amy Thompson who dreamed of marrying the paralyzed young man, were strongly attracted to him. He had lost the ability to move, but he had lost neither his good looks nor his charm and throughout his life women saw in John Allen a manly man. It's not difficult, looking at the pictures of him sitting in the wheelchair on the porch of the home place and between his two aunts in the yard, to understand the feelings of Amy Thompson and others. Had he not been injured in all likelihood one woman would have ultimately won John Allen; now, since he would be courting no one, all were welcome to share his company. There's no way to know how many entertained romantic fantasies about John Allen, but it's certain that some did.

One close friend through the years was Martha Winburn England, older sister of William Winburn, left halfback of the Badger football team when John Allen was injured and daughter of Dr. Hardy Winburn, prominent Baptist minister and civic leader in Arkadelphia. After graduating from Ouachita Baptist College, Martha attended Radcliffe Institute for Advanced study at Harvard where she received a Masters and PhD in comparative literature. Following graduation she joined the faculty of Smith College in Northampton, Massachusetts, and later taught for many years at Queens College in New York City where she was a scholar and translator of Italian opera, actively involved in academia and the arts. While Amy Thompson was young, Martha was older and married, but she clearly had strong feelings for John Allen dating back to the time she visited him with her brother after his injury.

She wrote the twenty-nine-year-old John Allen from Blytheville, Arkansas, in 1948:

Dear John Allen-

I don't like writing to you just now. It's got to be all are nothing with us—I have always written so from the heart to you. I do not have time or energy to write what I want you to know. And I wonder—do you really want to know? Would you rather remain at a distance? I understand that, too—for there is something a little indecent about such grief and pain. Something not at all attractive.

You know I love you. I will put on my Sunday manners when I come and do my best to tell you good bye calmly. And leave you your realistic literature.

But if you have a mind to get your teeth on a *real* problem, to know about *real* love and pain and joy and death and loneliness and *real* life – then I will tell you, if opportunity arises. I have always preferred the raw material to the finished product on paper. I don't like stories. They all sound silly to me. Always did. But I know a *real* love story. From start to finish now. And do you know – they seem to be rather rare? Much rarer than you are led to believe. So you should be glad to know Farmer and me.

. . . .

I'll be home the 20th – 26th I expect. Nancy and Bill with me. I have written to mother that I'll go see John Allen and *no* one else.

Love,
Martha

At the time she wrote this letter, in her late thirties, she was in Arkansas with her husband, Farmer England, apparently a prominent citizen in Blytheville. She mentions in one of her letters that the town was dedicating a portion of the library there in his name and in another that they were going to Memphis to see a musical, "Rio Rita," starring Farmer's cousin, Barbara Walker who had won the Miss America contest in 1947.

The letter above is cryptic; only the sender and receiver would fully understand the elliptical references, but it seems clear that Martha's feelings for John Allen were strong. Their relationship is one of a number of mysteries I discovered in the boxes of letters. Was she married to Farmer England when she visited the injured John Allen with her brother William? Though older than John, was she, like the young Amy Thompson, smitten by the handsome young man lying paralyzed in bed? Whatever her feelings, her resolve to tell him good bye was never acted on and her commitment to him was lasting, for they continued their friendship for years.

Knowing John Allen it's safe to say that if her feelings for him had been outside the bounds of her solid Baptist upbringing he would have been kind and understanding and would have helped her avoid embarrassment, staying all the while, like he said of his great-grandmother Elizabeth Scott Horton, within the lines of rectitude. It is a rare thing in biographical research to find a subject such as John Allen who, after all the interviews, testimonials, and correspondence have been carefully sifted, can never be found to have struck a discordant note or to have stepped over the line.

Martha England and W.S McNutt were just two of John Allen's friends who provided him windows on the wider world. Both were for a time in Cambridge with access to the Harvard library and the other intellectual and cultural riches of that region, though neither of them mentions the other in their correspondence. But thanks to these two close friends he could experience vicariously walks near Walden Pond and get cultural reports from New York City on Maria Callas' performance at the Met.

Martha encouraged John Allen in his poetry writing, offering him knowledgeable advice on composition and prosody while sharing his poems with her colleagues and students at Smith. It's interesting to note that she, after years of intensive graduate studies in literature, and John Allen, after his own reading and home schooling with help from local mentors such as Amy Jean Greene, were on equal footing when it came to discussing literature and ideas. Martha could casually include lines from Wordsworth's "Ode on Intimations of Immortality" assured that her friend in Arkadelphia would recognize them. They exchanged thoughts on many literary figures—Emily Dickenson, W.B. Yeats, Gerard Manley Hopkins, T.S. Eliot and others. She once humorously reminded him that she was now a doctor, but she well understood that when it came to knowledge of literature and ideas her friend was her equal.

By 1955 Martha's husband was dead. She had always chided John Allen about his agnosticism, and in the following letter she shares her thoughts on death, on her family and on the faith that had sustained her during times of trial. She recalls her father, Dr. Hardy Winburn's death, that of her husband, Farmer, and tells of the problems of her brother "Fuzzy" and his long-suffering wife, Helen. She begins the letter by remarking on the recent passing of B.W. McCormick, the dear friend and benefactor of John Allen who had been head of the Big Brothers Association when they committed themselves to helping the young football player who had broken his neck. That was October 1936; Martha's father had died the month before.

Jan 1955   Smith College Northampton, MA

Dear John Allen —

. . . .

I was sad to hear about Mr. McCormick—and my first – or at least my second thought—was of you. I know what you have lost. What a beautiful life his was. And how lucky we are to have known him. But you and I cannot see eye to eye on the subject of death, because you keep forgetting that death, while it is all those things, is merely seeing Farmer and Dad again. The Caddo Coffee Shop where they used to forgather, could not hold the joy of Dad and Mr. McCormick getting together again relieved of the infirmities of the flesh, and unworried about what will happen to their dear little friend, John Allen—because now they know more than we do and know enough not to worry, because God has his eye on you. Not a sparrow falleth. . .

You think sometimes that you can say: Behold and see if there be any sorrow like my sorrow . . . and goodness knows, sometimes I think the same of you. I do know and understand as far as I can the burdens you bear. The burdens you bear for others, and the sorrow of your heart for those around you. And your own. But John Allen, I watched Aunt Carrie Wallis, that saint of the Lord, die a lingering death with cancer, and I watched her faith unshaken through it all. Now, why should she suffer so? Do you think I have any answer for that? No—but her very life as it wasted away was an answer to *something.* And I, though I cannot put it into words, I will not forget it.

I wish you would write me about Fuzzy—anything that might give me a clue of what to do, at least. To suffer and endure—spare a thought for Helen when you think of that, as well as for him. Oh, God when I think of how my feeble spirit would have broken under what she has known, it takes away any possibility of spiritual pride, I hope. How do people find the strength to live through such things?

Because—and you must know this to know the whole sorrow—she loves him and always has. And he loves her. And always has. Now, John Allen, how can you think that there would be no heaven to reward such patience and courage and love? I know you set for yourself the cold standard of perfection, and think that you fail when you do not reach it. But God is kinder than you. He knoweth the frame. He remembereth that we are dust.

Little by little, in tiny sparks in the dark, the transforming miracle of love is with us—or sometimes is a clear warm glow as in Mr. McCormick.

I will tell you something else. Fuzzy loves me. I can still see that face, distorted with drink and grief before Farmer's funeral. Poor darling, he sat on the bed saying between sobs, "But I love you, sister. I would help you if I could. I have always loved you, but I never knew before how much." All right, so he was drunk and embarrassing me before my friends. I just was not embarrassed. I will take love as best I can get it, and by gosh, I never felt more so than then. I just rared back and gloried in my brother's love—that he had known me so long and so well and still loved me. He would help me if he could. He would help us all if he could. He would be strong, a man to lean on, if he could be. He would be your rock, your comfort, if he could. And God knows it. He longs to help you. He loves you, too.

I have never fought the desperate fight. Oh yes, I have been given up for lost lots of times in my illness, but that is not the same thing. And I have seen my father die, and Farmer—but I have never lost them, as Fuzzy may feel he has at times. The last thing Dad said to me was, "Old Fuz hasn't turned out the way we hoped." But he loved him, and died with him on his heart, and in the fullness of time God will answer Dad's dying prayer, and mother's and mine. And I say it—no matter what happens. My faith is not in Fuzzy, and my hope is not in him. They are for him.

You write me any news. Remember I am up here breaking my heart over the whole matter. And tell him I love him. Tell him every day.   And you.   M.

From this letter we learn that Fuzzy, (most likely the William Winburn who was left halfback on John Allen's football team), lived in Arkadelphia and no doubt, like many other friends, stopped by the home place from time to time to do business with and talk to his former teammate. Fuzzy may not have been strong, but John Allen was; he was a man people could lean on.

Martha's letters reveal, as do those from others in the boxes of materials Joy Adams entrusted to me, that people felt safe writing and talking to John Allen, that they trusted him and sought his guidance. Some people pursue careers as counselors, priests, pastors, analysts—all honorable professions—but for John Allen compassion was not a profession, it was the essence of who he was. This is not to say that for those seeking his counsel he would break out the crying towels—far from it. In fact his informal consultations generally consisted of light hearted conversation punctuated with wit and laughter. He possessed a quality all too rare among human beings— he was a good listener. He was also a clear-headed realist with a keen sense of humor and irony. All those who ever spent time with him could attest to the positive value of his company.

Clay Costner, one of his former student workers, wrote him from Campbell College in North Carolina where he coached athletics, "I miss those conversations with you and your thoughtful comments—hand on chin & head bowed— slow to speak yet always the most logical thought when you did speak." Clay, lonesome in his first job away from Arkadelphia, wrote to John Allen throughout his first year of teaching, letters which reveal a wide range of reading and intellectual curiosity and reflect clearly the influence of his former employer.

Another former Ouachita student, Jay Curlin, who had been introduced to the poetry of John Allen by his English professor, Dr. John Wink, wrote me of a casual scene in the book store which, in just a brief moment, captures the character of the proprietor.

> I was doing my usual browsing while Mr. Adams listened politely to two elderly men best described as "old timers." They seemed odd incongruities in the academic atmosphere of surrounding bookshelves, pleasant characters extracted from a Rockwell painting of a game of checkers at the general store. They were doing their best to speak of things literary but making their ignorance obvious with every remark. When one of the men attempted to talk of Yeats, pronouncing the name as "Yeets," I looked at Mr. Adams and found his expression revealed nothing but polite interest. I, young and immaturely intolerant of ignorance, immediately cursed my own lack of tolerance and thought to myself, "Ah, what a kind, tolerant man!"

For every personal letter to John Allen there were no doubt countless unrecorded face-to-face discussions with friends and customers, conducted during the early years in his bedroom office at the home place and later at his book store on Main Street. I learned of the therapeutic value of visits to Adams Book Store shortly after arriving in Arkadelphia.

Many customers, like Jay Curlin, perceived quickly the remarkable nature of the bookseller and poet, as did the young woman who wrote him a long letter which reads in part:

Mr. Adams,

I doubt that you remember me – because although I frequented your book store, and felt a peace there – as if a combination of compassion, understanding & suffering had made those walls a special haven - - - I never had the courage to ask you for a few minutes of your time.

My friend Johnny Wink has sent me excerpts from your book, *I Walk Toward the Sound of My Days,* and today I got a package – he had sent me a copy, an autographed copy! It is a special treasure to me.

The writer goes on to tell her story. She was an honor high school student from a comfortable family who came to Arkadelphia to attend Ouachita Baptist University. There she was invited by a friend to join a prison ministry and joined the group on a visit to the notorious Tucker Prison. She said with that visit her whole world changed. She says, "I became acquainted with true human suffering, as men entrusted their aches & fears & lives into my confidence." She goes on to explain how she felt herself cast into prison with the men she came to know and how she began to exchange letters with one of those men, a correspondence that lasted a year and a half. Six days after graduating from OBU she and the inmate were married. She tells John Allen she was able to hold her husband only once after the ceremony before the guards "pulled him away."

The young woman goes on to discuss a number of John Allen's poems in detail telling him how they were especially meaningful to her while undergoing the challenges she faced. And she tells him:

> You are in another kind of prison—life in prison. And you've suffered things—both imaginable and unimaginable to us. We don't pretend to understand, just like you wouldn't pretend to understand ours. But we feel a closeness—especially now through your poems. And like [my husband] has, you have overcome.

> Men like you inspire—those whose courage and zeal enable them to reach out to others. Thank you. I admire you greatly, Mr. John Allen Adams; your poems have made my life a better place to be.

It would be impertinent to inquire how this marriage that took place three decades ago turned out, but there's no doubt that John Allen wished them well and stood ready to help them any way he could. There seems to be here some similarity between this young woman's love for a man she could not physically hold and Martha England's love for John Allen. Such platonic affairs can be pure and powerful while at the same time escaping the tangles and heartaches that often accompany everyday romantic relationships.

The compassion John Allen showed others from early on, as when he ran all the way from De Soto Bluff to town carrying the boy with a lacerated foot, he extended to all mankind. An article in the *Southern Standard* during World War II concerning a food drive for the hungry overseas noted that he while lying paralyzed in his bed was the first to make a contribution. Unlike most of mankind John Allen seemed unable to shut out tragic news from afar. Distance did not desensitize him to suffering, a characteristic which goes far in explaining his later energetic opposition to the war in Vietnam.

Perhaps the people most influenced by him were the college students who worked in his book store over two decades. I have known several of them, had a couple of them as students and read letters from others. All give similar accounts of their experiences working for John Allen. One of them, Jim Larkin, wrote to him from Lonoke, Arkansas, where he was teaching physics and chemistry in high school while his wife, Barbara, was doing art work in the mornings and teaching piano in the afternoons. He says in the letter, "Every time I see somebody from Arkadelphia, I ask about you, and it's strange how often it is that whoever it might be has often just recently been in the book store."

One can clearly detect John Allen's influence on Jim who quotes from, *Manas,* one of the poet's favorite progressive periodicals dedicated to living simply and harmoniously with the earth, and when he describes the work he and his wife have been doing with a youth ranch outside Hot Springs and their plans to offer programs there in arts and crafts and nature studies. The idealism of the young couple is also reflected in their hopes to develop a year-round school for exceptional children. Then, near the end of the letter Jim writes,

> I have never really told you what a large role you have played in shaping my life. Somebody asked me not long ago what person or persons have made the greatest influence on me, and four people immediately came to mind—Jesus Christ, Gandhi, Thoreau, and John Allen Adams. That's pretty heavy company,

huh! But it is true. You have an independent, practical philosophy of life that is in tune with the universe, one which makes people stop and consider their own philosophy of life. I guess that, plus my love for books, is why I always enjoyed working in the store for you and Miss Bessie.

After his funeral another former assistant to John Allen, Sandy Hays, wrote a poem in his memory which I found in the boxes of materials from Joy. It reads in part:

. . .
The sun had come out
from behind the clouds
Hope, maybe
Then at last I saw the sign
Adams' Book Store
. . . .
I went there
looking for him
knowing he was not there
. . . .
. . . we had tea together
. . . .
You had to place his cup
at a certain angle, see
so he could hold it
I was not told
I observed and made
a special effort
to perfect that angle

I would turn the gas heater on
at his request
before I left
to keep him warm
. . . .
Molasses and milk
Honey and tea
I fixed them for him
And homemade bread and cheese
sliced
Turned pages, opened drawers
Changed the spoon
in the leather strap
. . . .
I said once
"Sometimes I don't think
you even need an assistant,
sometimes I think
you just want the company."
And he smiled
. . . .
We laughed about his chair
when it began making noise
"An ungodly noise" he said
"Transmission problems" said I
And he laughed and agreed
I removed a bit of sleep
from his lash once
He seemed touched
He loved classical music
and so do I

I put tapes and records on
We were a team there
in the Book Store
. . . .
Looking for him
on the way back
I felt
part of him in me
his eyes containing endlessness
cannot have ceased
The endlessness remains
I salute you
John Allen Adams
Because you lived
and live still
in me

If all the former collegiate acolytes from Adams Book Store were brought together I have no doubt they could compose a remarkable book detailing the profound influence John Allen had on their lives. Every one of them I'm aware of went on to successful careers and productive lives; some pursued advanced degrees, like a former student of mine, Sarah Sullivan, who earned a PhD in biochemistry and then went on to receive an MD, all the while living a life of service reflecting John Allen's influence. No academic course those young people took in college could have had the transformational influence that working in Adams Book Store provided; every one of them, I believe, would acknowledge that to be true.

For over two decades John Allen and his Aunt Bessie followed their daily routine at the home place on 3rd and Clinton

Streets, their income deriving from his growing magazine subscription service, the monthly rent from roomers and the continued generous support of Big Brothers and local churches and civic groups. Bessie and her nephew's physical restriction to the house near the river was lightened, however, by his business activities, and by regular visits from friends, family and customers. For fourteen years the two of them labored every day, on their own or with assistance from paid help or volunteers, to care for John Allen's paralyzed body.

Then in 1950 the two innovations arrived at the home place that contributed greatly to John Allen's mobility and eased the burden for Bessie and opened up a new chapter in their lives— the hydraulic lift invented by fellow quadriplegic and friend, Ted Hoyer and the motorized chair donated by family and local citizens.

Sadly, only four years after receiving Hoyer's life-enhancing invention came word of his death. The following letter is from Ted's wife, Marie:

Dear John Allen:

Thank you so much for your wonderful letter of sympathy. . . .

Ted considered you as one of his best friends and always felt that you were the one who really helped him start his life's work of helping handicapped people become rehabilitated. . . .

I am carrying on the office work as Ted would have wished me to do. I am trying to do the very best I can. His wonderful spirit of helping others is going to help me carry on too. I never realized how many lives he touched until he passed away. The letters I have been receiving are a wonderful memorial to him. In our short two years of married life we certainly packed every bit of happiness into it that we could and I know God is going to help me carry on in these days of loneliness that are ahead. I hope you will keep on corresponding when you have time.

With best wishes to you and your Aunt.

Cordially yours,
Marie Hoyer

Ted Hoyer's genius and dedication is evident in the letterhead stationery which is embossed with a picture of his handsome new factory in Oshkosh, Wisconsin, constructed sometime in the brief four years since he visited Arkadelphia.

Hoyer, his wife, Marie, his cousin and the others who helped the young inventor realize his dream were successful beyond what anyone could have imagined back in 1950. Almost sixty years later a quick search of the Internet reveals that Ted Hoyer & Company is today a major player in developing and supplying a wide assortment of devices and equipment for the handicapped. It is remarkable that two young men the same age suffering from the same devastating injury who first met in John Allen's bedroom at the home place in Arkadelphia could each in his own way, in spite of his severe handicap, go on to touch so many people and exert such a positive influence in the world.

Unfortunately Ted Hoyer's exceptional gifts could not protect him from the vulnerabilities of his condition; his death at thirty five, at the peak of his creativity, though not an unusual lifespan for quadriplegics at that time, was a tragic loss. His inventions and contributions in his short life, however, would insure that many handicapped who came after him could live longer and more productive lives.

Ted and John Allen met at the start of the decade which opened with the Korean War and closed in the age of rock and roll, an era remembered by some as "Happy Days." While the threat of nuclear war hung over the country during the 1950's, the fear of annihilation served merely as background noise for Americans as they busily went about reaping the rewards of the booming economy that followed World War II. After he took office in January 1953, President Eisenhower kept his word and went to Korea to help bring that war to an end thereby enabling Americans to focus once more on the pursuit of creature comforts. Levittown, Pennsylvania, became the model for sprawling suburbs that sprang up around the country during this time of growing prosperity, and even the smoldering Cold War contributed by spawning a vigorous boom in the military-industrial complex and the construction of fallout shelters. After the long lean years of the Great Depression and the severe sacrifices of World War II, Americans were ready to feather their nests and that's what they were busy doing in the 1950's leading John Kenneth Galbraith to give a name to what he saw around him with his book, the *Affluent Society*.

But, just as Arkadelphians had been somewhat cushioned from the Depression thanks to their practical survival skills, so were they unswayed by the exuberance of the Affluent Society.

As for John Allen, his admiration of Thoreau helped him steer a steady course through bad times and good, for both he and Aunt Bessie followed the Concord philosopher's dictum of making themselves rich by making their wants few and supplying those wants, in so far as they could, themselves.

John Allen had all he needed—his books, his business and his friends—and one of those constant friends was his former schoolmate and fellow Boy Scout, W.S McNutt, who was now pursuing graduate studies in California. These two men carried on a remarkable lifetime correspondence in which they shared with wit and humor their intimate personal experiences as well as their struggles with life's big questions. The range of their reading and exchange of ideas was distinguished, not only by its breadth, but by its quality.

In July 1954 McNutt wrote from Caltech in Pasadena, where he was pursuing studies in biochemistry, that he had been reading Trevelyan's Social History of England and a book of essays by Elmer Davis. He remarks, "Trevelyan is very fine and is both human and modest. Elmer Davis doesn't say anything new, but he says it so much better than anyone else that one rediscovers what he already knows." He writes of the concerns of a Tufts professor Sturdivant about radioactive fallout and complains there "is an underlying fear and distrust of intelligence in the minds of a great many people these days. Most of the people who shout the loudest about being 100% Americans have somehow lost faith in American institutions." He tells John Allen of his upcoming marriage to a cousin who teaches at Skidmore College in New York, that he is working hard in his graduate studies (post-doctoral?) leaving little time for drawing, sculpting, and reading. He says he's planning a six-day hike in the High Sierras with five men from the Institute and concludes, "Hope to see you in the fall. Dub"

Five months later he wrote again and put his finger on the spirit, or lack of spirit, of the times: "There seems to be a general desire to rest a while. Perhaps America has suddenly grown old. Even the young people–they want to rest too, and enjoy our prosperity."

Things were not restful at the home place, however, since the battles between the two sisters continued off and on throughout the decade. But as it turned out Bessie had hatched a plan to escape. She surprised her sister and the town in 1960 when she bought a house two blocks away at the corner at 4th and Main, the house that would become Adams Book Store. In 1957 John Allen had started to sell a few books from his room at the home place and to order others for his customers; after the move to Main Street he was able to expand the book side of his business and ultimately erect a sign proudly proclaiming the advent of Adams Book Store, an establishment which would become a community resource Rebecca Hall Fulmer would later describe as "an oasis of integrity, a nurturer of peace and compassion and freedom, a center for the arts and sciences, a last 'inpost' of enlightenment."

But all were not happy with Bessie and John Allen's move to new quarters. Bennie Jean Bledsoe told me that some people in Arkadelphia who had been contributing to Bessie and her nephew over the years were upset that she had been able to put aside enough money to buy the house on Main Street. Some said that if they had known she had all that money they would not have been so generous. But most were happy for Bessie and John Allen. And if the others had understood what a difference the move would make in the quality of life for John Allen they would likely have approved too.

So now in his new location with his hydraulic lift, motorized chair, and his self designed desk with phone, typewriter, and convenient pigeon holes for his papers and notes, John Allen was ready to carry on his practical business and personal correspondence and pursue the interests dear to his heart.

* * *

CHAPTER 10

Communities of Love and Thought

———— ■ ————

etween April and August of 1984 I conducted several informal interviews with Vernon and Joy in the room of the book store next to John Allen's bedroom. Vernon's ample frame filled the chair across from me while Joy sitting at my side stroked her long-haired black and white domino cat until it jumped from her lap and left the room with its bad rear leg dangling.

Although he had been dead several months now, John Allen's presence could be felt in everything around us. Through the open door his hospital style bed was visible with the hydraulic lift brought by Ted Hoyer thirty four years earlier still in place. On the other side of the wall that separated us from his room were shelves of some of his favorite books arranged so he could see them from his bed, the private library he had collected over the years—Thoreau, Emerson, Whitman, Melville, Shakespeare, the British Romantics, Thomas Hardy, Einstein, Tolstoy, Gandhi, Frost, and numerous others from the Adams pantheon. The pride he took in his collections as a boy never left him, the operative criterion always being quality, whether stamps, butterflies, artifacts or books.

Today Vernon and Joy are no longer resources for me, and as I look at the names in John Allen's high school yearbooks I realize that most if not all of his contemporaries are gone as well, so all I have are my notes from the interviews conducted back then, my memories and the contents of the boxes Joy entrusted to me. As I shuffle through these Horton family relics I am reminded of Lawrence Ferlinghetti's words that came to John Allen as he sifted through Aunt Bessie's old letters and photographs—"pictures of a gone world."

By now I've lived long enough to see for myself how short life is, to hold in memory pictures of several gone worlds, to understand how generation succeeds generation as trees on De Soto Bluff and all along the Ouachita yield season after season to implacable spring torrents to be replaced by burgeoning new growth. The present world is fleeting; most worlds are gone worlds—the Caddo Indian village that once thrived across the river, the unpainted clapboard buildings and houses that once lined the dirt road to the river in the settlement that would become Arkadelphia, the steamboat landing at the bottom of Main Street, the Horton plantation at Fairview and the parlor that proudly displayed Priscilla's piano from New Orleans, the Union and Confederate armies bivouacked along the Ouachita, John Allen and his friends of Troop 23 swimming in the river, those same friends as young men hugging their families at the train depot as they departed for World War II, a depot which is now a museum exhibiting artifacts and pictures from "gone worlds."

If it's not possible to trace all the names and track down all the leads from my notes and the boxes of Horton family papers, such is always the case in pursuing the fugitive details of past lives, for the webs of human relationships are complex. Gone worlds slip through our fingers like quicksilver and the most we can hope for is to hold on to some of those things we value by capturing them in words and stories in an attempt to save them from oblivion. Since time draws a curtain on the past through which we see but dimly, history presents us with mystery. Even with many questions unanswered, however, there remains ample evidence from the testimony of those who knew him and from the Horton correspondence and family relics, that John Allen Adams was a singular man possessed of remarkable intellect, spirit, good humor, strength and compassion, a man worthy of remembering.

Those were the qualities which drew people to him. Over his lifetime he had many circles of friends as he remarks in his farewell letter to Arkadelphia, people of "caring hearts and minds." In a sense, because of John Allen's wide range of interests, his friends over time can be thought of as comprising different "communities" centered around those interests: the quest for world peace; respect for the earth and the environment; literature and the craft of poetry; music; philosophy; science; religion—Judeo Christian, Eastern and pagan; living naturally; food, nutrition and the culinary arts; bird watching and squirrel watching; and most of all, friendship—mutual compassion and concern.

These communities overlapped in focus and evolved over time with the only qualification for membership being interest in one or more of the subjects and the love of conversation, sometimes carried on in the book store and sometimes through correspondence. Many of John Allen's friends belonged to more than one group, though none would have been aware of his membership since no charter for the communities was ever drawn up and no membership cards issued. Even John Allen, the spirit and focal point of the various groups, did not realize he was the magnetic center of these informal communities of love and thought, for he was innocent of any sense of his own importance, unaware of the influence he wielded with friends and customers.

One of the qualities that made John Allen attractive was the fact that he was a manly man, strong, principled and solid, one loved by many people but especially throughout his life by women—his mother and grandmother, Bessie and Gertrude, young Amy Thompson, his female classmates, and older admirers like Martha England and Martha and Amy Jean Greene. He won the hearts of a number of women who saw in him qualities not common in other men and who realized they could love him fully and freely, safe from physical entanglements, for polygamy is permissible in platonic relationships.

Three years after the John Allen Adams Scholarship was established in 1985 the modest goal of $5,000 had been exceeded by more than a thousand dollars. In 1988 I received a letter from the law firm Magruder, Montgomery, Brocato & Hoseman in Jackson, Mississippi, containing a check for $10,000 from the estate of Mary Elizabeth Thomas. On the letterhead were the names of twenty-one associates of the firm and the address of their Gulf Coast office in Biloxi; the letter was signed James T. Thomas, IV, her executor. Thomas had called me days earlier wanting to know who John Allen Adams was and what his connection had been to his great aunt Elizabeth.

Included in the letter were two pages of Elizabeth Thomas' will, the second of which contained the pertinent scholarship bequest. That page also contained other bequests: $200,000 to the Elizabeth Jones Library in Grenada, Mississippi, and thousands more to the Massachusetts SPCA; the University of the South, Sewanee, Tennessee; Americans for Middle East Understanding, Inc.; Princeton University—all of these on slightly more than one page of a will undoubtedly of some length. It was clear from the two pages I received that Ms. Thomas had been a woman of property. An Egyptologist and student of Eastern cultures with whom he had shared the most intimate details of his life, Elizabeth had been John Allen's dear friend for over thirty years.

Going through her letters I found one she wrote John Allen in November, 1976, encouraging him to write that novel he found in Aunt Bessie's trunk. In that letter she tells him, "I've felt you to be one of the most interesting people I've been privileged to know and have regretted the miles between us." The next letter from her is dated October 1954 from Princeton, New Jersey, in which she remarks that it has been seven years since she heard from John Allen.

From their correspondence it's not clear how the two met and became such good friends. There is mention of Frances, a mutual friend, perhaps Vernon's ex-wife, Mrs. Dan Whelchel, who pursued graduate studies at the University of Arkansas and traveled about in her studies; but when I interviewed Vernon and Joy in the book store after John Allen's death I didn't know enough about Elizabeth Thomas to ask questions. I did, however, write her along with others in 1984 for information about John Allen and she kindly responded by sending Joy Adams copies of his letters to her which Joy entrusted to me.

There have been many other questions that the letters and items in the boxes have raised that Vernon and Joy could have answered, but I didn't know to ask them twenty-three years ago when we talked. One thing I do know is that Vernon would have held back nothing; he freely shared with me, not only details of John Allen's life and Horton sibling conflicts, but unsolicited accounts of his own personal history including the story of "the red-headed bastard" who caused the breakup of his marriage with Frances.

However they met the bonds that held Elizabeth and John Allen together through the years was strengthened by the many interests they shared and the mutual respect they had for one another. She was the confidant to whom he wrote describing his dreams and his attempt to end his life when Aunt Bessie was committed to the TB sanitarium. She was another of those friends who enabled the poet to travel vicariously far beyond the confines of Adams Book Store. If W.S McNutt could take him hiking in the Sierra Madres, skiing in New England, and tramping the woods near Walden Pond, and Martha England could conduct him around the campus at Harvard and introduce him to students and faculty of Smith College as well as the literati of New York City, Elizabeth could transport John Allen to a land far away in both space and time, a land that was the lifetime focus of her studies— ancient Egypt.

A number of John Allen's poems were inspired by his friends; the following owes its existence to Elizabeth Thomas:

From an Antique Land

I fling no dust on my head;
there is dust enough in the heart,
a dryness no Nile ever touches.
Nor do I chant
"come and return to us!" –
knowing how weary you were,
how much in pain.
Do not resume those flaccid arms,
those flimsy knees;
here, I will help you sever
clinging flesh from bone–
I know how hard it is, how hard.

Re has folded his brightness;
how cold it is in the temple!
I will walk the fields where the fellah
sings to his creaking shadoof
and splashes his pittance of water.
Through flax grown ripe for pulling,
I walk toward the sound of my days.

The title of the poem, borrowed from the first line of Percy
Bysshe Shelly's well-known sonnet, "Ozymandias," ("I met a
traveler from an antique land"), is perfectly apt since Elizabeth
traveled to Egypt on several occasions in her studies where she
witnessed scenes depicted in John Allen's poem. "Antique"
describes as well the thirty-five century old desiccated mummy
of Ozymandias, the Greek name of Ramses the Great, Pharaoh
of the nineteenth dynasty of ancient Egypt, who lived to be

ninety years old. But for all the elaborate ceremony to outwit death and preserve the royal flesh, and in spite of the terrible human cost of constructing the colossal pyramids and monuments, Ramses was no more successful in outsmarting death than any other mortal. Though we retain his remains, he remains dead.

The major theme of Shelly's poem is the absurdity of overweening pride and the futility of the quest for immortality. The inscription on Ramses' fallen statue reads, "Look on my works, ye mighty, and despair!" The Pharaoh sought to cheat death, not only by having his tomb provisioned with all the wealth and comforts to ease his way through the underworld, but by leaving his likeness in stone, his monuments on earth to eternally remind those who followed of his greatness. The sonnet concludes,

> Nothing beside remains. Round the decay
> Of that colossal wreck, boundless and bare
> The lone level sands stretch far away.

John Allen's poem goes beyond the theme of hubris of the mighty and dramatizes the folly of all attempts to cling to life beyond the natural span, recognizing the wisdom and necessity of letting go when time has run out. Accepting mortality is not easy, of course, and it's natural to feel grief at life's end, but at long last Ramses must be released from the afflictions of the flesh. Death is the natural and proper end of human life.

The poem's persona rejects the ancient Eastern ritual of mourning, throwing dust on one's head, for he has, he says, a dryness in his heart "no Nile ever touches." The poet brings together the dryness of Egypt, the mummy, the tomb, the dryness of death itself, connecting these things with a spiritual aridity which no physical river can assuage. So what is to be done?

Like the Thoreauvean antidote to man's travails prescribed at the end of Voltaire's *Candide*, "to cultivate one's garden," and as in Adams' closing lines of "From a Space Capsule,"

> See the earth as it turns—
> And when its old simplicities of weight
> Draw us back to rock and frond
> We walk as men

the poet here calls us back to the things of this world. So, in the closing lines of "From an Antique Land," the focus turns from death to life, not life of the great and mighty, but of the humble peasant farmer, the fellah:

> I will walk the fields where the fellah
> sings to his creaking shadoof
> and splashes his pittance of water.

Even Re, or Ra, or Horah, the Egyptian deity whose longevity surpassed that of any other man-born god, at last had to fold his brightness and yield to his own mortality. The poem turns from the ancient realm of death to the world of the living where the fellah irrigates his fields with a shadoof. This most ancient of machines, made by balancing a long pole see-saw like with a bucket or skin bag on one end and a counter weight on the other atop an upright frame, enables the operator to dip water from a river or stream and swing it about to pour into the runnels of an irrigation system with minimum effort. While dynasties with their hubris and grandeur have come and gone, the lowly peasant has been wielding the "creaking shadoof" in his fields in Mesopotamia and throughout Africa and the Middle East for more than four thousand years.

John Allen, who could not walk and had never seen a field of flax, concludes his poem:

Through flax grown ripe for pulling
I walk toward the sound of my days.

His friends and his reading freed John Allen from the confines of his wheelchair and his book store on Main Street, restoring to him in imagination the supple-limbed world of his youth, where now in exotic lands he once more is able to walk. The last line of the poem becomes the title for his book of poetry.

Our worlds grow through empathy and imagination, and because John Allen was a consummate reader and listener he was able to share vividly world experiences with friends far away. He learned of the shadoof through Elizabeth who sent him rough sketches and a photocopy from an Egyptian tomb painting of the device so he could clearly envision the scene he was describing in the poem. The two exchanged many letters on Eastern culture and religion—Egyptology, the Tibetan Book of the Dead, on Hinduism and the Bhagavad Gita, and on Buddhism. John Allen got up-to-date reports on D. T. Suzuki, the octogenarian Zen master whose lectures Elizabeth attended at Princeton.

Rather than being removed by six degrees of separation, for John Allen his distance from some of those he most admired was in some cases only two degrees, thanks to friends in interesting places. He was no doubt moved when Elizabeth told him of seeing Albert Einstein in the closing months of his life still preoccupied no doubt with his elusive dream of a unified field theory. In 1954 she adds a handwritten note at the end of a long typewritten letter: "Now and again I've seen Einstein walking to and from the Institute. It is always an 'occasion,' for he is surely one of the top men, as well as brains, now with us, don't you think?" John Allen would certainly concur, admiring the man even more for his efforts to bring about world disarmament than for his scientific genius.

Only five months after Elizabeth wrote telling John Allen of seeing Einstein came word of the great man's death; just one week before he died he had written the British philosopher and mathematician, Bertrand Russell, agreeing to have his name added to a manifesto calling for all nations to give up nuclear weapons. As the alien Klaatu did in the movie *The Day the Earth Stood Still,* and as his earthly avatar John Allen was doing in his poems and correspondence, Einstein had been for ten years warning the world of the folly and dangers of the nuclear arms race. But though the influence of the Arkadelphia poet and bookseller could not match the reach of Hollywood or the fame of the great scientist, his dedication to the cause of world peace was no less passionate.

If Elizabeth provided John Allen with news of Egypt and archaeology, the lectures of the Zen master D.T. Suzuki and glimpses of Albert Einstein walking from the Institute at Princeton, his life-long friend, Martha England, from her vantage point in New York City, was able to share with him scenes from some of the exciting cultural life in that great metropolis. While some of the letters from John Allen to Elizabeth Thomas are contained in the boxes of Horton materials, because she returned them at my request to Joy who entrusted them to me, I don't have his letters to Martha. But her letters to him provide a fairly clear window into their decades-long relationship.

Martha's letters are filled with names of the leading operas, plays and personalities of the day, and it's clear she is not merely name-dropping or trying to impress. Her Radcliffe PhD and accomplished friends never blind her to her Arkadelphia roots which she clearly values as she does her relationship with John Allen, a friendship which survived her 1948 declaration of love for him and resolve to tell him good bye. Her letters through the years clearly reveal that she needed to share her exciting life with him, that she in fact never stopped loving him.

The following, from a letter she wrote in 1958, begins by telling John Allen about a book she is writing, and then describes the distractions:

> And I do get tempted out. People know I love the theater, and call me to say they have extra tickets and can I go? So I can usually—saw *Two for the Seesaw* Tues.—Henry Fonda's new play with two characters. A girl named Ann Bancroft is the other, and the play is, amazingly enough, about love. . . .Last night saw Cocteau's *The Infernal Machine,* the retelling of the Oedipus story in which the hero is, naturally, neither wise nor brave. . . .he is a cruel young sprout. John Kerr plays it—June Havoc is Jocasta. . . .

Vann Woodward is coming Wednesday to take me
to lunch, but I think I will ask the Joneses and have
lunch here. After all, he is frightfully famous and I
should have <u>him</u> to lunch. I am not really sure I know
him at all—but he was part of Arkadelphia scenery
and I have read his books for fifteen years with as
much pride as if I could remember him. I wish you
could come—the real reason he wants to see me is that
I will talk. No one will talk these days about the segregation, and I, of course, have all things figured out.
. . He sounds just like home over the telephone—and
I'm eager to see him. Bring Amy and come. OK?

One of the preeminent American historians of the post World
War II era, C. Vann Woodward was another of those people
like Thoreau and Abraham Lincoln who rose above the prejudices of his region and time and in so doing placed himself
on the right side of history. While taking graduate courses
at Colombia University in 1931 Woodward met Langston
Hughes and was influenced by the literary and artistic movement known as the Harlem Renaissance. His landmark book,
The Strange Career of Jim Crow, Martin Luther King Jr. called
"the historical bible of the civil rights movement." He won
the Bancroft Prize for *The Origins of the New South* and in 1982
the Pulitzer Prize for *Mary Chesnut's Civil War.*

Woodward at that time had not yet moved to Yale where
he would spend most of his professional career, but was teaching at Johns Hopkins in Baltimore and enjoying his most
productive period as an historian of the American South. The
"Amy" Martha refers to in her letter is Amy Jean Greene,
John Allen's former teacher and the classmate of Woodward's
at Henderson College who stood up with him to protest the

autocratic policies of President Clifford Hornaday, an act which provides early evidence that confronting injustice came naturally to him.

When Woodward made the phone call to Martha the Little Rock High School desegregation crisis was dominating national news. It may be that Woodward called because he wanted to discuss with Martha the Little Rock School crisis, but more likely he wanted to visit with a cultivated citizen from back home and exchange thoughts on their common history and swap news of their mutual friends. It's clear from her letters that she shared Woodward's attitudes toward racial injustice. She had, after all, taught at Smith before coming to Queens College, and Smith continues to this day to be one of the most progressive, some would say radical, campuses in the country.

She goes on in the letter to mention other notables she has recently encountered:

Feb. 21. Mr. Ashmore is giving the first Neiman lecture at Harvard and I am going to hear it. Will visit my friends the Aherens—Bob is mg ed of the *Boston Globe* and is so absolutely fascinated by Mr. Ashmore that he is asking him to a dinner with the Globe folks and Hal and Elma Martin. Can you come to that too? . . .

I wish I could see you. . . . I really do hope I have a chance to see Mr. A in action with that Boston gang. I know all of them—some pretty smart cookies. Otto Zaussamer, whom you may get in the *Atlantic Monthly*, is a very good friend of mine. As far as the Yankees and the foreign intellectuals and the South are concerned, I am myself a one-man desegregation movement. Bob Aherens is Boston Irish Catholic. John Taylor, Boston blue-blood. Otto from Vienna came by the most devious ways to the USA during the recent unpleasantness there for the Jews. Of course you know all about Hal Martin. If not—ask Amy. She knows a good many of these folks, I think.

The first Neiman lecturer referred to here is Harry Ashmore, "Mr. A," the editor of the *Arkansas Gazette* who supported the integration of Central High and confronted Governor Faubus in front page editorials. While Ashmore was celebrated in many places throughout the country including Harvard, his newspaper was boycotted in Arkansas and he was the subject of numerous physical threats from outraged segregationists. His presentation of the Neiman lecture coincided with the Pulitzer Prize he was awarded that year for his courageous stand.

Martha concluded the letter,

Love you, honey. Now don't you go off and join the KKK. M.

While there was no chance of John Allen doing that, it is interesting to consider his physical and historical situation regarding the question of race.

Bessie's racism was unwavering. The attitudes she absorbed at her Grandmother Elizabeth Horton's knee about the Damn Yankees who used her mahogany dresser drawers to feed their horses never left her, and she would brook no arguments on the subject of race. So John Allen grew up with that. And there were the Civil War atrocities in which W.S.

Horton, John Allen's slave-owning great grandfather, was possibly involved—the massacre of black Union soldiers at Poison Spring and the murder of black teamsters and escaping slaves at Marks' Mills. Some in the family believed that John Allen's grandfather, Louis Horton, was murdered by a black man. So the Hortons' entanglements in the question of race corresponded with those of many other white families throughout the South. No one would have been more familiar with these realities of Southern history than C. Vann Woodward.

A related strain of prejudice was introduced into the family by John Allen's prosperous uncle Rodney. In one of his letters Vernon complains of his brother's anti-Semitic rants, views he likely picked up while working for the Ford Motor Company in Detroit, views reflecting the influence of the founder Henry Ford. There is no evidence, however, that the infection spread beyond Rodney within the Horton family. Vernon was certainly scornful of those views.

But for John Allen, as with Woodward and Martha England, history was not fate. Where American slaves were set free with Lincoln's Emancipation Proclamation, John Allen freed himself from regional prejudices through his reading reinforced by the positive influence of enlightened friends. As Robert Frost says in "Poetry and School," Once we have learned to read the rest can be trusted to add itself to us." The quality of the reader will determine the quality of the reading, and John Allen in his life-long searching found his way to the very best writers and thinkers and acquired in the process a deep understanding of life, all while sitting in his quiet, still place.

Martha England's life in contrast was anything but quiet and still. She was an active scholar who, in addition to leading an exciting social life published studies on various literary figures while pursuing her interests in music, specifically religious hymns and opera. She combined those interests when she along with a colleague, John Sparrow, published *Hymns Unbidden; Donne, Herbert, Blake, Emily Dickinson, and the Hymnographers* and when she worked with a fellow opera lover, James Durbin, translating Rossini's opera, *Cenerentola* (Cinderella) into English.

But mostly, it seems, judging from her letters, Martha enjoyed her life—not that she did not feel others' pain, for in the following letter she begins by sharing at length with John Allen her concerns for her ailing sister, Nancy, much as she had shared her concerns years earlier about her brother, Fuzzy. Then she turns to her exciting life in New York, beginning with her elation over the publishing success of three of her Harvard professors and describing a recent visit to that campus and the reaction of her professors to a book she was working on.

Oct 17, 1963

. . .I spent 9 days in Cambridge, opening and closing the library—but running into many playmates in the course of the day and loving it every minute. Widener closes at 5:30 Sat and is locked Sun, so I did prowl about the countryside, and such color as was never seen adorns Mass this year. Coffee at Bakers', tea at Bush's, dinner at Martin's and lunch every day at the fac club with one pal or another. Elena Levin one day. . .Bush is really pleased with what I'm doing, Baker is really excited, said "I would read such a bk right away even if you had not written it. . ." And Bate. . .issued a command for me to get myself to his office where we could talk in peace—honestly flipped! He is not 'interested." He is thrilled—and thrilled with all I have done up to date. So why wouldn't I be happy?

Back to NY in time for dress rehearsal of Aida. My two dear friends since Cambridge days, Nat Merrill and Bob O'Hearn, had the season opening at the Met with a new production of Aida—which opera we had done together in Colorado, so I was especially involved. Had planned to work till midnight opening night then go to the cast party (for tickets are 50.00) and bless me if Mr. Bing didn't punch a ticket for me—which means it was free. I shall save the stub because of the price tag. Director's box. 650.00. You heard me. 300 admission, 350 contribution.

The Met not only gave the boys opening, but second night as well, with their Meistersinger which was declared the glory of the entire Bing regime last yr. So with two such shows wired back to back, we have simply declared Merrill-O'Hearn week. Nothing is left but to crown them with diamonds on top of the Empire State Bldg.

Martha goes on to tell how her friends Merrill and O'Hearn entertained her and her sister Nancy when they had taken the opera to Colorado, how they drank Champaign "like water." They had such a great time she says that when they left New Mexico, "I was not singing Aida, but that old hymn, 'Oh, they tell me of an unclouded day.' It was a golden time, a time out of this world almost. . . I have no idea if it helps or hurts Nancy that I write her hourly of new achievements. Many who were at that picnic are in the news pictures—audience and stage." She concludes,

> This golden week has taken color from that time in Col which was for me literally a foretaste of heaven— an unclouded day in the sense the hymn meant it. I feel her with me—but what that heroic gal feels, I do not know. Do what you can. Love. M

In spite of her Radcliffe PhD, her Harvard mentors and Metropolitan Opera associates, it's clear in this letter that Martha remains the daughter of her Baptist preacher father, Dr. Hardy Winburn, and that her years in church with her family and chapel at Ouachita Baptist retain their influence. No matter what happens to us later in life or how our religious views may change, the hymns we sing in our youth remain indelibly in our hearts. They are part of who we are.

The Mr. Bing who "punched her ticket" was of course the celebrated and charismatic Rudolph Bing, General Manager of the Metropolitan Opera for over two decades, the man who spearheaded the movement to construct the modern opera house which is now the central feature of Lincoln Center in New York. Of his many accomplishments, one that will always bring him distinction is that he was the first to bring an African American, Marion Anderson, to perform at the Met.

Ten years after her "unclouded day" Martha was still writing to John Allen (and now to his wife Joy as well) about beautiful people and exciting performances in New York City.

Tues I heard Maria Callas sing at Carnegie Hall, just after the sudden death a few hours before of Sol Hurok, who was manager of the event. The concert was dedicated to his memory by her and Di Stephano. It was great! Of course her voice is not what it was 20 yrs ago. Who cares? She is marvelous, and he played to her in fine style. He has sung better too – has had a cold. But it was an exciting event.

Martha's schedule is chock full. On Wednesday she had attended an opera by Donizetti, *Parisana d'este*. The next event she describes for John Allen and Joy is an exclusive dinner for the promising young pianist, James Tocco and his beautiful wife. She pictures in detail one of the guests, a celebrated Persian beauty, Lily, wife of American playboy Bunty Laurenz.

Last night I went to dinner in honor of James Tocco, a young pianist who will make a big mark in the music world, I am told. I shall have a chance to hear him soon for myself for he will be playing in and near NY. He and his wife are a very handsome young couple. I had my first sight of Lily. It was a small dinner—nine people. Everybody but me knew Lily—she is Mrs. Bunty Laurenz and he is charming, all-American play boy and fine amateur golfer. But I must tell you about Lily.

She is beautiful. Wore low-heeled white satin slippers, and from there upwards nothing visible though I think she had on a body thing with invisible stockings.

Then she had on a shirt like a man's—white satin. Period. Now she did wear tiny little white satin pants, Joy—once in a while they were visible. Black black long hair. Black black eyes. And skin! Wow! She is as lovely as I had been told she was. She wore several rings, one large one made of many rubies and turquoises, very Persian. AND one 62 carat diamond. Can you ever think of how big it would be? Very lovely. Gift of her father who is uncle (I think) of the Shah of Iran and owns the oil wells the Shah does not own. She was sent to school in England and then in Switzerland. I lost count of her languages and much of the conversation went on in Russian and Persian. Mrs. Tocco is Persian. And Lily has brains, and make no mistake about it. She spent as much time admiring my ring as I spent admiring her diamond—it is a lovely ring, and came to me from my father, and is an Arkansas pearl. Lily wanted to talk about Richard III, a much-maligned saint in her opinion, and she is very knowledgeable about the Tudors and Plantagenets. She also wanted to talk about the Kennedy assassination, another sinister plot in her opinion, and on this too she is very well informed (if mistaken).

What was it about Martha that elicited invitations from wealthy and cultivated notables? What I believe can be clearly inferred from her letters is that, among her other qualities, she must have been a sparkling conversationalist. She acknowledges that Vann Woodward possibly invited her to lunch because she liked to talk. And with her PhD in comparative literature, her work with the Metropolitan

Opera, and her Southern and Arkansas roots, she was certainly equipped with a wealth and depth of conversational material. She proved prescient in her remark that James Tocco would make a big mark in the music world since he went on to play with great acclaim in just about every major venue around the world. And it's interesting to note that Lily was as fascinated by Martha's Arkansas pearl as Martha was by her 62 carat diamond. It seems each of these women saw the other as exotic.

Martha's detailed descriptions of her exciting social life and the cultural events she attended show how important it was for her to share those experiences with John Allen and suggest how much she would have loved it if they could have shared them together. There's no way to know whether her declaration of love for him when he was in his twenties and she in her thirties explains her life-long dedication, but it's not unreasonable to think so. Whatever the nature of her feelings at the time of that declaration, they had since clearly been sublimated into an enduring and valued friendship.

No doubt Martha had Joy in mind when she included the detailed description of Lily's exquisite ensemble knowing that Joy, while far removed from such elegant society herself, worked for some time in a factory sewing women's clothes and as a woman would be interested in such things. For John Allen there were Martha's long letters detailing literary and cultural activities that were surely of more interest to him, letters which enabled him to share experiences his restricted circumstances prohibited. Unfortunately, his letters to her were not found in the boxes of family materials.

Although John Allen was loved by a number of women his injury obviated any rivalry on their part, and he could safely and with clear conscience be faithful to them all. Joy could freely share him with Amy Jean and Martha Greene, his high school coeds, Martha England, Elizabeth Thomas and all his female admirers. Aunt Bessie was the only exception; only she demanded primary rights.

While Elizabeth Thomas and Martha England were two important people in his life, many other talented and caring friends moved in orbit around John Allen and his book store. One of the many people he corresponded with through the years was Chet Dawson, an aspiring poet teaching at a small college in Brazil. They shared some common enthusiasms and friends and exchanged views on various poems and works of literature, but I'm not sure how John Allen viewed Chet's fanciful rhetoric. Here's a sample from a letter he wrote in early 1980:

My best friend bears the name of Plato. Another dear buddy, Aristotle. Still another is one less antique, Plutarch. All of these, but not to overlook the most persuasive, beautiful, and true playwright ever born on earth: Aeschylus. Of these I sing. With these I daily and forever and dearly associate. Nothing Christian; O yes, why not? I read some four months ago the Protestant equivalent of the Catholic Divine Comedy: Pilgrim's Progress, both of which are astounding in the skill and wisdom and exquisite language—but Dante, of course, far exceeding Bunyan. And while I have read all of the plays of Sophocles,

I cannot seem to get excited about either Euripides or Aristophanes—especially the latter. I don't go much for comedy anyway. And, to round out what might be a boring summation, the ecstasy of being comes from my almost daily driving far off the road, into the untrodden ways (to beg fr Wordsworth) and parking my car, hike the dry riverbeds, scale the hills, upturn large rocks to see who's sleeping under, and ponder the beauty of a world so intricate and so intelligent that I go thru life exalted and stunned. God? Well—slashing at theological foundations—I speak thereof as "The Central Intelligence," borrowed from Einstein. To this I kneel, yes.

Enuf. Are you laughing? Ah—surely not. I have only sought to be honest, to limn a reasonably accurate portrait. Did I fail?

Chet Dawson

He would not have been laughing at Chet any more than he laughed at the old timer who pronounced Yeats, "Yeets." Not that he lacked a sense of humor or an incisive sense of irony, but because he was always tolerant toward those who mean no harm reserving his scorn for deserving targets. And he and Chet shared many enthusiasms, including admiration for Thoreau and other anti-war and eco-friendly people and publications like *Manas* and Mildred Loomis' *Green Revolution*. Dawson had originally sought John Allen out to help him promote his book of poetry, "Seedlings." It's not known what success Adams Book Store had in moving that book off the shelves.

John Allen had a bright sense of humor and liked to play games. The student assistant who wrote the poem remembering him after his death, Sandy Hays, said he was the only other person she knew besides herself who liked to play the game, "Authors." She suspected he could run the store by himself and hired college students only to keep him company; clearly they enjoyed his. He liked to play a game with his last student assistant, Sarah Sullivan, an excellent speller, by challenging her with difficult words to spell. If he hadn't died Sarah said she wouldn't have left Adams Book Store to attend graduate school. Because their boss was always pleasant and comfortable to be around and the book store was a welcoming place, the young people working for him actually looked forward to reporting for duty.

While some in far places were vital members of his circle of friends, there were many others nearby who paid regular visits to the book store and exchanged news and ideas with him, not by letter, but in conversation. Once he and Joy got their van they were able to visit friends, sometimes having been invited over for dinner. Always interested in nutrition and food, John Allen would occasionally act the host himself, one time humorously fancying himself an epicure. He wrote to his close friend, Mrs. Boulware Ohls, about a great cheese experiment:

> The cheese came today—a ball of Edam . . . made in Holland, and a pound of English Stilton. I spent Moritz's [Mr. Ohls] Christmas present for the cheese,

thinking the Ohls and Amy Jean could come some night for a late snack; we can see whether we are really gourmets or mere dreamers. You will have to be well and hardy before encountering the Stilton. We took one deep breath and hastily put it in the refrigerator; but I fear it is already far along the road of all mortality. After a tiny nibble I began to think that the trick of becoming a gourmet probably lies in one learning to swallow while holding his breath. In his article on cheeses in the current *Holiday* Clifton Fadiman speaks of Stilton with deep feeling: "Of Stilton it is hard to speak without emotion. Its azure veins avouching its noble lineage, it thrones it as the world's most regal Blue, exerting, like any true aristocrat, authority without aggressiveness."

Even though John Allen could not share Fadiman's emotional enthusiasm over Stilton cheese, he had always been enthusiastic about his natural surroundings, and now with Joy able to drive them about in the van he was able to see once more the wonders of springtime in Arkansas. He saw again the flowers he had come to know in his youth on his jaunts down the hill on Clinton Street as he headed for the river—starflowers, henbit, dead nettle, wild onion, and dandelions. Joy drove him out into the countryside to see the jonquils in bloom and around Arkadelphia to see the dogwoods and azaleas.

One hot July afternoon she and a friend drove him to Lake DeGray, an inviting twenty-two mile long lake dotted with pine-covered islands. The lake, a fairly recent project of the U.S. Corps of Engineers, was created when the Caddo River was dammed shortly before it flowed into the Ouachita near Caddo Valley. John Allen along with other environmentalists had opposed the dam because it blocked one of the few free-flowing rivers left in the state and the resulting lake would cover the wooded, rugged cliffs along the most scenic stretch of the river. But there it was in front of him now, and he could not deny its beauty. He was so affected by the outing that he later typed out a brief account of the experience.

After a pleasant picnic lunch the two women took advantage of the sandy beach and went for a swim leaving John Allen sitting in his wheelchair to enjoy the view. It had been 96 degrees that day but now the red sun was sliding behind the hills at the far end of the lake and an evening breeze was coming across the water to cool his cheeks. He watched as a bird hopped to the lake's edge to take its last sip for the day and he could see from time to time on the rosy shine of the water a turtle's head pop up to take a gulp of air. In the distance there was the dark silhouette of four fishermen in a boat hoping for one last bit of luck before heading back to shore. On a nearby point two pine trees stood black against the pink, mother-of-pearl sky in the west. John Allen had to concede that "even tamed nature offers something healing" though he held to Thoreau's sentiment that "in wildness is the preservation of the world."

His love for the natural beauty of Arkansas had been awakened when as an eight-year-old he left the carnival circuit and came to live with Aunt Bessie at the home place. It was there as he stood amid the privet and poke weed on the banks of the Ouachita and watched the current glide by on its way to the Mississippi that he was first exposed to the inexorable flow of time and the river, though as a child he could have been only dimly aware of the consequences of being caught in that stream. Now John Allen, after having become one of the longest-lived quadriplegics in the country, fully understood, as he had understood for years, the terms of nature's imperatives and accepted what was to come as calmly as the picnickers that evening accepted the darkness that was descending on Lake DeGray.

* * *

CHAPTER 11

Concord Philosophers

———————■———————

John Allen was a man for all seasons, one with a broad range of interests evident in the friends he communicated with through the years. For perspectives beyond Aunt Bessie's Presbyterianism and Arkadelphia's strong Baptist fundamentalism he had Elizabeth Thomas whose work in Egyptian antiquities and Eastern religions fed his imagination. To free himself from his wheelchair-bound, provincial small town confinements, he had Martha England with her Harvard education and New York glitterati friends to provide him reports of Metropolitan Opera performances and goings on among the literary elite in that great city.

He loved music, particularly classical music. He wrote Mike Vogler, "I'm listening to piano, flute and guitar music by Mozart, Handel, and Bach. . . .Good music requires as much attention as a book." Not only did John Allen show early talent on the piano, but one of the last things he wrote his parents before he was injured was that he had signed up for Choir. Joy mentioned that he liked to sing to her. I never heard him sing but I would bet that, even with his limited lung capacity, his singing voice, like his speaking voice, would have been pleasant to the ear. Martha England, expansive, romantic, and unbothered by "the big questions," in addition to being a valuable source of news concerning the music scene in New York City, was an erudite literary companion and a skilled critic of his poetry. John Allen had enlightened and cultivated friends both near and far, but when he wanted to cut to the quick of life he turned to W.S "Dub" McNutt.

As he noted in his posthumous letter to the people of Arkadelphia, he acquired many new friends over the years, but since his youth the one closest to him spiritually and intellectually was schoolmate and fellow member of Mr. Huddleston's Boy Scout Troop 23, Dub McNutt. For over three decades they shared their experiences and ideas, mostly through correspondence, and while I have many of McNutt's letters to John Allen, four years after I contacted him he responded telling me he had no intention of releasing the letters John Allen had written to him. He wrote:

> The superficial aspects of John Allen's life do not concern me in the least. What I find so moving is what he has confided in me, letter by letter throughout his life. I have boxes of them.

> Such intimate details of his life are not matters he would care to have published, I gather, and which I am certain about. I had no intention, at the time, of sorting through them, page by page, and censoring section after section.

I am not offended by McNutt's statement at the end of the letter—that he was astonished there were some in Arkadelphia (me) as stupid as some he had to deal with there in Concord. I am in fact grateful for his letters which Joy Adams entrusted to me, letters remarkable for their intelligence, refreshing honesty, wisdom and wit. They remind me of something someone said of Mark Twain, that he was incapable of writing a dull sentence.

Professor McNutt's attempt to protect his friend is understandable though, I believe, misguided. What dark secrets did John Allen share with him that were not known to Joy, Gertrude, Vernon and the other family and friends I talked to? Of course, along with their many distinctions there was a dark side to the Horton family—the suicides of John Allen's mother and grandfather and his attempt to end his own life. There were also questions surrounding John Allen's birth: Was Louise pregnant when she married Al? Was she still married to Frank Hurt at the time and thus guilty of bigamy? Why did she for years conceal the fact that she was John Allen's mother? Perhaps these secrets were the reason Martha Greene and others did not want to answer my questions about his family history.

I'm not sure how much of this history McNutt was aware of, but I do know he knew of the fierce battles between the Horton sisters. Because John Allen had to live in the midst of those conflicts they would have been the most likely subjects of his personal revelations to his friend. It is possible beyond that, that there were discussions of mutual friends McNutt felt should not be divulged. Some such discussions are included in his letters. But whatever his motive for withholding the letters there's no question that his action deprived the John Allen story a valuable resource. Nothing the letters might have revealed, I believe, could have damaged John Allen for I am convinced that the dark shadows in his family background serve only to make his character stand out more brightly. I also believe we live in a more enlightened time than even twenty or thirty years ago. Surely no follower of Jesus today would be troubled by questions surrounding the birth of a good man.

Still, even though a crucial half of their correspondence is missing, McNutt's letters provide an invaluable window into the relationship of the two men by revealing the topics of their conversations through the years and the focus of many of John Allen's intellectual interests and concerns.

Adult friendships have a different quality when they have endured from childhood and that quality is evident in McNutt's letters to John Allen. You can hear in his words to his friend echoes of conversations that would have been heard around campfires with Mr. Huddleston along the Ouachita and at the Boy Scout Jamborees at Camp Bonanza. Both men had since those days grown considerably in knowledge and matured in the ways of the world while holding on to youthful ways of addressing one another. Together they studied the great books and tackled big philosophical problems exchanging news and ideas often in the language of the teenagers they had once been. Example:

> I have more money, man. Pick out a volume of Icelandic Sagas, Richard Burton's early history of Virginia, and the letters of Felix Mendelssohn and mail them to me. I will pay you, man!

The miles between them were never a barrier to their friendship. They shared their lives in letters and during McNutt's periodic visits to Arkadelphia. While in graduate school at

Cal Tech he reported not only on his camping treks into the Sierra Madres but on his political activities in support of Adlai Stevenson, a man he admired for his intellect and wit. In the mid 1950's he wrote about American complacency: "There seems to be a general desire to rest a while. Perhaps America has suddenly grown old. Even the young people—they want to rest too, and enjoy our prosperity."

In the spring of 1956 he wrote from Pasadena that he was working a precinct for Stevenson and complained, "Here in southern California there is a feeling that things are so close to perfect that only troublesome people quibble about changing anything." Eisenhower, he said, "has done very poorly in his excessive earnestness over moderation." The Brown vs. Board of Education ruling was stirring things up in the South at the time and he asked about the so-called. "Citizens Committees" and whether there were any such groups in Arkadelphia. He remarked on John Allen's "ripostes" to the *Arkansas Gazette* on the topic, and though I don't have those letters it's certain they were in opposition to the hateful racist sentiments flying about the state at that time.

President Eisenhower did come through, however, defending the constitution by sending the National Guard to insure that the court order to integrate Central High in Little Rock was carried out. It was during this period that Martha England was entertaining C. Vann Woodward in New York and attending the Harvard lecture by the *Gazette* Editor, Harry Ashmore.

It's interesting to note that McNutt never discussed his scientific studies and accomplishments with John Allen even though those studies must have consumed the great majority of his time. The reason, I believe, was because their friendship nourished part of him that science could not. McNutt went on to a long and successful career as researcher in biochemistry and an academic professor and scholar, but the world of science for him was not sufficient.

He had told John Allen earlier about marrying his cousin, Jessie, who taught at Skidmore College for women in Saratoga Springs, New York. By 1965 the family had moved to Newton Center, Massachusetts, where he was teaching at Tufts University Medical School. He wrote at the end of that year about his experiences with fatherhood, with his two sons, Malcolm, who was eleven, and Ronnie, who was nine. Of his younger son he said, "Two years ago he thought that he was in charge and well able to run the world by himself. But, alas, he is now learning (as all Americans are learning) that even with all their power the world cannot really be controlled, and that even to mitigate certain problems is by no means easy."

The parenthetical reference in the letter was to the Vietnam War, an issue of crucial importance to John Allen. It's sad to note that, even into the first decade of the twenty-first century, America had yet to learn the lesson Ronnie was learning. McNutt also mentioned in the letter that his older son, Malcolm, was studying cello under a member of the Boston Symphony Orchestra.

In one of his letters it sounds as though McNutt may have purchased Britannica's *Great Books* through John Allen. He wrote, "Advise me, my friend, what should I read? Believe me, I still dig it out of those Great Books; that's the best deal yet I got off you. Do you have some other buys?" Another time he tells his friend,

> . . . making great progress in the world of the Great
> Books. If one will only put two ½ hour trolley rides

to proper use, as classical a knowledge may be gained in this way as that recommended by Lord Chesterfield to his son! It has proven so useful to me that I have decided to improve upon it. I am moving to Concord (two miles from Walden Pond) which means that ¾ of an hour will be required each way. The cost will be greater, but it is only fair to expect that a classical education should cost *something*. Also I shall have a lodge (in addition to the house) where I can carve in marble…and a blessed absence of neighbors to complain of my noise.

It's hard to think that Dub McNutt didn't have his friend in mind when he moved close to Walden Pond. In June, 1966, he wrote, "We are now well established at Concord. Each morning and evening I take a stroll along Thoreau St. to and from the train station."

As noted before few people care to look much below the surface of life. To do so is a lot of trouble and can be disconcerting and even frightening, so most are content to cushion themselves with social conventions and traditional beliefs and go on with their lives. Why go to the trouble to examine things for yourself when others before you have done the work and offer readymade and comfortable answers?

But W.S McNutt, like Thoreau and John Allen, marched to a different drum beat. It's true that the earlier Concord philosopher, while challenging convention at every turn, was basically a practical handy man who kept both feet on the ground while questioning the values by which most men live their lives. Being unflinchingly honest, however, he did from time to time confront the existential strangeness that operates below the surface of things, or in one case the strangeness he discovered atop earth's surface on the heights of Mount Ktaadn. He describes that other-worldly experience in his book, *The Maine Woods*.

Having left his hiking friends below, he found himself disoriented in an alien landscape of giant boulders and stunted vegetation lit by shifting beams of sunlight breaking through low scudding clouds:

> It reminded me of the creations of the old epic and dramatic poets, of Atlas, Vulcan, the Cyclops, and Prometheus. Such was Caucasus and the rock where Prometheus was bound. Aeschylus had no doubt visited such scenery as this. It was vast, Titanic, and such as man never inhabits. Some part of the beholder, even some vital part, seems to escape through the loose grating of his ribs as he ascends. He is more lone than you can imagine.

Thoreau's contemporary Herman Melville goes even further in *Moby Dick* confronting man's existential predicament, his "aloneness," in what he calls "the heartless immensities of the universe." Little Pip, the black cabin boy, experiences that isolation traumatically when he is tossed out of a whaleboat during a chase and left bobbing alone on the great expanse of ocean. Unlike Conrad Aiken's Senlin who nonchalantly stands before the mirror and ties his tie as he spins through the incomprehensible vastness of space, Pip, more immediately aware of his dire circumstance, is struck with panic. Emptiness is a frightening thing.

Ishmael, the narrator of Melville's epic novel, also reflects on emptiness when he considers the whiteness of the whale—whiteness, the color of nothingness, the color of the sepulcher, the color of death; bizarrely, whiteness is the total absence of color which results when all colors combine. Colors themselves, he knows, are merely phantoms, various wave lengths of light that trick our eyes and deceive our brains. Ahab, captain of the doomed *Pequod*, sees malevolence behind the whiteness of the whale and determines to strike it; Ishmael sees an even more fearsome possibility—that there is nothing behind the phenomenological world we experience—the azure sky, the verdant woods, the vibrant allure of all earth's flora and fauna. Behind the beautiful mask is blankness; all nature, he concludes, paints like the harlot.

Dub McNutt, John Allen and all the Scouts of Troop 23 sat at night along the Ouachita and told scary stories, their emotions intensified by the darkness of the gloomy pine trees that surrounded the small circle of light from their campfires, just as De Soto's desperate band of adventurers and the Caddo Indians across the river had done before them. In that image is the whole story of man from the beginning, his attempt to expand his circle of light into the darkness, a darkness that has always been inhabited by terrors, real and imagined.

Nature has provided man with real terrors, from sabertoothed tigers and other prehistoric predators to contemporary man-eating carnivores and venomous creatures, such as vipers, poisonous spiders and insects. Earthquakes, volcanoes, and storms have also been perennial dangers, but the greatest mortal threat for man has forever been his own kind. It was not wild beasts that led to the extirpation of Caddo villages along the Ouachita or to the removal of Native Americans from the Southeastern states and the tragedy known as the Trail of Tears or to the Civil War slaughter in which W.S. Horton found himself a participant or the carnage of World War II that Buddy Whitten, Billy Gill East and other of John Allen's classmates found themselves caught up in. Wars, tribal and national, have been from the beginning the greatest scourge of mankind.

And as if all these external dangers were not sufficient, man has added to the terrors of life with his fevered imagination. It's not only natural and human threats that roam the darkness outside our circle of light, but horrors of our own making—ghosts, evil spirits, witches, chimeras of all descriptions as well as theological horrors inflicted by vengeful gods, torments such as the Apocalypse, Armageddon and the infernos of Hell and Hades awaiting us beyond the grave.

But perhaps the most shocking horror of life is a reality we live with every day giving it little thought, one we see in *Moby Dick* when the crew of the *Pequod* watch one night in the light of lamps suspended over the ship's side as sharks in a violent feeding frenzy tear at the carcass of a recently harpooned whale. As the crew slash at the boiling voracious sharks with sharp cutting spades eviscerating them and watching them devour their own entrails, the second mate Stubb, the killer of the whale, looks down at the thundering, bloody feast below having just enjoyed his own rare whale steak.

The Fiji Islander and first harpooner, Queequeg, looking on the carnage remarks, "wedder Feejee god or Nantucket god, but de god wat made shark must be one dam Ingin."

The shark may be the epitome of savagery, but in nature there is no more efficient killing machine than man. The horrible reality we accept with little thought and as a matter of course is that life feeds on life and that man is as involved in the process as the shark—but it is not just for food that man kills. Here we are presented with a daunting theological problem because, as Queequeg points out, the creator of it all must have had something to do with this arrangement.

Such issues as the universal cannibalism of life are not for Sunday school lessons or conventional polite discourse and would never have been broached in John Allen's correspondence with Elizabeth Thomas, Martha England, or even Chet Dawson. It was the other Concord philosopher that tackled such elemental problems, though not without irony and humor.

Here is McNutt on the subject writing from his home on the Old Road to Nine Acres Corners in Concord:

April 10, 1971.
Dear John,

It was good of you to call and make inquiries whether I had died. Actually I had not; it only seemed that way. And if you could have seen me in action on the ski slopes you would have wondered even more why I hadn't.

I am now working quite hard at being a good parent and only very casually at discovering the meaning of life. It seems a long, long time ago that I worked full-time at "know thyself" and such-like. I was never able to convince myself that a breakthrough was imminent. That cooled me down a lot and caused me to turn my thoughts elsewhere. Also I was never able to approve the way the universe was set up in the first place. Specifically, this business of higher animals eating those socially inferior to themselves in order to sustain their physiology is particularly reprehensible to me. It is so horrible that I still have difficulty believing it is really so. And I wish all to know that I am playing under protest.

I disapprove of it on moral grounds each time I enjoy a beefsteak, and brood gloomily over the fact that my views were neither asked for nor acted upon. With so much going on in opposition to my wishes I cannot avoid the feeling that I am somehow serving time. But for what? That is a horrible thought. No. 2: We are serving time whether we are guilty or not.

In view of the set-up, it is amazing that people are not worse than they actually are. How could any kindness have arisen at all? There must somehow be a way to derive selfish gain from it. Is there a point in evolution beyond which pure and unalloyed ruthlessness no longer insures survival best? Is man's perfectibility just another example of evolutionary necessity? If this is so it is every bit as humiliating to us as our low descent, for it says that the only reason we have any kindness to us at all is because we can't help it. That's a pretty poor excuse.

Needless to say, parenthood with all its problems is one hell of a lot simpler than cracking the philosophical code, and I am plenty glad that having other people dependent on me takes up so much of my time and keeps me working so hard to come up with the needed financial backing.

Thus, I have arrived at a relatively painless way to serve out my time. Had I been required, like you, to turn in a solo performance I have no idea at all what the outcome might have been. In my opinion, your performance has been remarkable.

Sincerely yours, Dub

p.s. What's on your mind these days? Come on, quit your stalling. Out with it.

John Allen's scientist friend wrote with energy and wit and his letter here quoted in full is reflective of the quality of the correspondence between the two men over several decades.

McNutt left Arkansas to study biochemistry and found success as a scientific researcher, scholar and professor at Tufts University Medical School, and like Martha England he would always maintain his friendship and strong attachment to John Allen. It's clear from this and his other letters that, while the study of science offered him rewards, they were not sufficient. The human spirit requires more than empirical fact for sustenance, and for those needs he looked to his family, to nature in his camping and skiing excursions and his walks around Concord and Walden Pond, he looked to music and art, particularly his drawing and sculpting, and he looked to his friend John Allen to share views on religion, philosophy, literature, and the great books.

John Allen got from his friend in return a sense of the adventurous, physical experiences he would surely have enjoyed had they not been denied him. Dub wrote of his handball games and skiing outings, and once described an excursion that provided a healthy mixture of pleasure and pain.

> I was up in Nova Scotia two weeks ago. Miles and miles of beaches just picking shells alone. Not a soul in the water and I knew why. I actually got so cold I couldn't get my clothes back on. It was only after I got in the car and rolled the windows up and sat there an hour I got the shakes stopped. Those lobsters are a hardy beast, I tell you!

Strengthening their bond further were their shared experiences of growing up in Arkadelphia, their mutual friends and mentors who contributed to their remarkably positive development in those days that would come to be known as the Great Depression. The relationship between these two old friends proved to be a decades-long intimate colloquy.

The opening paragraph of the April letter apparently refers to a skiing accident McNutt suffered, and it was that favorite sport of his that inspired John Allen to write a Shakespearean sonnet about his life-long friend, one of his finest poems:

Philosopher on the Ski Slope
(For W.S McNutt)

No longer young and disinclined to chance
he chooses gentle inclines for his skiing;

and as he glides across the white expanse,
he muses on the quiddity of being.
"I ski therefore I am—it cuts as near
the core, perhaps, as that more famous thrust."
turning, he sees his children, blind to fear,
rush downward, laughing as they lace the crust
with patterns of their passing. "Joy allays
the chronic ache, but nothing cures; for when
that lengthy Archimedes lever pries
us loose from these inviting slopes—what then?
As darkness comes to end our sport, we go;
our tracings fading under evening's snow.

This is the poem that John Allen sent to McNutt along with one about Mr. Huddleston, both of which would later be included in his book under a section headed "Lineaments of Love." His friend responded:

My Dear John,

You have done my heart good and made me feel young again. Even though pictured old I feel immortal, for I am now preserved in poetry! Please, for heaven's sake, get it published and on the record, because I can see, now, the limited uses I shall be able to make of science!

Dub, like John Allen, had pretty much given up on cracking the philosophic code, but he had two sons now and was busy tackling the challenge of child rearing. He shares his theories on the subject with his friend:

Sept 21 1974
Dear John,

Thank you for your letter and the stimulating poetry. I was struck with how many of your poems are peopled with children. You are a married man; go ahead and have one. I always did; I mean I always wanted to have one; but Jessie had them all.

I have always felt cheated about that. I would give anything to know what it's like. Here's something else that really crushed me: She said it wasn't an especially uplifting experience, but very much as though she just defecated them. That's what I learn, too, the more narrowly I look into it. Nature is a real cheap woman–a lot cheaper, I believe, than the better sort of woman. What do you say, Philosopher?

Kids are great to have around once you get them toilet trained and past wetting their beds. It turns out they are easy to bring up no matter what you hear. For example, if you read them the poems you wrote they would love it. If you said they inspired them they would really squeal. That's just the way they are. They might not know one word of what you said, and it wouldn't matter any.

Kids just naturally start out thinking they do everything wrong no matter how they act. All you do is tell them they are doing great, in a way to make them think you mean it, and they'll love you all their lives. That's just how they are. Then when you get mad and tell them they are a failure, they won't believe you. It all works out. That's all there is to kids, so go ahead and have one.

That was a very fine letter. Thank you. As ever, Dub

P.S. I'm going on sabbatical leave Oct 1. I'll write you from Cleveland.

Apparently Dub McNutt and his wife Jessie were successful at child rearing for six years later he wrote:

Our younger son is now applying to law school; our older is in Sacramento getting his Naval Flight Officer's wings. He wanted to go to the moon but no one would supply him with a space vehicle which made me glad, never entirely trusting the things, and he is still damn mad. His disappointment proved a rather rough landing for him and his expectations are still so far up there he's an angry young man.

One perennial topic of their correspondence was the original Concord philosopher and thinker and ideas associated with his name. The following excerpt reveals the enquiring nature of McNutt's mind and the quality of his musings.

April 9 1982 Concord
Dear John Allen:

Thank you very much for your book about Concord and for the picture, but which, in my present mood, both serve to depress me. Perhaps it was the cantata by Buxtehude I just heard. People wrote much music in despair and listened to it from a like cause, and I doubt that we have changed. I haven't, and I suppose it's the natural state of man. In fact it's why I can't seem to write answers to your letters.

You speak of Thoreau. Recently, at the library, some notes he jotted down have been discovered in a magazine he left to the library. One had to do with Agassie, but I should not discuss him, I suppose. Agassie made the mistake of writing some letters in which he was trying to discover from associates why black men did not measure up to Europeans in certain regards. He did not question *whether* they were inferior but sought the answer *why*. I'm not sure if they know who he wrote to, but if they do he's in trouble too. What these people don't know is that the abolitionists didn't consider the black man their equal either. In fact, that's why they were so sorry for them. *More* sorry, in fact, than most people.

Anyway, Agassie interests me for a totally different reason. He was not a Darwinian. Agassie believed that woodpeckers were all descended from a woodpecker of whatever sort, wrens from a wren, etc. and that a wren, a woodpecker, etc. etc. were independent acts of creation.

That's not what has him in trouble, but that's what interests me; because Mr. Huddleston had that same idea. One day we were out digging for Indian pots

and he came out with that one. As I always say: Two
great minds!

I really must stop reading; it's beginning to get to me.
Do you realize that Thomas Jefferson, that soaring
genius of a man, never supposed the United States
would ever be anything other than a land of small
farmers? And James Audubon, himself a naturalist,
who though he saw the disappearance of certain spe-
cies, never believed the balance of nature would be
affected. That was only 120 years ago, and there are
now people living in Boston who take their children
to a zoo so they can say they have seen a cow.

There is something very depressing about *Homo
Sapiens*. Everyone who keeps insisting on how intelligent he is is a *Homo Sapiens*. What is needed is an
outside opinion. . . .

In almost all his letters McNutt thanks John Allen for his
"fine," letter or "splendid" letter leaving us to regret their absence from this story though thankful they are to some extent
reflected in those of his friend.

For more than three decades these two friends carried on
a warm personal correspondence exchanging condolences from
time to time over the deaths of family, Aunt Bessie and Dub's
mother, and mutual friends. He comments in one, "What a
slaughter it is among our friends—even Billy Gill East!" In
the spring of 1980 Dub laments the passing of another friend
and remarks on John Allen's book of poems that had recently
been published.

I must tell you how very grateful I am for your poems.
Between the two of us, I have had a very good cry.

. . . .

The poem I liked best, I think, is the one you took the
title from. The mother-hen feelings of the grounded
skier have the ring of authenticity! I am glad you have
a book to your name.

. . . .

Is the inscription yours? Can you wield the pen by
hand?

. . . .

John could in fact sign his name. The book of poems he
gave me is autographed; I didn't see him sign it but Linda
Wells, one of his former student assistants, told me he could
write by having her hold the paper firmly on his desk while
he took a pen in one hand and placed his other hand on
top to attain the strength and control to execute with both
hands a handsome cursive signature. What he was able to
do he did do.

Through the years the two friends exchanged views on the
topics of the day—the nuclear arms race, the Vietnam War,
the fall of Richard Nixon—and were in general agreement
on all the issues. McNutt also opposed the war but was able
to keep a more detached perspective than his friend: "I have
not been able to convince myself that democracy will soon
come to Vietnam whether elections are held soon or late," he
wrote. "If the generals are not democratic; if the Buddhists
are not democratic; if the Viet Cong are not democratic, what
element in that society is to provide the democratic spirit?"
Many people understood the problem, he said, but no one had

a solution. John Allen for his part could not distance himself from the suffering and was greatly disturbed by the carnage of the war.

His reaction to human suffering never changed. John Allen demonstrated throughout his life the same concern for others he showed when he ran all the way from De Soto Bluff into town carrying the boy with a lacerated foot to the doctor, or when during World War II he was first to donate to campaign for the hungry overseas. He was not only sensitive to the pain of those nearby, but, because he lacked the protective mechanism most of us have that shields us from suffering in distant places, the war in Vietnam tormented him. It was ironically television, the "vast wasteland" that he deplored, that graphically brought home to him and other Americans the devastation our nation was inflicting on a poor country seven thousand miles away, and he felt keenly the agony of those caught up in that conflict.

* * *

CHAPTER 12

War and Civil Disobedience

———————— ▬ ————————

The mass of men serve the State thus, not as men mainly, but as machines, with their bodies. They are the standing army, and the militia, jailers, constables, <u>posse comitatus</u>, etc. In most cases there is no free exercise whatever of the judgment or of the moral sense; but they put themselves on a level with wood and earth and stones; and wooden men can perhaps be manufactured that will serve the purpose as well.
—Henry David Thoreau

Still the numbing cadence rings, and still the polished boots march down that ancient road to nowhere—never at ease, never gaining ground. Why do old men send young men marching, and why do the young men march submissively?
—John Allen Adams

Only two-hundred feet from the back of the former Adams Book Store, up a flight of ten concrete steps, stand the double oak doors of the Clark County Courthouse completed in 1899. From his back porch John Allen had an unobstructed view of the three-story red-brick building with its clock and bell tower. At the east corner of the courthouse square on a tall pedestal stands the statue of a Confederate soldier with rifle and bedroll looking toward the nearby Ouachita, a memorial championed shortly after the turn of the century by Bessie's great aunt, Laura Scott Butler, and other patriotic citizens proud of their Confederate heritage. At the west corner of the square rises a convex wall, a triptych, inscribed with the names of Clark County men who served in the wars of the twentieth century, a number of them John Allen's former classmates. Behind the courthouse just one block west is the National Guard Armory where local guardsmen hold their regular meetings. Next to the vacant lot behind the book store and directly across the street facing the courthouse sits a small white frame building, a present-day law office with a bronze plaque on the front identifying it as the former law office of Governor Harris Flanagin. Flanagin, former state senator and veteran of the Mexican war, was captain of Company E, Second Arkansas Mounted Rifles in the Civil War and fought in the battles of Wilson's Creek and Pea Ridge. John Allen's great grandfather, W.S. Horton who joined the Arkansas volunteers and served throughout the war was believed to have fought in the later battles of Poison Spring and Mark's Mills.

John Allen's family had been intimately involved in wars fought by the United States for over a century and a half. His great-great uncle General Winfield Scott, son of a Revolutionary War soldier, devoted his life to the study of war and fought in every conflict from the War of 1812 to the Civil War. Scott was instrumental in removing Native Americans from their homelands in the Southeastern United States and sending them off on the tragic Trail of Tears. He helped relieve Mexico of forty percent of its territories with his victory at the battle of Vera Cruz and was the senior leader of the Union Army at the outset of the Civil War, a war which ironically found John Allen's great grandfather, W.S. Horton, fighting on the opposite side.

The Horton patriarch and Confederate soldier no doubt conducted himself bravely during that war, but at what cost? The shameful slaughter of the Kansas 2nd Colored Regiment at Poison Spring, the murder of hundreds of innocent Blacks at Mark's Mills, the loss of Horton's two brothers, John Allen's great uncles, were only a small part of the untold suffering brought on when in the Spring of 1861 the second horseman of the Apocalypse was set loose upon the land.

World War I, fought mostly in the muddy, bloody trenches of France, was one of the deadliest of wars, and though the United States arrived somewhat late to the battlefields, still both John Allen's dad, Al, and his Uncle Thad were among the millions who served in that conflict.

John Allen's generation's turn came with World War II. He missed that war only because he lay paralyzed at the home place. But he watched as his good friends and classmates heeded the call. His Uncle Vernon contributed to the war effort with his work on the proximity fuse while John Allen followed the war news closely reading the daily reports in the *Southern Standard* and listening to the radio. Many of Arkadelphia's young men became casualties of that war, a number of them John Allen's good friends. Billy Gill East and his close friend Buddy Whitten were wounded in the Normandy Invasion. Johnny Hall, the Badger right halfback who had shown so much concern for John Allen when he was lying on the ground with a broken neck, was killed in that same campaign on the 4th of July, 1944. Their names can now be found on the memorial wall at the courthouse.

I found no comments in John Allen's writings that reveal his attitude toward World War II or the one I served in, the Korean War. While justifications for the war in Korea are still debated, that's not the case for World War II. We were attacked at Pearl Harbor and the right of self defense is universally recognized. Furthermore, the evidence is overwhelming that Nazi Germany, Imperial Japan and their junior partner, Italy, constituted a true axis of evil, so if ever a war was justified, it was the Second World War. Still we might agree with Ernest Hemingway who said, "Never think that war, no matter how necessary or justified, is not a crime."

The war in Vietnam was one many people today believe was neither necessary nor justified. It was the first televised American war and the carnage delivered to living rooms, the "Rolling Thunder" bombings, free-fire zones, body counts, day after day, month after month, year after year drove home to John Allen and others the human cost of war. The violence and destruction he read about and saw in news reports stirred his conscience and gave him a cause to work for. In Thoreau he found a kindred spirit who had protested the Mexican War that his great-great uncle Winfield Scott had played such a significant part in, and now, like his exemplar, John Allen would speak out against America's actions in Vietnam.

The mature John Allen, who shared Thoreau's feelings about war and the military, remembered fondly his experiences in Mr. Huddleston's Troop 23, but he wondered if the Boy Scouts' quasi-military character brought to the organization by its founder, the Boer War veteran Robert Baden-Powell, might not have conveyed the wrong message to boys—the uniforms, bivouacs, bugle calls and regimentation. In 1968 he wrote to his fellow peace activist Mike Vogler who was in Federal prison for refusing to submit to the draft:

I went to town today for a haircut. [He could drive his electric wheelchair the few blocks to the barbershop] As I was driving on the walk near my house, I suddenly smelled something very familiar that brought me to a stop. I was passing under a large elm tree, and the walk and the ground were covered with brown and yellow leaves. It was the smell of Fall . . . and memories came crowding in. I was a boy (and a Boy Scout) in a small town and I spent much time hiking in the woods and along the river. They are good memories to have. Odors have a strange power to evoke the past.

Today I may have reservations about the Scouts as being an organization with something of a "paramilitary" flavor (wasn't Lord Baden Powell, the British founder, a military man?—I'm not sure), but if it still gets boys out in the (disappearing) woods, perhaps it does some good. Our scoutmaster was also the school principal, and I now realize that he devoted much of his time to us—taking us on overnight hikes etc. He was a simple man with a rural background, and he truly loved the outdoors. I remember he told me that as he grew older he became reluctant to take a gun and fishing rod to the woods.

It had no doubt been a long time since John had read the Boy Scout *Handbook,* so there's no reason to expect he would remember the organization's position on war. He would have been reassured, however, to discover how the 1932 edition, the one he read when he joined the Scouts, addressed that subject:

> War is one of the tragedies of the life of the world. In its wake stalk sorrow, poverty, disease, moral let-down, debt, hatred, fears.
>
> One-third of the taxation of the world is either to pay for past wars or prepare for new.
>
> Wars tear down civilizations. The effort of home, church, school and state is for us to guard life and respect property—war says kill and destroy (544).

The anti-war John Allen could have written those words himself. The *Handbook* goes on to enumerate the losses in life and treasure the United States had suffered in all its wars. So John Allen's opposition to war, specifically the Vietnam War, was perfectly consistent with the Boy Scout teachings of his youth.

Before he moved from the old home place John Allen had lived through several tumultuous episodes of American history—World War II, the Korean War, and the Little Rock School crisis. From his quiet new vantage point at Adams Book Store on Main Street he was to witness other crucial national events. In 1960, the year he moved into his new quarters, John F. Kennedy was elected President. In January 1963, only ten months before Kennedy's assassination, the Civil Rights march in Washington D.C. captured the world's attention and Martin Luther King's "I Have a Dream" speech touched the nation's conscience.

1964 was a year of triumph and tragedy for Kennedy's successor, Lyndon Johnson. That year he masterfully maneuvered the Civil Rights Act through Congress guaranteeing himself an honored place in history. He followed that success one month later with an act that would ultimately tarnish his name and drive him from office, the Gulf of Tonkin Resolution, a bill which he pushed through Congress with only two dissenting votes in the Senate. That resolution, based on a claim that U.S. ships had been attacked by North Vietnamese boats, a claim later proved to be false, was followed by a steep escalation of violence in Vietnam, a country whose millions of citizens lived mainly in rural villages and on small farms.

Events unfolding in Vietnam and at home at that time resonated with some of John Allen's long-held vital concerns and he began to speak out, typing letters at his desk with his rubber-tipped pencil to the *Arkansas Gazette* and other newspapers and periodicals around the country. He sought out and subscribed to publications that shared his interests, such as *Manas*, self-described as "a journal of independent inquiry, concerned with study of the principles which move world society on its present course, and with search for contrasting principles–that may be capable of supporting intelligent idealism under the conditions of life in the twentieth century." Many notable intellectuals of the day contributed articles to *Manas* in opposition to the Vietnam War and advocating world disarmament. John Allen over the next two years continued to follow closely the actions in Vietnam as the conflict heated up.

While the articles in *Manas* were generally secular-humanist in their arguments, other journals such as *Catholic Worker* and *Peacemaker*, derived their principles from Christian teachings, specifically Matthew 5:9, "Blessed are the peacemakers: for they shall be called the children of God." It is likely the agnostic John Allen was introduced to these publications by Mike Vogler, the anti-war activist and former seminarian who became his closest ally throughout this period. On October 15, 1967 he wrote his friend:

Dear Mike:

I tried to call you this afternoon, and I learned that you are in Fayetteville (I think) and that you go to Jonesboro tomorrow. I suppose you are on the speaking tour you mentioned.

I shall be interested in hearing more about your NY peace meeting. I think it is a fine thing—your decision to oppose Selective Service and war; and I hope you find the strength to face any difficulties that lie ahead.

This is truly a crucial point in history; and if we pass through it into a more civilized world, it will be achieved through the efforts of committed individuals. I have been reading Tolstoy's "The Kingdom of God is Within You"—it is the most exciting book I've read since I discovered "Walden" 25 years ago. It speaks to our condition today. If you don't have a copy, I want to send one to you. Even if you can't read it now, you will get around to it some day—maybe in jail!

Thanks for your long letter. I intended to write sooner but I've been short of help. Yesterday the new girl was telling me that her husband (of three months) will make a career of the army after graduating from

Henderson. He had spent all night on Henderson war games. Three of his men had been "killed" and he had stepped in a trap and had to run a mile as a penalty. He really "liked" his work and she found it "interesting" to hear him talk about it.

It depressed me—she was so bright and cheerful about it, as if it were some kind of sport her husband was engaged in. How do you awaken people—direct their attention to other possibilities? At infancy our culture fits us with blinders.

Anytime you can come, we should be able to have a visit. However, I'm usually occupied in getting on my chair from 1 to 3 p.m. —so from 10 to 1 or from 3 to late at night would be the best.

I'm glad that Jane and Steve are your neighbors. Give them my regards.

> Sincerely,
> John Allen

Mike left Catholic Seminary and enrolled at Little Rock University (today the University of Arkansas at Little Rock) in 1966 while the draft for the war in Vietnam was going strong. By the following year he was active in the anti-war movement attending peace conferences around the country and speaking out on college campuses against the war and the draft.

He wrote on October 20, 1967:

Dear John Allen,

I just have time to scribble a short note. Have just returned from a "Peace Tour" over the state of Ark. I traveled with Dave Nolan, founder of the Virginia Student Civil Rights Committee and presently editor of the New South Student from the Southern Student Organizing Committee. Bruce Smith, also a member of VSCRC & SSOC, went to Cuba this past summer and has previously studied Latin American History. Nancy Hodes spent from 1955-1960 in Peking where her father was teaching neurophysiology. They talked on Vietnam, Cuba, & China respectively. I spoke on the draft & non-cooperation. We spoke to over 1000 students at six Arkansas colleges including L.R.U., Hendrix, State College of Ark., Ark. Tech, U of A, & Ark. State U.

We were very well received & had pretty good discussions at all but A.S.U. At that God-forsaken place the president of the "University" called in two F.B.I. agents, and let it be known that we could not speak on campus, and, if we spoke off-campus, any student who attended would be expelled. Needless to say we have little regard for some people there who seemed willing to help but in the end were so intimidated by rumors & threats that they even helped remove us from campus by asking us quietly but emphatically that we leave. We have written a letter telling about our experience to Sen. Fulbright, Gov. Rockefeller, the Gazette, & radio & T.V. stations in Jonesboro. Maybe the police-state atmosphere can begin to be broken down at our newest "University" in Arkansas.

. . . .

Now I have a conference & peace tour to tell you about. Hope I see you before the non-cooperators conference in Chicago from Nov. 10-12. Then I won't be able to tell you everything in one day. Till then,

Mike

Even as he wrote Mike knew he was headed for prison. Realizing he was about to be called by the Selective Service he had written his draft board explaining that he could not submit to the draft. When he was offered alternative service he declined that opportunity on the grounds that even that action would violate his moral stand against the war. He had been denied conscientious objector status so, in the spirit of Thoreau, he decided to break the law, suffer the penalty, and let his body be a counter friction added to the rising national protests in an effort to stop the machine of war.

He told John Allen in the letter he was delighted to hear he was reading Tolstoy, for he was reading about the Russian writer himself, a two-volume biography that he hoped to finish before going to jail. Many anti-war activists were attracted to Tolstoy, not because he was widely considered the world's greatest novelist for masterpieces like *War and Peace*, and *Anna Karenina*, but for his later works on Christianity, most particularly, *The Kingdom of God is Within You*, a work advocating non resistance to evil by force based on Jesus'

"Sermon on the Mount," and written after he had repudiated his works of fiction. It is the book John Allen was reading and wanted to send to Mike.

Ten days after receiving the letter from Mike John Allen responded:

Dear Mike:

I read a little of the book this morning. My uncle had the TV on in the living room, and fragments of a sermon drifted in: "People of God...God's plan... The Church is Christ's body...the church is God's power...may the words of my mouth and...I believe in God the Father, God the...In Christ there is no East or West..."

The sermon seemed so unreal—Tolstoy was getting to the heart of the matter, while the pious claptrap sounded in the distance. The minister did make some passing mention of the brotherhood of man, and I believe he spoke of how the wonders of science and transportation have shrunk the earth—but never did he mention Vietnam. Bombs are falling and brothers are killing each other in Vietnam, and I am sure the minister was aware of this and concerned about it, and yet he never mentioned it. He did find time to defend the church against those he judged to be overly critical, and no doubt his congregation went home greatly comforted—but his silence preached a different, more apposite sermon which will not be found among his notes.

> While I have no faith in any dogma, I am perhaps beginning to have faith in certain ethical ideas and attitudes to be found in many religions. Tolstoy and Gandhi speak to my heart. . . .

In Vietnam the war continued to escalate. In 1966 President Johnson had ordered B52s to join the Rolling Thunder bombing campaign targeting the supply trails of the North Vietnamese, but by the end of 1967, after dropping unprecedented tons of ordnance into the jungle, Secretary of Defense Robert McNamara had to admit to a Senate subcommittee that the bombing campaign had not cut off supplies to Vietcong forces in the South.

Shortly afterward the combined Communist forces celebrated the New Year by launching the deadly Tet Offensive catching Americans off guard and wreaking the greatest damage to our forces since the United States had entered the war. In addition to the wide-spread destruction, loss of life and suffering on both sides from that offensive, the Vietnamese saw Hue, one of their holiest cities, laid waste, its beautiful temples and wide tree-lined avenues, shattered. Following that costly battle General Westmorland told Washington that he would need an additional 260,000 troops.

These events were unfolding early in 1968 as Mike Vogler was entering prison at Springfield, Missouri. That year continued to be eventful. Following the Tet Offensive and the further escalation of the war, the rising tide of opposition in this country led President Johnson to announce in March that he would not run for another term. He was helped toward that decision after anti-war candidate, Eugene McCarthy, received surprisingly strong support in the New Hampshire primary.

The following month Martin Luther King Jr., who had earlier begun to speak out against the war, was murdered in Memphis. In June Bobby Kennedy, who had entered the presidential race and was also speaking out against United States policies in Vietnam, was assassinated in Los Angles. These traumatic events played out against a backdrop of growing national unrest, of increasingly violent anti-war protests and demonstrations. In November Richard Nixon won a decisive victory against George McGovern and the Democrats promising the nation he would bring "peace with honor" to Vietnam.

During the two years Mike was in prison, he and John Allen exchanged long, highly literate and thoughtful letters on a wide range of subjects, but mostly on the war and their circle of friends working to oppose the war. It's interesting to note the avenue each followed to reach his anti-war position. Mike found in the teachings of Jesus support for his opposition to war; the strength from his Christian faith helped lighten the burden of his years in prison. John Allen, by contrast, was a secular humanist; though influenced by religious thinkers such as Tolstoy and Gandhi, his anti-war reasoning followed more closely the ideas of Thoreau, Einstein, Bertrand Russell and Noam Chomsky. But both John Allen and Mike had come to the same conclusion: The war in Vietnam was morally indefensible.

Because of his age and his condition John Allen was denied the chance to demonstrate his convictions by refusing to submit to the draft, but Mike Vogler was provided that opportunity. In mid January, 1968 he wrote his Arkadelphia friend:

Last Monday, Jan 15, I was to report to the local board to receive orders for alternative service. I went down, but refused to accept the orders, taking about 1 ½ hours to talk to the clerk and a couple of others giving the reasons for my actions. I also returned my draft cards. So as of then, I am subject to arrest at any time. I would really like to see you before then, but of course no one knows how fast they will act, and more than likely I will have no chance to get to Arkadelphia. My car has broken down and because of that I am not free to take off to see you any time I can. If I do get a chance I will notify you as before by calling for myself long-distance to your house.

He was soon arrested, held in the Little Rock jail and assigned a court appointed lawyer, Ronald May, who was opposed to the war and sympathetic to his cause. Mike tried to explain why he didn't want a lawyer; still May did what he could though his efforts to obtain conscientious objector status for Mike were unsuccessful. When John Allen next heard from his friend in late April he was in a Missouri federal prison.

Left L.R. on April 17 early in the morning and the marshal took me through the Ozarks to my new home. Spring came late to the Ozarks, and the trees were just getting ready to dress themselves with green. The dogwood was already beautiful in white. The whole panorama reminded me of "Spring" in *Walden.*

Afraid I broke up the regular admittance-orientation program by getting myself taken to administrative segregation—better known as the "hole." This developed when I refused to take leather shoes at clothes issue because I am a vegetarian. But I soon decided that I did not want to spend three years in that place, and after three days I accepted shoes. Excitement wherever I go.

Prisons are designed to rob a man of his spirit–his very soul. And this place is no exception.

Mike was apparently troubled, as was W.S McNutt, by the universal cannibalism of life, but rather than eat steak with a guilty conscience, he became a vegetarian. John Allen, like Thoreau, preferred plant food—vegetables, fruit, grains and nuts—but more for reasons of health than revulsion at the natural order. He and his best friend, Buddy Whitten, had taken their guns to the woods in search of quail though without success. And Thoreau ate the fish he caught in Walden Pond, and once with no compunction killed and ate a woodchuck that was raiding his bean patch. He believed hunting was good for young boys like John Allen and Buddy, for it got them out into the woods, but as they grew up he said they should, like Mr. Huddleston, put aside their guns and hunt for bigger game. His philosophy is expressed in his remark that "in wildness is the preservation of the world," a view that would include the sharks in their feeding frenzy as they attacked the whale carcass and perhaps even the crew of the *Pequod* as well.

If John Allen didn't share Mike's religious faith or his strict vegetarian regimen, both were in total agreement on the war in Vietnam. His admiration was unstinting for Mike and other young draft resisters who were speaking out against the war and demonstrating their convictions with acts of civil disobedience. He shared his feelings with his friend in prison:

At best, there is—inescapably— an adequate amount of suffering and tragedy in our lives; but the needless suffering we inflict on one another, it is this wanton horror that sucks joy from the present and pillages our future. Why—to take the most extreme example—do we expend time (which is life itself), and wealth, and gifted minds on more effective means to destroy ourselves? It is estimated that there are "100 billion lethal doses of nerve gas manufactured and stored at Rocky Mountain Arsenal." And you and I—businessman and minister, farmer and blue-collar laborer, teacher and housewife—we all quietly support horrors such as this.

If it is security we seek, how real a refuge is military power, when the two most powerful nations feel so insecure that they commit aggression against weaker peoples? However delicately we balance the balance of terror, still our fears consume us—our fears wear down our heritage to stones, and time runs out for us.

It is beautiful—*beautiful*, I say that there are young men who feel so compelled by their conscience that they must choose jail rather than take part in these horrors. Their courage is no less than that of those who fight and die in this unspeakable war, and they support the better cause.

Denounce them as draft dodgers (a misnomer) and hippies, if you wish, or look on their waywardness with parental concern, and even disown them (as some parents have done); but in the conscience and courage of these young men–in this questing ray of sanity–lies whatever honor America may salvage from our moral debacle.

John Allen was particularly appalled by the readiness and even eagerness with which his Christian neighbors took up the call to war. They seemed to follow more closely the vengeful examples from the Old Testament rather than the teachings of Jesus. In a letter to Mike, John Allen cites one example he ran across in the newspaper:

> On page 18 is an article about Redfield, a small Arkansas community with seven boys in Vietnam. Their Baptist minister is reassuring: "There's no fanaticism against the war," in his town. He sometimes teaches "Bible truths about wars and rumors of wars before the return of Christ. Our time is no exception to the past. Every century I can remember had its share of war. In other words, men are prone to fight."

"And," John Allen remarks, "men are prone to play it cool and utter nonsense from high places."

Those who were not actively for the war mostly looked the other way like the T.V. preacher Vernon listened to who spoke of the role of the church but never mentioned the destruction and death taking place in Vietnam.

Rising from pulpits all across the country were prayers
for our men in the service and for the successful prosecution
of the war in Vietnam. But John Allen, Mike Vogler, and
their friends in the anti-war movement saw beyond the flag-
waving ceremonies, patriotic prayers, speeches and parades,
to the human cost of war just as Mark Twain did in his "War
Prayer" written shortly before his death. In his story a strange
old man enters a church after one such patriotic prayer was
delivered and announces to the congregation that he was sent
by one in authority to deliver the unspoken part of the prayer
they had just heard. They listened to the old man in stunned
silence as he prayed:

> O Lord our Father, our young patriots, idols of our
> hearts, go forth to battle – be Thou near them! With
> them – in spirit – we also go forth from the sweet
> peace of our beloved firesides to smite the foe. O Lord
> our God, help us to tear their soldiers to bloody shreds
> with our shells; help us to cover their smiling fields
> with the pale forms of their patriot dead; help us to
> drown the thunder of the guns with the shrieks of
> their wounded, writhing in pain; help us to lay waste
> their humble homes with a hurricane of fire; help us to
> wring the hearts of their unoffending widows with un-
> availing grief; help us to turn them out roofless with
> little children to wander unfriended the wastes of their
> desolated land in rags and hunger and thirst, sports of
> the sun flames of summer and the icy winds of winter,
> broken in spirit, worn with travail, imploring Thee for
> the refuge of the grave and denied it—for our sakes
> who adore Thee, Lord, blast their hopes, blight their

lives, protract their bitter pilgrimage, make heavy their steps, water their way with their tears, stain the white snow with the blood of their wounded feet! We ask it, in the spirit of love, of Him Who is the Source of Love, and Who is the ever-faithful refuge and friend of all that are sore beset and seek His aid with humble and contrite hearts. Amen.

Wars are often launched in high spirits. After the firing on Fort Sumter, excitement ran high in both North and South. Families around Washington D. C. took picnic lunches in wagons to watch the First Battle of Bull Run, the tinglings of fear they felt just adding to the excitement. W.S. Horton and young men of Clark and Dallas Counties must have felt their pulses quicken as they galloped from farm to farm spreading the word of the impending conflict. It would, most thought, be a brief and glorious war; each side knowing they would triumph because the divinity smiled on their cause. No one anticipated what would follow, the four-year affliction detailed in the Drew Faust's recent book, *This Republic of Suffering: Death and the American Civil War.*

We seem never to learn the lessons of war having recently seen our president in a flight suit striding across an aircraft carrier deck to cheer the crew and quicken the hearts of Americans by speaking triumphantly of the success of his campaign of "Shock and Awe" under the banner, "Mission Accomplished." Seven years later the human costs for that moment of glory are still being tallied.

At the book store John Allen took every opportunity to share his thoughts on the war with his customers, listening to their views while employing the Socratic method of discourse in an effort to lead them toward the light, but not always with success. To Mike he recounts one such case:

> This morning I talked with a customer, an elderly man who is a minister and who still teaches philosophy in an obscure seminary in a Southern state–Mississippi, I think. As we talked, I told him of reading Tolstoy. In his best classroom manner he rather reluctantly agreed that non-violence might be one of the chief Christian teachings; but on the other hand–so thought our philosopher–he could see the danger of non-violence carried to "extremism." Yes, a nuclear war would kill vast numbers and leave a stone-age society; on the other hand he didn't want to live in a world taken over by the godless Communists.
>
> He was a man of little imagination. I wonder if he bored or impressed his students.

The old minister was more in tune with bellicose public sentiment in Arkansas than some Vietnam veterans. John Allen describes one's experience in Little Rock:

> Last week I talked with a young man who had spent 18 months in Vietnam. He said he wouldn't return under any circumstances–he has served his three years and is discharged. He expressed his views in a café (L.R.) to some young hawks; the café owner had him arrested and he was fined $25. I understand that there was no violence, nor was he asked to leave the café–so I don't see how he could have been fined.

Vernon told me that if John Allen had been young and able bodied he would have burned his draft card and become a hippie. I don't agree with the hippie part. I believe had he not been injured he would have served honorably with his classmates in World War II showing the leadership and courage he demonstrated throughout his school years. Whether he would have come to the strong anti-war position he later adopted cannot be known, but I believe the insanity of the nuclear arms race and the bloody conflict in Vietnam likely would have led him to the same conviction and that had he been of draft age he would, like Mike, have refused to serve in the war and gone to jail.

But neither he nor Mike would have become hippies. Both John Allen and Mike lamented the fact that so much of the anti-war movement was marked by the drug culture, that so many young people had heeded Dr. Timothy Leary's call to "tune in, turn on, and drop out." They believed such indulgences turned away many who were otherwise sympathetic to the anti-war cause.

Still, in some important ways American youth had made progress. Just ten years earlier mobs of hateful teenagers and their parents were taunting nine black students at Little Rock Central High hurling racial epithets and chanting "Two, Four, Six, Eight—We don't want to integrate!" Now black and white American young men were fighting and dying side-by-side in the jungles of Vietnam, while other youth of both sexes and all races had found in Washington D.C. a different target for their anger. Gathered along the fence in front of the White House they were chanting, "Hey! Hey! LBJ! How many kids did you kill today?"

John Allen was not able to attend anti-war rallies around the country, but with his typewriter and telephone he did everything he could to oppose the war in Vietnam. The only regional source for peace buttons, Adams Book Store became a base and refuge for anti-war activists in the area, something like a safe house for the Underground Railroad in the days of slavery. Through Mike he came to know many conscientious objectors, and at every opportunity he offered them encouragement, keeping up with their activities and legal struggles while providing free reading materials and financial support from his limited resources. He wrote Mike only weeks after his arrest:

> What can I say? I hope you find the strength to carry you these difficult times. If there's anything I can do, please let me know.
>
> . . . .
>
> I was happy to have your friends come to see me. Chuck, Paul, and Patricia are fine people. And two days ago a girl from Fayetteville came in–I think her last name was Willowsby. I liked her too.

Mike too had sympathetic visitors in prison. Arla Elston, campus minister for the University of Arkansas Christian Church and Sister Elizabeth Blattell, a nun he had gone to school with in Little Rock, brought news of friends who were active in the anti-war movement. He said their visits lifted his spirits out of a two-week depression.

There was a glimmer of optimism when in May 1968 peace talks began in Paris. All hoped the bloodshed could be stopped, but after the talks had gone on a while John Allen wrote his friend:

Each day brings less and less hope that there will be any settlement at all through the negotiations in Paris. But I see that Britain and Soviet Union perhaps could reconvene the Geneva Conference on S.E. Asia. To me that seems like a much more sensible thing to do than to continue with the fiasco in Paris.

John Allen was solicitous of his friend in prison regularly sending him books and reading materials and money for his incidental expenses, and always asking what more he could do. Mike responded:

You ask me what you can do. You are already doing so much. Ever since I met you I tell all who will listen about a beautiful man in Arkadelphia. You have been and certainly will continue to be a source of immense inspiration to me. I can not ask any more of you than you have already given. That would be impossible.

Whenever John Allen got news of fellow activists he shared it with Mike. They kept up with their friends through anti-war publications such as *Peacemaker* and *Catholic Worker*:

I've received letters from Patricia Glover and Betty Elwell saying that Paul received a letter I wrote to him. He isn't allowed to write to everyone. They say he is all right and expect trial in June. I sent him three books last week–maybe he can have them.

I also received a copy of *Catholic Worker* with an article written about your arrest and trial written by Pat

_____(I forgot her last name, and I sent the newspaper to a friend. But it must be the young woman who came with Chuck and Paul. I suppose she sent the CW to me.)

I think I read–reprinted in *Peacemaker*–some fine letters you received from your NY friends; but, again, I've given the publication away–though I intended to keep it. Are you receiving *Peacemaker*? Could I send *Manas* to you for a few months (a subscription)? I think you would like it.

Any word from Chuck? He is an impressive person and I hope to see him again.

. . . .

Through the two years Mike was in prison the friends corresponded regularly, each confined by circumstance, Mike to his cell and John Allen to his bed and wheelchair. As the young Ouachita graduate who married the Tucker Prison inmate pointed out, John Allen was in his own kind of prison. His earlier letter explained that it took two hours for him and Aunt Bessie to go through their rigorous morning routine that got him from bed and situated in his chair, and an equal time at night to get him from chair to bed. The fact that both men accepted the constraints imposed on them with serenity brings to mind words of the poet, Richard Lovelace: "Stone walls do not a prison make, / Nor iron bars a cage; / Minds innocent and quiet take / That for an hermitage." Both men made good use of their time writing friends and reading news in anti-war publications, such as *Catholic Worker, Peacemaker, Ramparts* and

Manas along with the non-violent teachings of writers like Tolstoy, Gandhi, Thoreau, Einstein and Schweitzer.

Mike was permitted to spend some time outside on pretty days and recalls former pleasant outings with friends and underprivileged kids he worked with.

> Last summer a group of us in L.R. got into the habit of having a picnic every week or so. All Saturday or Sunday afternoon would be spent roasting hot dogs & marshmallows over a campfire, singing while someone played a guitar, having a game of football, holding hands with a beautiful person while taking a refreshing walk into surrounding nature. It seems so long in the past and so long in the future. We would take up a collection from everyone in order to buy necessary picnic items. We always collected exactly enough.

> Those still are beautiful days. The days were spent working with a group of kids in South L.R. They were so beautiful, and we had a great time. Every one of the boys over twelve had a juvenile record. And most were at least as big, or bigger, as me. But there was no trouble during the entire summer.

John Allen had pleasant days as well. He always had visitors, family and friends around. Over the years the bitter battles between the two sisters had subsided, especially after John Allen and Bessie moved out, and now Gertrude could walk the two blocks from the home place to visit. With Vernon often present in the book store, the survivors of the Horton clan were having more amicable gatherings than anyone could remember.

In good weather John Allen, Aunt Bessie and friends like Martha and Amy Jean Greene and Boulware Ohls would sometimes sit on the front porch, Bessie and friends in the swing by her heirloom roses and he in his wheelchair facing them, talking of goings on about town, the weather, or perhaps their flowers and trees—the japonica at the corner of the house, the dogwood and redbuds in the yard, whose flowering they took much pleasure in. The war in Vietnam, however, would not have been a topic of their conversations.

Sometimes Bessie would follow John Allen down the wheelchair ramp on the front porch to the sidewalk where they would circle around the corner on 4th Street to their backyard to sit in the sun near the fig trees at the side of the garage, always empty since they had no car, and enjoy beautiful weather. Honeysuckle grew thick on the chain link fence that separated their yard from the former Civil War armory and Freedman's Bureau next door where Joy Salisbury and her husband Tom lived. From their spot in the yard Bessie and John Allen had a clear view of the courthouse and the memorial wall with the engraved names of Clark County war veterans and opposite that on the east corner of the courthouse square the stalwart Confederate soldier gazing ever steadily toward the Ouachita. Sometimes they could see crows circling the clock tower and hear small planes revving their engines as they began their approach to the nearby airfield just off Highway 67. In spring the sweet smell of honeysuckle and privet hung in the air and stirred memories of a supple-limbed world, of carefree days when John Allen, Buddy Whitten and friends from Troop 23 swam in the river and roamed its banks all the way up to De Soto Bluff and beyond.

But while the Vietnam War did not weigh heavily on Aunt Bessie and her friends, John Allen was unable to get the destruction and killing off his mind. His concern was intensified one Sunday each month when he heard young National Guardsmen calling cadence as they marched around the courthouse square. He wrote a short poem capturing the occasion, the young men passing in front of the courthouse as if on parade:

> . . . .
> While the Confederate soldier
> Patiently reviews these green recruits
> Who barrage their neighborhood—
> HUP! HOO! HEE! HORE!
> HUP! HOO! HEE! HORE! Grapeshot rattles in the
> trees. . . .

It was a never-ending story.

That old men start wars and send young men off to fight angered John Allen. He believed much of the blame for our martial enthusiasms lay with deficiencies within our educational system, that the older generation failed to teach young people the true cost of war, that the lessons spelled out in the Boy Scout *Handbook* of his youth had yet to be learned. Like Mark Twain, John Allen saw clearly in his mind's eye the horrors that inevitably follow outbursts of patriotic war fever.

If he could not physically attend protests or refuse the draft, he could follow those who did, write them, support and encourage them, and when possible intercede in their behalf. He wrote Mike in July, 1968:

> The new *Peacemaker* came three or four days ago, and
> I read a report on Chuck and Bram Luckom. They

have been arrested in Rawlins, Wyoming, for hitch-hiking. After serving 15 days, Bram was released; but Chuck is still in jail and seems to have had a rather bad time. By going to the governor, Maurice McCrackin managed to visit Chuck. I called the sheriff–thinking that it might be of some value if the authorities knew that their bearded guest had a real square, crew-cut American for a friend. The sheriff was "on vacation," but I talked with a deputy there. I introduced myself as operating a book store here, then I inquired about Chuck's health, saying that I heard that he had received some abuse and that there was talk about sending him to a mental institution. He denied the abuse, but admitted that there had been some thought of transferring him to a mental hospital–"this boy acts real strange sometimes." The deputy seemed a little surprised that I had so much information. He said I couldn't talk with Chuck, but I could write to him. I wrote to Chuck. –I tell you this, in case you don't receive PM regularly.

This is only one of the many instances when John Allen, at his own expense, attempted to exert influence in order to help those working to stop the war. He sent many books and periodicals free of charge to draft resisters who were incarcerated and exchanged intelligence on the whereabouts and activities of others within his circle of contacts. He kept a steady stream of impassioned and informed protest letters going to the *Arkansas Gazette* and other publications, never hesitating to pick up the phone to call an editor and make a point. He was, in fact, considered by many to be a gadfly, and he caught the attention of some in Arkadelphia who were displeased with his activities. One banker attached the following note to his magazine subscription renewal:

> I do feel that I should tell you, John Allen, that I very definitely disagree with your thinking on the moratorium, Vietnam and other matters of public controversy. It occurs to me that it might serve your purpose better if you did not take such an active public stand. This is, of course, something for you to determine, and you can well realize that I am not letting this influence me in continuing to subscribe to magazines through your office. It is not my purpose in any way to indicate that you do not have a perfect right to your own thoughts and opinions.

If the banker had known him a little better he would have understood John Allen would not be intimidated by such warnings. John Allen's response was that a man can only follow his conscience, and he soon launched another campaign, this one against a proposal to introduce a Junior ROTC program into Arkadelphia public schools. He wrote Mike:

> Two weeks ago a Henderson ROTC officer addressed the local Chamber of Commerce and told the men about the virtues of the Junior ROTC. I read of it in the local newspaper. Later I read the Hot Springs JROTC was invited to parade at the HSU homecoming game. Being of a suspicious nature, tonight I called the new superintendent of schools and asked if the local

schools were thinking of starting a JROTC. Yes, it was being considered for next year; it had worked well in his former school. It appeals to the non-academic type of student. They meet class every day, march once a week, receive one credit for three years' work. Uniforms and guns (22's) are provided. No pay.

Mr. Stephens was a little surprised when I expressed opposition to the JROTC; I was the only one he had heard oppose it. To give me hope, I suppose, he said that 100 students had to sign up, and there was doubt there would be that many interested. I asked him to send me any printed material available (I'm sure the ROTC provides glossy brochures).

It may be a foolish boondoggle, but I think I shall try to get signatures to a petition opposing a military unit in the public schools. I can think of some people who might sign it. We could send copies to the school board members and the newspaper.

John Allen attempted to stop the JROTC program for Arkadelphia public schools by writing to the local paper and presenting his arguments to anyone who would listen. When he saw a newscast about a program promoting military training in the public schools of Arkansas supported by the governor, Sid McMath, he fired off a letter to the *Arkansas Gazette*. The editor declined to print the letter, perhaps because of the prominent citizens John Allen took to task in the following paragraphs:

I saw the TV film "Sid's Kids," a slickly produced program showing off Catholic High's Marine Junior ROTC unit. Mr. McMath, the governor, generals, priests–they all appeared, all joining in praise of the marching lads. And loving mothers were there too. It seems that the ROTC makes boys neat in their habits. One priest was "gung ho" for the program; another said that it makes "real men" of the boys. Flags flying, bands playing, snappy uniforms, guns–we were given the whole mind-numbing works that man has foisted on himself for centuries.

Is there any justification for our fostering uniformed, marching, gun-toting children? It should not be necessary to remind school authorities–especially those of a religious school–that "Sid's Kids" are also God's kids; and that the aims of military instruction and the aims of education are forever opposed. As Thoreau wrote: "It is impossible to give the soldier a good education, without making him a deserter."

After the *Gazette* refused to publish the letter John told Mike he was thinking about sending it to the *Democrat*. "I'm curious," he wrote, "to see if these views can be expressed in this community."

The truth was that expressing such views in Arkansas at that time was not only difficult, but doing so exacted a price. It perhaps takes more courage to stand up to patriotic neighbors strongly in support of a war than it does to face an armed enemy. In the first instance you face the angry multitude alone, and they are your neighbors and friends; in the second you enter battle with trusted comrades at your side while those you fight are trying to kill you.

John Allen's efforts to stop the JROTC program in public schools likely had little effect state-wide, but he may have had some success locally. Whether or not his efforts were a factor in the school board's decision, the program for Arkadelphia was abandoned.

In Vietnam the killing continued. In 1969 Nixon began the secret bombing of Cambodia and word of the My Lai Massacre reached the United States, the shameful incident where American soldiers lined up between three-hundred and five-hundred Vietnamese civilians, old people, women and children, and gunned them down. These revelations were followed by protests in growing numbers and greater intensity. On the 4th of May, 1970, National Guard troops on the campus of Kent State University shot and killed four students and wounded eight setting off even more wide-spread protests and acts of civil disobedience. A week later a hundred thousand protesters converged on Washington D.C.

But the killing didn't end. Once the machine of war is set in motion its lumbering inertia carries it hurtling forward like a runaway train which cannot be stopped before it reaches a grade of human suffering so steep, a cost in human blood and treasure so great, that its own unbearable weight and the friction of public revulsion bring it to its sad conclusion. Then are we left to look back on the destruction left in its wake. So it was with America's tragic military adventure in Vietnam.

In 1972 President Nixon ordered B52 bombing raids on Hanoi while stepping up efforts to arrange for a cease-fire. An agreement was ultimately signed in Paris that took effect January 1973 after which time the U.S. began withdrawing its forces from the country. Two years later violence erupted once more between the warring sides this time resulting in Communist North Vietnamese taking control of the entire country. The final toll of the war was 58,000 U.S. servicemen and between one and two million Vietnamese killed, and untold numbers, many civilian women and children, maimed and wounded.

As long as the United States continued its military actions John Allen's anti-war efforts never flagged. He used whatever tools available to speak out against the war in Vietnam and to support conscientious objectors like Mike Vogler, who courageously went to prison rather than take part in what they considered an unjust war. Their correspondence while Mike was in prison is remarkable, not only for the dedication and idealism it reveals, but for depth and breadth of their reading and quality of their intellectual exchanges. A listing of the authors and works they read and discussed could fill the curricula of several graduate seminars; for Mike his imprisonment proved educational in more ways than one.

Before he was set free he again expressed his gratitude to his friend John Allen in Arkadelphia:

> Your courage, personal strength–Your plain old beautiful beingness–these help me to remain a human. It is a constant reminder that all men at least have the potential–a potential that can only be realized through love.

After being released from prison Mike married his sweetheart, Dana, and together they traveled to Vermont to pick apples. There he could relish his freedom and return to the simple basics of life he so much enjoyed. Later, discovering Dana was pregnant, the young couple left for Cincinnati where the baby could be delivered by natural childbirth. In the last letter I have from Mike, dated 1971, he tells John Allen he and Dana are homesick for Arkansas and will be returning and that they look forward to visiting with him when they get there. Whatever the future had waiting for Mike, it's a safe bet that service to others would remain his guiding principle.

About the war in Vietnam John Allen and Mike were right, and about wars in general Thoreau and Twain and Tolstoy and the many voices down through history that have spoken out against the evils of war have been right. The Boy Scout *Handbook* of 1932 accurately describes war as one of the great tragedies of life, a destroyer of civilizations. "The effort of home, church, school and state is for us to guard life and respect property—war says kill and destroy." Surely all rational people must agree with this proposition. So we're left with the question, "Why can't mankind put an end to war? Why does the killing go on?"

The answer seems to be that war, like the biblical curse of original sin, is part of our genetic inheritance; it is woven into our DNA. The human propensity for group conflict cannot be sanded away like a blemish on a board; it is a knothole in our family tree that goes all the way through. The ability to reason, which resides in the most recent evolutionary layer of the human brain, the cerebral cortex, is fragile and easily over-powered by the primordial emotions of fear and hate which lie coiled in the deeper folds of our brains, the limbic system. We have a Grendel sleeping in our basement which, so long as not aroused, permits our lives to go along peacefully. But when awakened by clamor and conflict, by a call to battle from leaders and neighbors, it comes raging forth drowning voices of moderation and eclipsing the light of reason.

The evolutionary explanations for such collective reactions seem straightforward: In the struggle for survival proto-human and early human hunters and gatherer clans and tribes competed for hunting grounds, for territory that could sustain their families. No doubt there were long periods of peace and cooperation between early human communities, but when a group felt its existence or livelihood threatened by another the tools developed for hunting quickly became weapons of war. It's not difficult to see the survival advantage for the group that responded instantly to threat, rallying around its leader and entering a conflict passionately and in force contrasted to a group without a dominant leader, one that preferred submitting the question of war for discussion before entering the fray.

Those tribes with strong and decisive leaders and brave and skillful young warriors clearly had a survival advantage, and abilities honed in the hunt and in sports and games were the same ones called upon in combat. Many team sports are thinly disguised forms of ritualized combat and their popularity with the young, particularly males, goes back to dim antiquity. Boys naturally love to run and throw things—rocks, spears, baseballs and footballs. They love contests of strength and skill, such as boxing and wrestling, and at the height of their physical strength in their late teens and early twenties with the sap of youth flowing strong many are primed for a call to action.

We don't have to look very deep to see an underlying pattern of human behavior that connects sports and warfare, to see the relationship for example between the Arkadelphia High Badger football team in 1936 in high spirits on their way up Highway 67 to challenge Malvern and the forces of Union General Steele in the spring of 1864 with its long train of soldiers and animals, of cannons, caissons and supply wagons, headed down that same route toward Arkadelphia and a grim rendezvous with General Price's Confederate forces waiting along the Ouachita.

John Allen was right in his belief that old men start wars and send young men off to fight, but he was mistaken in believing young men march off submissively, for often they want to be tested, are ready for the contest and eager to join the ranks. The young National Guardsmen marching around the courthouse square were not conscripts, but volunteers. If some were there to avoid the draft, many were there because the challenge of military life attracted them. In high school John Allen himself had thought seriously about applying for admission to the Naval Academy to further his education. In 1938, three years before Pearl Harbor, his best friend Buddy Whitten who planned to apply to Annapolis with him, joined the Arkansas National Guard. Six years later hunkered deep in a hole in a French farmer's field Lieutenant Whitten no doubt had second thoughts about the attractions of military life as he listened to the Messerschmitt begin its power dive.

Although John Allen vigorously opposed the war in Vietnam, his own family history was punctuated by wars. To a great extent all human history is a chronicle of warfare. The predisposition to respond emotionally and collectively to per-ceived threats that provided a survival advantage for primitive tribes and clans, however, has itself become one of the greatest threats to mankind. Like some prehistoric reptile struggling to carry the weight of massive armor and huge tusks to defend against enemies that no longer exist, we are burdened with our own obsolescent genetic inheritance. This innate tropism for violent conflict which has wreaked havoc on civilizations throughout history, today, because of our greatly improved killing technology, poses an even graver threat, and that threat haunted John Allen. In a letter to Mike Vogler he laments, "This unspeakable war and the old ways prevail today, and one wonders whether we have the intelligence, the courage, the love to struggle forth into the light," calling to mind the closing lines of Matthew Arnold's poem, "Dover Beach."

> And we are here as on a darkling plain Swept with confused alarms of struggle and flight, Where ignorant armies clash by night.

It very well may take man a long time to find his way out of the darkness. Our struggle toward the light is made more difficult because we glorify warfare. Our genetic predisposition for violent conflict is reinforced by cultures which honor warriors and celebrate battles in story and song, from Homer and the Bible to Tom Clancy, from Achilles and Odysseus, Joshua and Samson, to "The Ballad of the Green Berets." We remember and perpetuate the glory and forget the horrors.

When John Allen and Aunt Bessie sat in the backyard enjoying the warm spring weather, much of their family's history, their state's and their country's history, was represented in the scene before them—the memorial wall of Clark County heroes to the right, a block behind that the National Guard Armory, straight ahead the courthouse, on their left the former law office of Governor Flanagin and across the street from it the stalwart Confederate soldier.

Bessie's Great Aunt Laura Scott Butler, niece of General Winfield Scott and member of the Harris Flanagin Chapter of the United Daughters of the Confederacy, was a leader in the campaign to have the memorial erected. Bessie and Gertrude were proud of their family's role in the Civil War and believed in their hearts the truth of the inscriptions on the pedestal: "The Principles for which they fought are eternal," the cause for which they fought was "glorious," and both would have added their voices to the prayer, "When the last trumpet is sounded may each one answer the roll call of the heavenly army." Here even the fallen cannot escape the ranks; God has been conscripted and heaven itself become an army camp.

Behind the comforting words on the monument and on similar monuments across the country and around the world lies the suffering and devastation left in the aftermath of every war. The American Civil War took 620,000 lives, more killed than in all the wars of the country from the Revolutionary War through Korea. It laid waste vast swaths of the country, particularly the South, and left destruction and starvation in its wake. The war that so many thought would be quick and glorious lasted four horrendous years; no one was prepared for the disease that swept through the army camps or for the thousands of dead that lay unburied for days and even weeks on the blasted battlefields—Antietam, Gettysburg, Cold Harbor, and countless others. The country during those four years truly became "This Republic of Suffering."

The great tragedy of war arises from the paradoxical human condition that enables us to love one another and kill one another. If killing were all there is to war there would be no tragedy. But the death of every soldier grievously wounds the hearts of those who love him. War memorials around the world are testimonials of love, and reminders of the human hurt we inflict on one another, a hurt we attempt to cover with comforting words like those on the pedestal of the Clark County Confederate soldier:

> On fame's eternal camping ground
> Their silent tents are spread
> And glory guards with silent rounds
> The bivouac of the dead.

Finding no comfort in such sentimental consolations, John Allen launched his own campaign against the war in Vietnam—but it was an uneven battle. When he, Mike Vogler and their anti-war activist friends sallied forth in an attempt to stop the killing their only weapons were their voices and their bodies; the fields of battle were college campuses, newspaper editorial pages, forums wherever they could be found, and ultimately, federal prisons. But their arguments, based on reason and compassion, on the principles of Jesus' Sermon on the Mount, on Thoreau's "Civil Disobedience," on the teachings of Gandhi, Einstein and Tolstoy, were no match for the collective response of a nation in the grip of fear and anger and driven by determined leaders and misguided national pride.

So the war ground on for ten years—the longest in U.S. History.

* * *

CHAPTER 13

Weaver of Words

———————■———————

Merlyn

See how I gather song from the air?
See how I harvest roses?
See what effortless skill I have,
deftly assaying the glint of your hair
and the worth of the sun as it rises?

Out of the selfsame stream I seine
fingerling stars and lovers—
this is the cunning I give to you,
this my store of legerdemain
only to true believers.

Wise in the weaver's ways,
I finger the web,
the rough of the warp I feel;
and the robe that was old
in Camelot's youth
I wear to the end of the world.

When John Allen came to live at the home place after eight nomadic years with traveling carnivals—the Ziedman and Pollie Shows, Barker Shows, and Leon Broughton Shows—he was ready to settle down. As any child would have been, the "Curly-headed Carney punk/ sure-footed darter through crowds," was for a time caught up in the excitement of carnival life, the lights, the rides, the earth-shaking music of the calliope, the "sawdust lots bannered with promises/ of marvels and rare delights." He would have been a favorite among his playmates there, his pals the other "road boys," as he later proved a favorite among his school mates in Arkadelphia. Early on, however, he had seen, behind the grease paint and gaudy veneer of the traveling shows, the hardscrabble lives of the troupe that made it go, of carneys like his mother and father, Louise and Al. Not much to look forward to there. But that life was all he knew before he met Grandma Amy and his Horton kin in Arkadelphia. In them, especially in Aunt Gertrude and Aunt Bessie, he found an unexpected path to a better future.

By the time he entered school in Arkadelphia John Allen had seen more of the United States than his classmates would see in their lifetimes. Now he would find new friends and discover new worlds to explore, some in books and others along the Ouachita. He had faithfully kept up with his studies while on the road and, in spite of Louise's hatred of school and indifference to books, her son developed a love for reading that would shape his future. Evidence of that love appeared early when Bessie's neighbor, Alberta Culbertson, wrote Louise about her ten-year-old son and told her, "John Allen is fine and happy; he is a sweet good child. No one can help but love him." She goes on to report that John Allen and her daughter Helen, who was about the same age, spent much time in the nearby library and read "the biggest part of their time." To be sure, both Louise and Al encouraged their son in his studies and were proud of his academic achievements, but it was Louise's sisters, specifically Bessie, who guided John Allen through his school years and helped him realize his intellectual and creative potential.

In the Arkadelphia of 1927, before the world had become virtual, before television, cell phones, iPods, and computer games, children and their neighborhood friends filled their free hours with reading, with outdoor games and explorations of the surrounding natural world. For John Allen, only three blocks away, there was the Ouachita. As he played along its banks, waded on its sandbars and skipped rocks across the water, it's not likely he recognized any connection between his own life and the river, between the minutes, hours and days slipping away and the unrelenting current of the Ouachita sliding under the iron railroad bridge near Caddo Street on its way past the site of the old Fairview Plantation, through the former campgrounds of General Price's Confederate soldiers near Camden before surrendering its identity to the Black River, the Mississippi, and finding rest at last in the waters of the Gulf of Mexico.

John Allen, however, would have become aware sooner than most that the long summer carefree days of his youth were fleeting. Stories he read of earlier days in books, such as *Ivanhoe, The Last of the Mohicans, Tom Sawyer, Huckleberry Finn*, along with the pleasure they gave him, would have impressed on him two realities: that everything we see about us is evanescent and that the only way to hold on to experiences we value is to somehow capture them in words. We are able to preserve bits of our past in narratives, in histories, biographies, poetry and song. God may have created the great universe out of nothing, but we create our own small worlds with language; it is by virtue of our ability to tell stories that we are the only creatures not condemned to surrender all to time. Thoreau said, "Time is but the stream I go a-fishing in." John Allen's Merlyn seined from that "self-same stream . . . fingerling stars and lovers." If we hope to save things we value from the flood our nets must be woven of language and our "catch," the experiences and epiphanies we want to hold on to, must be preserved in words. John Allen thought about it—

> But how commit to paper daily chaff
> That's better tossed on air—the common way
> We hide ourselves; or how find space enough
> To scribble what we really want to say.

Like many youth John Allen began to write poetry in high school, but those early efforts, according to his own testimony, were "mercifully lost." After he was injured, finding himself with "an uncommon amount of leisure," with a paralyzed body but clear vision, sharp hearing and a head full of thoughts he once more set about to capture his desultory observations and reflections in words and fashion them into poems. For him at this time the phrase "the life of the mind" took on a special meaning.

It was after Mr. Huddleston helped him get started in the magazine subscription business at the home place that John Allen resumed his efforts at poetic composition. There in his bedroom-office he learned to type with the rubber-tipped pencils in order to take care of business and, when not taking care of customers or visiting with friends, found he was often left alone with his typewriter. He took advantage of those opportunities to peck out words and phrases that caught his imagination on the reverse sides of old business correspondence, advertisements and pamphlets. He was a pioneer in recycling paper long before the rest of the nation awakened to the need, and he followed that frugal practice throughout his life.

As he said in his posthumous letter to Arkadelphia, he and Aunt Bessie had many supportive friends following his accident, and, while some passed on and some moved away others, captivated by his exemplary character, his humor, intelligence, and kindness, were added to his circle of friends and admirers. For twenty years after his injury while he and Bessie lived at the home place his closest friends would have included many of his high-school classmates and teachers, such as Buddy Whitten, W.S McNutt, Martha England, Amy Jean Greene and Martha Greene. Thanks to his magazine subscription service and his budding book sales, however, he steadily acquired new friends, many of them students and faculty from the nearby colleges.

John Allen's attempts to write poetry at that time, however, were no doubt often disrupted by the battles between Bessie and Gertrude, each of whom would seek his sympathy and attempt to enlist him on her side. One of the greatest testaments to his strength is the fact that over the years, with his calm nature and soft voice, he mediated the battles between his two aunts without ever losing the love and respect of either. Thankfully the Horton wars greatly abated after he and Bessie moved into the house at the corner of 4th and Main. There John Allen continued to expand his communities of love and thought as new customers arrived to discover the pleasant and stimulating atmosphere of Adams Book Store, and there also he was able to focus his attention more intently on poetry.

The first requirement for a would-be poet is to love poetry and the second is to understand that writing poetry is a craft that must be studied and mastered. John Allen began with a genuine love of poetry and had the determination and talent to study and learn the craft. In a letter he told Mike Vogler, "I know a good deal of poetry by heart, and some mornings when I wake early it gives me pleasure to lie there and recite some. Beautiful words give a strange satisfaction." He not only studied poetry on his own but sought out mentors, the first were no doubt his high school English teachers, but later there were his knowledgeable friends, such as Elizabeth Thomas, Martha England, and later the poet Jack Butler. He exchanged many letters with those friends which reflect a sophisticated yet practical knowledge of prosody on the part of all correspondents.

Though he could no longer tramp the banks of the Ouachita John Allen found that, if he could not explore widely, he could look closely. He discovered within his compass at the home place and later at the book store many of nature's remarkable commonplaces. He liked to sit on the porch of the home place where he could see the seasons change—the pink-tinged white star-flowers that blanketed the lawn like snow in early spring mingled with henbit, dead nettle, clover and wild onions whose sharp, green tang blended with the damp loamy smell of the warming earth. There on the porch when the weather was cool Bessie would cover his shoulders and legs with blankets so he could spend more time outside.

In warmer weather she would place damp towels on the back of his neck and on his brow so he could be cooled with the passing breezes.

Had he not been injured he likely would have traveled broadly both during World War II and after, but since he could not he took comfort from Ralph Waldo Emerson who believed travel is a "fool's paradise," and from Thoreau who stuck close to home declaring with some pride, "I have traveled a good deal in Concord." Both men believed nature's laws applied everywhere and that, if the world cannot be found in a grain of sand, the mysterious operations of the universe can be found at one's doorstep. The reclusive Emily Dickenson proved with her discerning eye and fertile imagination that nature's unremarked miracles were waiting to be uncovered close by—in the seclusion of her father's house in Amherst and the confines of her own backyard garden. She saw wonders in the ordinary:

> A bird came down the walk.
> He did not know I saw.
> He bit an angleworm in half,
> And ate the fellow raw.

The birds that showed up in John Allen's yard were the usual Arkansas suspects—at the feeders, chickadees, titmice, cardinals and sparrows, scouring the ground, robins, juncos, and more sparrows. He especially loved sitting on the porch on warm spring days and listening to the soothing voices of mourning doves; their soft *oowoo-woo-woo-woo*, evoked memories of earlier supple-limbed spring days along the Ouachita. Woodpeckers—the small downy and hairy, the mid-sized red-bellied, and the occasional large pileated—would visit his yard and he could see from their common behavior, the dipping flight patterns, their preference for backing down tree trunks, how Mr. Huddleston came to the conclusion that all woodpeckers descended from one ur-woodpecker. He took mental note of all his feathered visitors as assiduously as he had pursued his hobbies as a Boy Scout. For John Allen, as with all birdwatchers, it was novelty that grabbed his attention, the rare rose-breasted grosbeak, the gaudy yellow, white, and black evening grosbeak, the flocks of masked cedar waxwings in early spring that swept down in funnels to plunder every red berry in sight. In his poem for Aunt Bessie, "Star Walk," the mockingbird along with her heirloom roses connects the old woman sitting on the porch swing at Adams Book Store with the young girl she had been during those long-ago idyllic days with her adored grandfather at Fairview Plantation.

In "Collage for Ted," apparently written for a familiar figure, a former customer or a departed friend, John Allen acknowledges other feathered visitors to his yard.

> I hear the bluejay
> rasping the last frost
> from this rimed morning.
> He is busy about his work,
> while I—I watch the sun,
> sliced by slant blinds,
> garnish my bacon and eggs.
> > *Memento vivere!*

John Allen is alive to hear the raucous voice of the blue jay this sunny winter morning and he thinks of Ted who is gone.

> (Ted, Old Boy, thou art one
> with rock and tree and me
> wheeling in the Whereless Now. . . .)

In these lines that echo Aiken's "Senlin" and Wordsworth's "A Slumber did my Spirit Seal," John Allen fixes for a moment on the curious fact that he is alive and sensate, able to enjoy the bird's call and the sunlight on his breakfast plate, while Ted cannot. *Memento vivere!* "Remember you are alive! Remember you will die!" The lesson here is *carpe diem*, seize the moment—enjoy the breakfast; seize the day; enjoy the birds that visit your yard, even when they come dressed in widow's weeds:

> Outside the window
> a sudden gust precipitates
> blackbirds—
> a funereal company
> (with secret gauds
> of green and blue),
> they find sleekness
> in winter's dry litter.

The iridescent blackbirds feed their "sleekness" in "winter's dry litter" while the omnivorous poet on this morning nourishes himself with bacon and eggs, a meal Mike Vogler would decline and W.S McNutt would ponder. There's no question, however, that John Allen too was troubled by the cannibalism of life as he makes clear in the following poem.

Man Gifted Above His Kin

Terrible in its beauty You have made,
my God, this clawed, mawed world
where even plants reach out
with hooks and gape for prey.
Bright singing wings
bear beaks that snap in air,
or fold to pounce and tear
the cringing flesh below.
One thousand fathoms down,
cold in its dark domain,
life stalks itself to feed
on succulence of pain.

Sucking the tender teat,
toothless and untaloned, man,
gifted above his kin,
refines the shape of fangs
and rends the web of life
with many weaponed hands.

Here John Allen addresses several of his life-long concerns, not only the issue that troubled his friend W.S McNutt, that life feeds on life, but the degree to which man with his technology has exceeded the destructive powers of his fellow creatures in this "clawed, mawed world." The synecdoche and imagery in lines 5 - 12 show the poet was well aware that the harmless birds that visited his yard sometimes met their fates in the talons of their raptor cousins and that sharks are not the only predators that swim in the sea; but this natural order, the wildness that Thoreau believed was essential for the "preservation of the world," John Allen accepted. What troubled him was that man has far surpassed all other creatures in rapaciousness using his "many weaponed hands" to unleash large-scale depredations against the natural world and to attack and slaughter his own kind.

In the following poem John Allen shows how technology has greatly multiplied man's predatory capabilities and stoked his lust for power:

Leadership Training

This is the muzzle, this is the grip,
and here insert the shining shell;
when you have worn it on the hip
a while, you feel your muscles swell.
We've made advances in the art,
since cavemen used a club to clout;
a rifle reaches far to part
their hair and proselyte their doubt.
It's true (and this we deprecate)
that some few innocents' demise
is brought about by guns and fate—
but freedom is a costly prize.

The violence and destruction taking place in Vietnam haunted John Allen but beyond that lurked the specter of all-out nuclear war. Throughout the years of the Cold War the fate of the world hung in the balance while the two super powers practiced the dark arts of brinksmanship. With a doomsday potential so horrible the only resource for the poet is irony:

Bending the Twig

My child, you do not understand;
be patient 'til your years increase—
we did not devastate their land
from malice, but to further peace.

Out of our tender love for you
came napalm, dragon ships—the rest;
we builded better than we knew,
but our intentions were the best.

And can't you see the silos full
of missiles tipped with bursts of sun
are torches lifted up with zeal
in freedom's cause whose race we run?

Goals are elusive, yes, but note:
we pay our taxes, go to church,
and when in doubt, we always vote
a larger budget for research.

John Allen deplored man's lethal inventions and harbored resentments against even some more benign technologies. He wrote a sonnet, "Sick Leave," in which he imagined that he called in sick to work, cut all the wires to the TV and telephone, sneaked out to the backyard on a moonless night when neighbors couldn't see, dug a hole and buried both infernal inventions. Following this ceremony of "exorcism" he returned to the house, sat on the floor with the blinds drawn and waited for the silence to close around him, waited to see if he could "track the thing he was." Technology he believed has distracted us; it has separated us from our true selves and we need to find some way to reconnect.

He did not live to see the age of the Internet, cell phones, and the digitization of the world. For both good and ill we modern folk have become in a sense cyborgs, inextricably bonded with a technology which has greatly expanded our horizons and multiplied our powers while simultaneously removing us farther from nature. As Emerson says in his essay, "Compensation," for everything gained something is lost. How do we measure what today's youth, absorbed in their cell phones, Internet communities and computer games, may be missing compared with their counterparts of the Great Depression who sat around campfires at night along the Ouachita listening to wind whispering through the pines as Mr. Huddleston told stories about Caddo Indians and the early days of Arkadelphia?

As regards the merits of the present versus the past, whichever way the scale might tip we know we can't turn back. Studies show the bond between humans today and their technology is so strong that when deprived of computers and cell phones people suffer withdrawal symptoms similar to those suffered by drug addicts when they go off drugs cold turkey. We are hooked.

Like all of us who become frustrated with technology, however, John Allen made exceptions. He loved his motorized wheelchair and the hydraulic lift Ted Hoyer had installed on his bed, and when electric typewriters became available he acquired one and found it much easier to use. The van the town bought for him and Joy enabled him to visit friends and see landscapes he had not seen since he was a Boy Scout and to watch Joy and her friend go swimming at Lake DeGray. Some of the greatest benefactors from technology today are those with spinal cord injuries, and there's no question that John Allen would have welcomed any invention that would have helped compensate for his handicap. It was primarily television and the telephone that provoked his ire.

In his opinion there was little on TV worth watching, and he was often compelled to endure shows that Bessie and Uncle Vernon chose to watch. He had no way to escape. He did, however, come to realize television's potential when the U.S. space program succeeded in taking man to the moon, a feat that enabled everyone to see, in John's words, "The bright haloed beauty of the world." And when Carl Sagan's *Cosmos* came to television he had to acknowledge that, when properly used, the medium had incredible power. In fact it was television that brought home to Americans the horrors of the war in Vietnam and reinforced the efforts of anti-war activists such as Mike Vogler and John Allen.

It was not only by writing letters to editors, providing support for war resistors, and protesting to local officials against military programs in public schools that John Allen contributed to the anti-war effort. He spoke out forcefully in his poetry against war and the war in Vietnam, although irony is a frail weapon against collective patriotic emotions grounded in anger and fear. On the personal level he attempted to reason with his pro-war customers such as the minister who taught philosophy in a small southern seminary, and he found it curious that so many Christians, followers of the "Prince of Peace," seemed so bellicose, so supportive of war. John Allen's views were well expressed by Gandhi who said, "I like your Christ, I do not like your Christians. Your Christians are so unlike your Christ."

In spite of a few not so subtle warnings that his activities could harm his business, John Allen used every avenue at his disposal to speak out against the war in Vietnam. It is testimony to his character and temperament that he was able to strongly oppose the predominant sentiment of his fellow citizens without forfeiting the high regard in which he was held by the community of Arkadelphia. The war in Vietnam, however, was not the only issue where he found himself out of step with his neighbors.

When he was a student Arkadelphia public schools were segregated and remained so for a quarter century after he was injured. Aunt Bessie, growing up under the strong Confederate influence of her grandparents, W.S. and Elizabeth Horton, was never able to free herself from the racial prejudice that infected the South of that day, but John Allen, with his open and questing mind, came to see the damage racial hatreds inflict on the human soul. Later he said his early years on the carnival circuit helped him grow up free of such attitudes. He learned he could not reason with his aunt on the subject, but he did share his views with college students who visited his store and was pleased to note over time their growing awareness of the evils of racism. But that ancient evil would not, he knew, be easy to eradicate:

Incantation

"Gog" or "Magog," "gook" or "geek"—
which is the magic word we seek?
Which syllables will exorcise
the evil ones whom we despise?
"An infidel," "uncircumcised,"
though passé now, were highly prized.
Both "chink" and "Jap" were good, and "frog,"
"Yankee imperialist," and "wog."
"nigger" is potent, it's alleged;
and "po white trash" is triple edged.
While "Communist" is serving well,
and "Jew" –a happy nonpareil,
obviously this age of jets
needs more effective epithets.
Could it be "honkey," "pig" or "slope?"
We seek the word, and live in hope.

Not all of John Allen's attention was devoted to the somber and serious concerns of war, racism and the environment. He had a genuine interest in and affection for people and was surrounded throughout most of his life with cheerful family and friends. Since he could never interest Amy Jean Greene in sad subjects, their conversations were light-hearted and full of humor, although as he told Martha England he believed Amy Jean's uniformly happy exterior concealed darker currents below. But she and her cousin, Martha, were frequent visitors at the book store coming by to share their adventures with John Allen and Bessie. They liked to go to Hot Springs to eat out and see movies, and when there was a children's movie they wanted to see they would take their young kinsman, Amy

Thompson, the girl who wanted to marry John Allen when she grew up, and use her for cover.

As a teenager John Allen seemed always in motion. When not swimming, he and his friends hiked miles along back roads and through the woods along the river. As do boys everywhere they loved taking dares and doing daring things, like rappelling without ropes down the sheer face of De Soto Bluff by clinging to tree roots and whatever scanty foliage they could grab on to. Football practice was grueling but he found the exercise and the shower afterward exhilarating. In his junior and final year of high school, in the regional track meet, he won the 440 yard dash and placed in the javelin keeping his parents, Al and Louise, informed of his physical development. He wrote them about running laps with Buddy Whitten and told them that after he warmed up he was able to stand, legs straight, and place both palms flat on the ground. He also told them that he then wore a size 11 shoe. At an early age he showed he was dedicated to taking care of his health.

When he was injured the world for him changed, but he continued throughout his life to attend to his health as best he could. The secret, as everyone knows, is no secret—diet and exercise. But now, since he could no longer exercise, the only thing left in his control was his diet. As in so many other areas, when it came to healthy eating John Allen was ahead of his time. Of course there have always been health faddists, those whose dietary recommendations are based on speculation and anecdotal testimonials unsupported by any scientific evidence. Thoreau had his own ideas, some of which were sound while others were not. He believed living on a simple vegetable diet while avoiding meat, spices, tea, coffee and alcohol would suppress his animal urges and energize him spiritually. Modern nutritionists believe strict adherence to his diet would omit some important nutrients, and studies have shown that coffee, tea, and alcohol, when consumed in moderation, can have beneficial effects.

Sandy Hays, his student assistant who wrote a poem for John Allen shortly after his death, revealed some of his dietary practices:

> . . . we had tea together
> . . . .
> You had to place his cup
> at a certain angle, see,
> so he could hold it.
> I was not told.
> I observed and made
> a special effort
> to perfect that angle.
> I would turn the gas heater on
> at his request
> before I left
> to keep him warm.
> . . . .
> Molasses and milk
> Honey and tea.
> I fixed them for him
> And homemade bread and cheese
> Sliced. . . .

Sometimes he would simply take hot water. His friend, the poet Jack Butler, who could scratch out a poem for the nonce as readily as Picasso could limn a form on a napkin, in one of his letters wrote a lean pattern poem for John Allen which read in part:

> . . . .
> You sip
> your cup of heat, your fare,
> spoon-dip
> by spoon, on pure calor-
> ic, and
> sing bone.
> sing on. . . .

So John Allen ate meat on occasion and dairy products, milk and cheese, and he drank tea, but he preferred natural, home grown foods. He could experiment and have fun with food as he did when he and Boulware Ohls tried the great cheese experiment; and he liked to toy with and think about gourmet dishes, but his approach to diet was informed and practical. He read *Prevention* and other health and nutrition publications and took what recommendations seemed solidly based and ignored the rest. But he preferred always fresh, organically grown foods, especially fruits and vegetables. And while white, fragrant, spongy bread dominated the market, he preferred whole grain, and when a friend baked him a loaf he repaid him with a poem:

Jess's Bread

I think of route men driving into the dawn,
their vans loaded with trays of bread
trailing a warm fragrance—

an incense which, in old days,
before the gods were banished,
rose from every hearth

Each in its colorful sheath
proclaiming its ideal whiteness
and the wonder of its sponginess
("the way children like it"),
their limp loaves make a frail staff
for our breakfast faring.

But Jess's honest loaf is a wayfarer's joy
rising from whole grain and his kneading,
dark with earth's goodness,
and preserved only by its integrity,
a sharp knife and a firm stroke
slice it for our need.
And I go forth into the day
leaning on Jess's pilgrim staff.

As can be expected with a John Allen poem, as with good poetry in general, the closer the reader looks the more he sees. Among other things waiting to be discovered in this modest poem of thanks for Jess's "staff of life," are the names of two of the poet's commercial targets whose artificial preservatives Jess has replaced with "integrity."

Commercialism was another frequent target of John Allen's satiric arrows. Although an entrepreneur himself, he was dismayed by America's fevered consumerism and the constant hyping of products and services he saw on television. He was with Thoreau in his belief that "trade curses everything it handles; and though you trade in messages from heaven, the whole curse of trade attaches to the business." Behind the assault on the earth's natural resources—its oceans, forests and wildlife—is the profit motive. This monster that has slouched its way to Bethlehem to be born has appeared as our new "Savior."

. . . .

Out of the depth of darkest night
he comes to comfort and endow!
behold him there so pure and bright!
all haloed and anointed now

with Johnson's Oil and DDT,
a loser graced with winning ways,
who serves the nation's GNP—
this only child the father spays.

The title of this poem in the section of his book, "The Children's Hour," is a bit of scripture taken from Isaiah, borrowed by Handel, and given a slight twist by John Allen Adams: "Unto Us A Child Is Had."

He doesn't shy away from aiming a little satire at himself. How did John Allen feel about his life that began with such momentum—eight years traveling the country, nine years in motion as an energetic student, Scout, and athlete, then finding himself confined for the rest of his life to two houses within a two-block radius in Arkadelphia? Might as well look for a little humor:

You Gotta Walk

They put you on Track 9
and promise you'll arrive on time—
and you do,
but it ain't where you wanna go,
you know?
it ain't where you wanna go.
So you buy a different ticket,
but every ticket's a round trip ticket,
and you end up Here,
and Here ain't where you wanna go,
you know?
I been to K.C. and all points West,
and I hit every burg in the East,
but the depots always look the same,
smell the same—just like Here.
I figger it this way,
if you wanna go There,
you gotta walk.
But you can't get there in Hush Puppies,
and I ain't seen no walking shoes
since—well, since '37.
I recollect seein' a pair
in old man Hollon's showwindow.
They looked like they'd been there 50 years,
saggin' and a bit faded (he marked them down),
but you could tell they was made
of good oak leather and would give lots of wear.
I still wish I'd bought 'em,
but money was tight in '37,
and I couldn't afford
even the marked down price.

Consider this: His neck was broken in October 1936 and he did not recover from surgery and the swirl of alarm, confusion and activity that surrounded him until the early months of 1937 when his future would be determined, a time when he, his family and the community still had some small hope he might regain use of his limbs. But when feeling and movement did not return all had finally to accept the painful reality that John Allen was a quadriplegic. The size 11 shoes he laced up before his last football game were the last ones he would ever walk in. From that point on Aunt Bessie would have to cover his feet with thick socks and blankets and, for those occasions when both needed to remind themselves that they were still feet, in soft shoes, such as Hush Puppies.

John Allen's predicament in the poem is that he is "Here" and he wants to go "There," but every time he buys a ticket to ride, the train brings him back to the same spot. If he'd got those walking shoes back in '37 he would have been all right, but now he's stuck "Here" and knows that the only way to break out of the circles he is going around in, the only way to escape, is to walk; but he knows he can't walk, that he'll never be able to get "There" in his Hush Puppies.

So he remained in one spot for forty-six years. But the range of his influence reached far beyond "Here," the two-block area in which he spent the rest of his life. Throughout those years the student worker acolytes who were touched by his kindness and wisdom departed to distant parts of this country and beyond to live their lives carrying with them lessons from his life and the heartening awareness that such a good man lived. His schoolmates who went off first to World War II and later to colleges and Ivy League schools and successful careers shared the same convictions, as did his many friends and customers. All who knew John Allen Adams understood he was extraordinary.

Five years before he died he selected a few poems from those he had written through the years and published them in a slender volume, *I Walk Toward the Sound of My Days.* He had for a long time been encouraged by Martha England, W.S McNutt and other friends and associates to publish a book of his poetry, always responding to those requests by saying the world didn't need another "third rate poet." But John Allen was no third-rate poet. He looked squarely at the world and captured in words his experiences and his distilled reflections on life in language always honest, vivid and apt. He understood what good poetry is and knew how to craft it.

Professor England assigned his poems in her literature classes at Smith College in Boston and Queens College, New York; they were published in the *Saturday Review of Literature,* the *New Orleans Review* and various newspapers and publications around the state. Among other recognitions he received was the Sybil Nash Abrams Award from the Poet's Roundtable of Arkansas for his poem about the Revolutionary patriot, Thomas Paine. Periodically throughout his life he was visited by reporters from various publications who wanted to tell the story of the Arkadelphia poet and bookseller.

Shortly after the publication of, *I Walk Toward the Sound of My Days*, a review by Jack Butler appeared in the *Arkansas Gazette.* Butler, a gifted poet who had published widely in national journals including *The New Yorker* and who would later become a successful novelist, was the Poet in Residence at Henderson State University in the early 1970's. When he came to Arkadelphia he brought poetry with him like Harold Hill brought music to River City. Butler is one of the rare practitioners of the art who not only writes exceptionally well but reads his poems with a natural expressiveness and power that commands attention. His presence on the two college campuses and in the public schools stimulated the creative spirit among many people in the area, and when he got to know John Allen and read some of his poetry he liked what he found. He refused to accept the "third-rate poet" line and joined Martha England, W.S McNutt and others in encouraging John Allen to publish his poems and his influence no doubt played a significant part in bringing about the publication of *I Walk Toward the Sound of My Days*. Though he was a genuinely modest man, John Allen naturally cared about the products of his creative efforts, and now he could take justifiable pride in his book of poems.

In his review Butler describes Adams as a "Thoreauvian of rare sincerity—a lover of simplicity, a hater of hatred and violence, a resister of conformity and dullness—with yet a tense ironic turn." While acknowledging that not all the poems in the collection are flawless, Butler says that there are a dozen poems he believes "deserve ranking with Crabbe or John Clare—or perhaps even George Herbert. Certainly they have wit, grace, and concern equivalent to Herbert's." He cites passages from several poems to illustrate his point then discusses one poem in full. He says of John Allen, "He is a metricist of occasionally formidable deftness," and offers as an example the following sonnet:

Winter Landscape

These winter days befit the wintered mind;
the brittle branches clawing sleeted skies,

and scouring winds that chill and blur the eyes,
are with a self-inclemency combined.
The inner weather and the outer find
unwonted consonance today, and these
attuned antiphonal austerities
are fitting music for the unresigned.

Nature's abiding cycle slowly yields
alleviation for its wintering,
however cold it is, however long;
but what assures the heart's denuded fields
the green assuaging of a second spring
to resurrect the singer and the song?

"This is an old theme," Butler acknowledges, "but what superb handling! The sound and the image of the third line are exactly right. And how few formal poets can handle phrases like 'self-inclemency' or 'unwonted consonance' and make them not only sing precisely but mean precisely. This is not to mention the outrageous seventh line of the octave, which gulps five neat feet in three big alliterating bites. Maybe that's too much of a display. I don't know. I love it."

Butler singles out another poem for praise, one that was a favorite of Martha England:

The Inner Man Alone

The inner man alone,
Homunculus of lime,
Will come into his own
In time, in time.

Ironic liegeman! He
Who pliantly sustains
The weaker one's decree
Knows, while he feigns,

Abrasive years install
This unbraided one
To eminence, and—all
Submission's done.

This pallid peroration
The centuries assay,
The limy consummation
Of the clay,

No logic of the mind
Resolves—how reconcile
The rigid grin behind
The agile smile.

Of "The Inner Man Alone," Butler says:

Some of it may make for difficult reading at first, but
look up the exact meanings and etymologies of such
words as "homunculus"—the ironies that ripple from
that word in this poem!—and "peroration." And if
thinking of medieval theories of generation, of the
frequent topic of medieval sermons, of how limestone,
and something else, is made of $CaCO_3$—if thinking
of these things doesn't bring the grim secret of this
poem across, let me urge the first large section of

Gray's Anatomy upon you. I don't know where the movements of the speaking mouth have been put to better use in a poem than in "the rigid grin behind/ the agile smile," or where a second reading has freed more meaning from deliberate ambiguity than "in time, in time" of the first stanza. This poem underlies the whole frame of the book. The poet has met "the rigid grin" unflinchingly, and earned the symmetry, sympathy and grace he reports."

John Allen never flinched from hard realities such as the one he saw daily in the mirror, reflections of his own body which likely gave rise to this poem. As falling sand in an hourglass measures the passage of time, his diminishing flesh through the years marked for him the passing of his own life and, toward the end, the approach of its conclusion. If he could confront his paralysis with humor in his poems he could with equal serenity look death in the face. More importantly, through it all, John Allen never lost his ability to enjoy life.

Perhaps the happiest period for him as a poet came following Jack Butler's review in the *Arkansas Gazette* and reviews in local papers. People wanted to meet the poet and hear his poetry. The Henderson State University English Club met at his book store for group poetry readings. He was invited to give readings in local schools and in nearby communities and told his friend Mike Vogler he was becoming a traveling troubadour. As before noted he had a beautiful speaking (and singing) voice, but because of diminished lung capacity he was unable to speak long or project far. He overcame those difficulties by taping his readings in the book store, then having Joy drive him, his books and tape player to his performances where he would then talk to those assembled, play his poems and respond to questions. When those fortunate listeners saw him wheel into the room with a big smile on his face, they were set to hear, not only a skilled poet read his fine poems, but to witness in John Allen Adams, the Arkadelphia poet and bookseller, a living example of how the most difficult challenges in life can be met with humor, courage and grace.

* * *

CHAPTER 14

Gone Worlds

———————————

This Cup of Water

This cup of water
has passed through heaven
and the veined earth
oh many times, many times—
anointing the dust,
then rising again
to the blue heaven
which I drink and what I was
becomes part of me.
. . . . .
this in remembrance I do.
May those who drink me
in a future time
taste what they are in me
and I in them—
the rarest vintage in the winery!

Not long before he died John Allen wrote a letter to his wife,
Joy:

These eleven years have been the richest in my life. We've shared some good times—at home, at the lake, at church, eating at the Becker's, at Bowens, etc. I have no regrets; I hope you don't. I've made new friends, written a few more poems and published my little book. And all of this would not have been possible without you. Thank you, Joy, for the bonuses— love and the unexpected years.

You will understand better than anyone how unendurable my life has become. It's terminal quadriplegia; the body can't endure 46 years of this condition. I won't regain the automatic bladder, I have a bad curvature that makes it difficult to sit erect, my arms and shoulders are giving me much trouble. I think I have a rupture and other problems. I can't face going back to a condition like that in the early years when I was weak and bedfast. I haven't been able to run the store properly most of the year.

I love you and the girls and their families—they have been good to me. And I love Vernon, and Aunt Gertrude, Jessie and Evelyn, and many others—and Sarah and Joel. . . but the list is too long. . . .

The remainder of the letter is devoted to suggestions for his funeral and instructions for taking care of the store and personal business. He says he gave up the idea of cremation and, since Joy would want to be buried in Rose Hill by her first husband, Tom, the little country cemetery at Sardis in Dallas County where Bessie, his uncle Thad and grandfather Louis and other members of the Horton family were buried would be fine; but Rose Hill in Arkadelphia, he said, would be all right as well. He asked for an inexpensive coffin and funeral and a simple headstone with his name and the inscription, "A Bookseller and Poet." He asked that the only music at his funeral be the slow movement from Mozart's Piano Concerto 21 which he had on a cassette.

While John Allen faced his difficult life and death as courageously as any human could, he was not immune to sadness, depression, and fear. He wrote Mike Vogler:

> As I get older, I seem not to mind using the word [God] occasionally ("in a loose humanistic sense"). I try to be a seeker after whatever "reality" may lie behind this (strange? fantastic? amazing?—there is no word) life of ours. And with my limitations I've had no notable success. Sometimes—listening to beautiful music, or sitting in the sun, or reading beautiful words (Camus' essay is great)—I feel a pleasure that approaches happiness. I am grateful and receptive at these periods. Other times I am depressed, dispersed, empty of strength. I used to think I had no fear of death, but that was youthful ego. To die aware and serene—that is to have lived well—that must be the rarest and highest art. Judging by his sister, Thoreau died well. Socrates, of course; Schweitzer, probably. Was Christ doubtful and disturbed at the end?

In his letter to Joy, John Allen accurately described his condition and foresaw his own imminent death. His quadriplegia was, as he said, terminal and his paralyzed body had sustained his mind and spirit as long as it could.

On February 27th 1984 both Joy and the last of his college student acolytes, Sarah Sullivan, recognized his precipitous decline. The customers who stopped by the book store that day were unwitting distractions for the two women who were completely focused on John Allen. After they closed the store John told Sarah she should go home and, though not wanting to leave him, she reluctantly complied.

Joy in her vigil by John Allen's bed that night saw what was coming but could not bring herself to accept it. She was comforted when at midnight he agreed to take some food after which he seemed to drift off. At two in the morning he woke and asked the time and told Joy to go to bed. "No" was her response as she kissed him on the cheek. "I have hoed some rough rows," he said, "but this is the roughest yet." He then told her if he was not better by morning to call Dr. Taylor at the hospital. Those were the last words he spoke before slipping from consciousness. Joy, distraught, stepped into the bathroom and stood praying, "Lord, make him better—Yet, Lord, not my will, but Thine."

When she stepped back into the room the change in him was startling. She ran around his bed, flipped the light switch and yelled, "John!" He turned his head and looked at her as though he had come back one last time, then his breathing lapsed into irregular gasps, his eyes glazed, the breathing stopped—John Allen was gone.

* * *

Two months later I sat with Joy and Vernon in the book store by the open door to her late husband's bedroom while she stroked the long-haired domino cat in her lap. John Allen was gone but Joy and Vernon, his family and friends were not ready to let him go, so she brought me boxes of old letters, newspaper clippings and photographs hoping we might be able to fit the pieces together and preserve his story. I conducted several interviews with the two of them there over the next couple of months and compiled a substantial list of people and places that were important in his life and family history. Without question the most formative place for the Horton sisters who raised John Allen was the site of the old Fairview Plantation in Dallas County.

So in the middle of May I drove down Highway 7, the same route John Allen's mother Louise and her parents had come up the year of Halley's Comet when they brought all their belongings in horse-drawn wagons from Fairview to their new home place in Arkadelphia. When I arrived at what I thought was the general vicinity of the old plantation I knocked on several doors in that rural community and asked questions but was told by the first few residents I talked to that they had not lived there long and knew nothing about Fairview or the Hortons. I saw a two-story white house which I thought could be the one built by his Uncle Thad that John Allen had written his parents about. If it was the occupants, also recent arrivals, knew nothing about the house's history. Continuing my search at last I saw a man standing in front of a white-frame house by an outbuilding in his yard. I drove up, got out and introduced myself and explained my purpose. Yes, he said, he knew the Hortons and told me the place where we were standing was still called Fairview. He told me the site of the old plantation was nearby. His name was John D. Wilkins, a stocky, weathered, active 71 year-old saw mill operator.

Mr. Wilkins declined to be interviewed on tape because he still had friends in the Horton family. And besides, he quoted an old timer, "two things you won't hear around here are the sound of good meat frying and the truth." He had had dealings with "Mr. Thad" over many years and no doubt could have told me a great deal but he was clearly cautious and not given to loose talk with strangers. Still he was courteous and helpful and gladly offered to show me about Fairview and the former Horton property.

We drove in my car about a half mile down a gravel road across from his house and stopped in a wooded area where, according to Mr. Wilkins, Mr. Thad's father, Louis Horton, had burned to death in a chicken house seventy years earlier. We tramped through poison ivy and tangles of honeysuckle looking for an old oak tree and a rise in the ground where Mr. Wilkins remembered a concrete slab marked the area where Louis was attempting to build a new house after his divorce from Amy in 1914. We found the concrete slab and the remains of the well Louis had dug; the big oak tree, though still standing, was dead and covered with moss. As expected, there was no trace of the chicken house, the spot where Louis had sat outside reading, listening to the call of the chuck-wills-widows and the pulsating songs of tree frogs that hot August night of his death, a mystery which remains unsolved. Was it suicide as the family generally believed, was it the black man that Thad and Pete ran out of the county, or could Louis's death have resulted from something more sinister?

Thad had been Justice of Peace at Fairview where his grandfather, W.S. Horton, had been Postmaster. He had a reputation for being tight with a dollar and crafty in financial dealings with his neighbors. "Mr. Thad," as he was known around those parts, also had a reputation, as did a number of the Hortons, for a hot temper which would, on occasion, flame into violence. There had been bad blood between Thad and his father when his parents divorced and no doubt that was why Pete later shifted his suspicion from the black man to his brother. But Louis, the prodigal son of W.S. Horton, had threatened to kill himself so suicide remained the prevailing theory. Still questions remain. How and why would a man committing suicide take such elaborate precautions to destroy the evidence by fire?

The plantation house of W.S. and Elizabeth Horton was gone and that was just as well since no actual place could ever live up to the nostalgic recollections of Elizabeth's younger sister, Laura, or the childhood memories of Bessie and Gertrude. Laura Scott Butler, historian, public school and college teacher for many years and a loyal Daughter of the Confederacy as well as the mother of John Allen's piano teacher, wrote glowingly of life with her courageous sister at Fairview Plantation during the hard years of the Civil War. Her great niece, Gertrude, remembered her grandparent's home in her tribute to her Aunt Elizabeth Priscilla Horton who died shortly after graduating college at the age of twenty-one in 1876. Buried at Fairview close to the family garden, Priscilla was, years later, joined in death by her father, W.S. Horton, whose last words were, "Bury me by my daughter at the back of the garden and I will be all happy and right." The white-marble monument, the ivy-covered lattice house over the grave "out of which rose a spire that seemed always reaching toward heaven," the stately parlor with Priscilla's piano and her beautiful artwork were all gone.

John Allen, who knew of his great-grandparents only from the stories of his two aunts, recreated the post-bellum Fairview farm in his poem for his Aunt Bessie, "Star Walk."

In going through Bessie's papers after her death he found letters from her grandmother that reveal why Elizabeth was so highly regarded in the family including her great-grandson who was only four years old when she died. He wrote Mike Vogler:

> Grandmother Horton (my great grandmother) was nearly blind in her last years, and her letters are difficult to read. One letter moved me to tears. A postscript wandering across the back of the last page says: "My health is good. Old Father Time seems to have forgotten me while using his reaping hook and has left me standing alone in old age, but am blessed with helping hands always extended ready to help as I need help. For which I am very thankful."

> . . . . After a life of rectitude (always within the rules), she was troubled by the meandering of her penciled words beyond the bold black lines love drew to guide her failing sight.

I left Mr. Wilkins at the site of the old Fairview Plantation and farm and drove to nearby Sparkman where Louise and Frank Hurt spent the one unhappy year of their ill-fated marriage. Just outside town I found the Sardis Methodist Church, a typical white-frame country church building, and its nearby cemetery where Aunt Bessie, her father, Louis, and other Hortons and Butlers are buried. As I walked across the newly mowed grass of the cemetery on that spring day the honeysuckle covering the surrounding fence wafted its sweet smell through oak, pine, sweet gum and cedars while a soft breeze stirred branches high overhead. On both sides of a dividing ravine marked with deer tracks were other names—Givens, Knights, Bryants, Greens, Walkers. On one headstone was a verse popular in cemeteries in days gone by.

Remember friends,
As you pass by,
As you are now,
So once was I;
As I am now
So shall you be,
So prepare for eternity.

I found the Horton graves I was looking for. Here was that of the prodigal son, Louis S. Horton, Jan 5, 1860-Aug 9, 1914. At the top of his tall headstone was the word "Hope," and below his name an inscription from 2nd Samuel 22:18-19:

He delivered me from my enemy and from them which hated me. For they were too strong for me. They prevented me in the day of my calamity. But the Lord was my stay.

Ever since Vernon had described his father's death to me I had been unable to get the image of Louis' charred skeleton fused with bed springs out of my mind. As I stood looking at his grave I wondered what an exhumation now seventy years later would reveal.

Four of Louis' and Amy's children are buried there, the two girls, Evelyn and Marjorie who died in childhood, Thaddeus George, Thad, who had died only a year and a half earlier at the age of ninety-one, and his wife, Iris. And there too was Aunt Bessie—Apr 1, 1887-Nov 9, 1975. It was with her that John Allen asked to be buried, though he told Joy Rose Hill Cemetery where her first husband and other Hortons were buried would be all right as well.

I concluded my tour of the Horton family's departed in Arkadelphia at Rose Hill Cemetery. Just through the Main Street entrance off to the right behind an old wrought iron fence are the graves of Amy Jean Greene and her family. Some distance to the west where the ground begins to descend toward a stream bed I found the graves of more of John Allen's family. There were the esteemed founders of the Arkansas clan, the Forty-Niner and Civil War veteran W.S. Horton and his wife Elizabeth Scott. Buried beside them was their beloved Priscilla, called "Betty" by her admiring nieces, whose body had been transplanted from near the garden at Fairview along with that of her father. Nearby were the graves of Amy and her troubled, gift-bearing daughter, Mary Louise Horton Adams, "Madam Justina." Joy had not had John Allen buried here with his mother or at Sardis with Aunt Bessie, but across the ravine on the upward slope in the newer part of Rose Hill. I would visit his grave later.

Vernon by now I had talked to many times. There was another of Louise's siblings available to me at that time, however, one who had played a critical role in John Allen's life that I needed to hear from—John Allen's Aunt Gertrude.

I called on her on June 15, 1984, my first visit to the old home place. The big old house had declined over the seventy-four years of Horton occupation to the point where anyone wanting to renovate it wouldn't know where to begin. I stepped across the warped and worn planking of the porch and knocked on the door and was greeted there by Gertrude's nurse and companion, Jo Knox, a neat, dark-haired strong-looking woman in gold-rimmed glasses. She invited me into the living room whose furniture had attained the status of antiques without ever changing hands, giving the room the aspect of a faded photograph of a parlor from an earlier era. There I met Gertrude Horton King seated in one of the antique chairs wearing a light, flowery print dress. She was smaller and fleshier than I had expected with round cheeks, a round nose and slight squint in her right eye, with short thin gray hair wisping straight down behind her head.

I told Mrs. King I was hoping to write a book about her nephew and she thought that was a worthy project. She wanted to talk about John Allen but warned me her memory was poor, explaining she would be ninety-six years old the 19th of July. She was more than happy to talk about her teaching career, however, and on that subject her memory seemed clear. She had always been proud of her education, the fact that she had come from the sticks at Fairview and entered public school at a late age and gone on to earn her college degree. She told me how, while practice teaching, she had impressed a school principal in Little Rock when she interceded with a teacher who became frustrated with a student with a "speech deficiency." Gertrude told the teacher that all the child needed was a hug and some attention; after the teacher followed her advice and got a hug in return from the student, the problem was resolved. The principal witnessing her positive intervention told Gertrude, "We must have you for a teacher." That was how she wound up teaching the "three R's" to third graders in Little Rock.

Gertrude showed me pictures of herself and her brothers when they were younger, she shared the family history she had written out in a spiral notebook and agreed to let me return later and go through her letters and photographs. She also offered to recite one of her own poems for me, "Crepe Myrtle," an offer I gladly accepted; from memory she then recited the entire poem with amazingly good diction and expression and without missing a word.

It was difficult to imagine, sitting across from this small, mild-mannered elderly woman, the ferocious family conflicts she had been part of, many having taken place in that very house and witnessed and mediated by the unfortunate John Allen. She did tell me that Bessie, a sickly child, had been the favorite of their father and that she, Gertrude, always had to do more than her share of household work, including washing Vernon's diapers. (Vernon said Gertrude had always been jealous of Bessie and never got over it.)

Before I left she told me John Allen had called her every day to see how she was doing and every day told her he loved her.

If with the passage of time the fire had died down in Gertrude, the same could not be said for Aunt Bessie. From the time of their marriage in 1971 until Bessie's death in 1975 John Allen and Joy had to endure her rage. Many of their close family and friends realized the couple was under siege and offered their moral support. Two who did were John Allen's dad, Al, and his wife, Mayrene.

Allen Frank Adams had remarried after Louise's death, this time to a woman who told him he would have to abandon his nomadic lifestyle and get a steady job; so he did. Always personable, Al got a job in sales and, so far as I've been able to determine, he and Mayrene enjoyed a long, happy and successful marriage. Through the years they remained close to John Allen and Bessie and visited them when they could. Knowing Bessie's health and strength were in decline they were relieved and happy, as were other friends and family, to learn John Allen and Joy were getting married. Few could have foreseen, however, the trouble that marriage would cause.

Bessie's treatment of Joy turned many of her old friends against her. One of those was Vernon's successful, well-educated ex-wife, Frances Alexander Whelchel. In the 1930's and 40's the two women had been close and corresponded regularly, even after Frances' and Vernon's rancorous divorce. Frances was the person Bessie wrote describing the elaborate preparations taking place in Arkadelphia for the 1936 Centennial celebration. As did many others, Frances loved John Allen, so when she learned of Bessie's vindictive behavior toward Joy she was furious. She wrote me in June, 1984:

> I think [John Allen] was a saint in his attitude toward Aunt Bessie after she turned against them. She did her devilish best to make life miserable for Joy and John Allen. But he refused to hate back.

> One hot afternoon as I drove from Little Rock to Hope I stopped by. Aunt Bessie was sitting in the backyard. John Allen insisted I go out and visit with her. He was gentle and loving and expected me to be the same.

The sharp contrast between that old woman eaten up with hate and John Allen's compassion was something I shall never forget. It was cloud and sunshine. I think I never loved John Allen more.

So what do we make of people? There was W.S. Horton and his wife Elizabeth and her sister Laura, upright, loving and even heroic, admirable folks all, sustained, even through the grimmest days of the Civil War, by slave labor. Laura wrote that Elizabeth's "negroes planted and cultivated as much land as when their master was home, but cultivated enough cotton to make clothing for the family, the negroes, and the soldiers. Corn, wheat, potatoes, sorghum, turnips, and other vegetables were raised in abundance." The survival of the Hortons at Fairview Plantation through those hard times was paid for with the sweat of the very people the South was fighting to keep in bondage. Slavery was the curse that led to the tragedy of the Civil War, a sin that John Allen's great-grandparents and his great aunt could never acknowledge. That curse tainted generations of Southerners of both races up to and including Aunt Bessie, a curse not to be found in the inscriptions beneath the soldier on the Confederate monument in front of the Clark County Courthouse.

John Allen said his great-grandmother Elizabeth lived "a life of rectitude (always within the rules)." Yet by the rules of the antebellum South humans were permitted to own other humans and live off the fruits of their labor. History confronts us with paradox. Clearly many of those who lived with those values were possessed of genuine virtues. How can we admire Robert E. Lee, for example, a man of virtue who dealt out death in defense of a Confederacy that supported slavery?

And what do we make of Aunt Bessie—bitter, bigoted, and abusive toward Joy? John Allen well understood that he owed his life to his aunt, that had it not been for her indomitable love he would not have had eleven good years with Joy, and would, in fact, never have made it through that first critical period when his life hung by a thread. A long life of dedicated labor counts for something, so love such as Aunt Bessie's must be given its due weight in the balance scales of a life.

A problem arises when we attempt to measure those who have gone before by the moral standards of our own day. The mass of men are blind to customary evils, and yet there are those few in each age who are able and courageous enough to stand above and outside their times and speak out against institutionalized injustice, people such as Emerson, Thoreau, Mark Twain, Martin Luther King Jr., and John Allen. The rest of us go along with what is given and wait for future generations to point out our moral blindness.

John Allen well understood that his influence was modest and greatly limited compared with those other voices, but he did not let that keep him from speaking out. Like Gandhi whom he admired, he was fully aware of the tragic dimensions of life (his own and the world's) yet maintained a pure love for life along with the ability to smile and laugh easily. His religious views are reflected, I believe, in James Wright's summation of Tolstoy's faith: "the one really essential thing is to love life because life is God and to love life is to love God."

In one of his letters to John Allen his Concord philosopher friend W.S McNutt wrote, "Religion is in much more serious difficulty than they are prepared to admit. Matters of mere scientific certitude or doubt regarding peripheral aspects of religion somehow miss the point. What I would like to know is whether there is anything left over after the error has been removed which has value and is true and has significance for our time. This is the question thinking men discover for themselves and with some pain, if, like myself, they grew up in a strong religious tradition." He concluded the letter with a question for John Allen, "What are you going to invent to save us?"

John Allen did have some ideas about that subject—religion. He wrote Mike Vogler: "Panoply and traditional ritual do not move me—and yet I might be willing to create my own ritual. I sometimes wonder how we could stir children to a reverence for life, to a feeling of love and responsibility for our earth, and it occurs to me that ritual might play some part—though the deeper need is for us to labor in love and to permeate our entire society with this reverence."

Carl Sagan's *Cosmos* filled John Allen with a sense of wonder for the universe and our place in it, "wheeling in the Whereless Now." In spite of his antipathy toward the medium, television provided him a window to the wider world as can be seen in another letter to Mike: "I sometimes see elements of joy—the delightful grace of seals swimming and playing under water, sea lions riding the surf, African lions playing in the sun. It is good to remember this side of our indescribable experience."

John Allen's longing for rituals that would connect man to the miracle of life on this living planet and to the real and unfathomable universe rather than religious rituals that focus on those long dead and imaginary future punishments and paradises, brings to mind a stanza of the poem "Sunday Morning" by Wallace Stevens:

7

Supple and turbulent, a ring of men
Shall chant in orgy on a summer morn
Their boisterous devotion to the sun,
Not as a god, but as a god might be,
Naked among them, like a savage source.
Their chant shall be a chant of paradise,
Out of their blood, returning to the sky;
And in their chant shall enter, voice by voice,
The windy lake wherein their lord delights,
The trees, like serafin, and echoing hills,
That choir among themselves long afterward.
They shall know well the heavenly fellowship
Of men that perish and of summer morn.
And whence they came and whither they shall go
The dew upon their feel shall manifest.

"Simplify. Simplify." Thoreau said, and John Allen imagined a simple, natural life:

> I sometimes dream of a group of like-minded people living on land near Arkadelphia and experimenting with cooperative living—several families. During the growing season they would produce enough food to supply most of their needs and a surplus to sell from door to door in town. They might also sell whole-grain flour and meal freshly ground. This would serve the health of the community and be an honest way to earn needed cash. I think that—when possible—food should be produced in the area where it is consumed.

He was, however, a realist, and adds: "It's a dream, of course; the history of communal efforts is an unbroken record of failure, I think, except for several that had a religious basis." But what if we had a religion such as the one both he and John Lennon imagined, one based on reverence for the miracle of life, for the natural world and our amazing universe? John Lennon was a dreamer; but he was not the only one.

One of the many writers John Allen and Mike Vogler discussed in their "seminars" while Mike was in prison was Albert Camus. In his essay, "The Almond Trees," Camus writes, "We must mend what has been torn apart, make justice imaginable again in a world so obviously unjust, give happiness a meaning once more to a peoples poisoned by the misery of the century. Naturally it is a superhuman task. But superhuman is the term for tasks men take a long time to accomplish, that's all."

Some day John Allen's dream of humans living in harmony with the natural world and with a sense of reverence for life may come to pass, but it will require superhuman effort. There are encouraging signs today that people are slowly waking up to the importance of caring for the earth, a growing awareness that all nations and all people must work together to clean up the environment, save the oceans and rain forests, and reduce global warming. One of John Allen's ideas seems to be getting some attention today— the growing of food near communities that consume it, a "buy local" movement called community supported agriculture or CSA.

His dream of a world living in peace will be much harder to realize since violence and conflict have played such a major role in man's evolutionary and historical past. John Allen witnessed many conflicts in his own family, always playing the role of peacemaker, and he did all he could to serve as a peacemaker for his country. Perhaps his most remarkable quality, however, was his gift for inspiring love.

What was behind Aunt Bessie's fury? Impaired faculties and advanced age may have contributed to her bad behavior but cannot explain it. Even though she could no longer take care of John Allen she could not let him go. To see Joy usurp her place as his companion and principal caregiver was, for Bessie, unthinkable. Her reaction to this new arrangement exposed the motive behind her life-long dedication to caring for her nephew. She had done so, not for family, not from altruistic, humanitarian impulses, but because of her fierce love for him. She had loved only two men in her life without reservations— her grandfather W.S. Horton and John Allen. She had lost her grandfather when she was a young woman and very nearly lost John Allen after his injury. But she kept him alive and made it possible for him to become the successful man he was. He had been her life, and she could not let him go.

John Allen had always been loved by women from the time, as a beautiful curly-headed boy, he came to live at the home place until his death. My colleagues, Bennie Bledsoe and Clarice Freeman who were his classmates, told me how he was admired by girls all through his school years. That admiration didn't stop with his injury. His female classmates could often be found around the stricken young athlete's bed cheering him with their company. The eight-year-old Amy Thomson wanted to marry him when she grew up so she could take care of him. For his ill-starred mother, Louise, John Allen was her one star of hope, her one good thing. He was the blessing Madam Justina, bestowed upon Bessie and all the Horton family.

Among female admirers was one a few years older than John Allen, Martha Winburn England. This Radcliffe PhD, professor and scholar, was a life-long friend and correspondent who opened doors for John Allen to Ivy League campuses and the glittering cultural life of New York City. In quoting from her correspondence to him I have made no attempt to characterize her feelings or their relationship beyond her own words. She was, in the early letters before he died, married to Farmer England, but her feelings for the young man who lay paralyzed in Arkadelphia were strong. She wrote John Allen, "You know I love you. I will put on my Sunday manners when I come and do my best to tell you good bye calmly. And leave you your realistic literature."

Martha's declaration here reveals an important contrast in their two natures. John Allen was, as she indicates, a realist, like Thoreau who said, we want to "work and wedge our feet downward through the mud and slush of opinion, and prejudice, and tradition, and delusion, and appearance . . . till we come to hard bottom and rocks in place, which we can call *reality*, and say, This is, and no mistake." Martha, by contrast, was an inveterate romantic who preferred fantasy over unpleasant fact. That propensity no doubt goes far in explaining her love of opera.

The contrast in their natures can be seen clearly in their approach to religion. John Allen made a serious study of the subject, reading the Bible through as a young man and exploring other major world religions before arriving at the conclusion that all were the creations of men and, while containing much of value as literature, philosophy and history, all, as Thomas Paine said, were hearsay. None were revelations from God.

Martha England as a romantic had no use for such rational analysis. Raised a good Baptist by a prominent Baptist minister and graduating from Ouachita Baptist University she had better things to do than parse scriptures or question the faith of her fathers. Her faith lived in the dimension of feeling. She loved church hymns and truly believed there would be an "Unclouded Day." She chided John Allen for his skepticism, reassuring him that death is not the end.

> . . . you and I cannot see eye to eye on the subject of death, because you keep forgetting that death, while it is all those things, is merely seeing Farmer and Dad again. The Caddo Coffee Shop where they used to forgather, could not hold the joy of Dad and Mr. McCormick getting together again relieved of the infirmities of the flesh, and unworried about what will happen to their dear little friend, John Allen—because now they know more than we do and know enough not to worry, because God has his eye on you.

Not a sparrow falleth. . .

When I first set out to write about John Allen in 1984 I didn't know who Martha England was. At that time I compiled a long list of his friends and family and her name was on the list, but it was just one of many and I didn't understand her significance. It was not until I recently resumed my effort to tell his story that I discovered her importance in his life, but it was too late. I Googled her name on the Internet and found the following obituary from the *New York Times*:

Martha Winburn England, Professor, 80
Published: December 28, 1989

Dr. Martha Winburn England, a retired English professor at Queens College and a writer and translator, died on Monday at the Parkway Nursing Center in Little Rock, Ark., where she lived. She was 80 years old.

Her writing included an English translation, with James Durbin Jr., of Rossini's opera "Cenerentola" (Cinderella).

Dr. England, a native of Arkadelphia, Ark., earned a bachelor's degree at Ouachita University there and master's and doctoral degrees in comparative literature at Radcliffe.

The most amazing thing about my belated discovery of Martha England was the fact that at the time of John Allen's death in 1984 she lived in an apartment only five blocks from Adams Book Store. She had, at the end, come home from the big city.

Martha was one of many women who loved and admired John Allen. I believe it's safe to say that all the coed assistants who worked for him admired and loved him, young women like Sarah Sullivan, Linda Wells, Teresa Young, and Sandy Hays who wrote the long poem honoring his memory. There were also many women customers who felt close to him through the years. Rebecca Fulmer wrote the local paper after his death, "John Allen Adams, you were a friend for me and you were a friend for this whirling, hovering, sweet planet Earth. Oh friend, goodbye!" The young Ouachita student who married a Tucker Prison inmate, though too shy to address him directly, clearly sensed his strength and compassion and wrote to tell him her story. She concluded, "Men like you inspire—those whose courage and zeal enable them to reach out to others. Thank you. I admire you greatly, Mr. John Allen Adams; your poems have made my life a better place to be."

If women could love him safely, the same could be said for men. Why did Professor McNutt react angrily to my inquiry concerning John Allen? Misguided as I believe his response was, it seems clear his intent was to protect his life-long friend from those who might do harm to his memory. In just a cursory reading of McNutt's letters his love for John Allen is evident. The same can be said of Mike Vogler's letters to John Allen, one of which concluded, "Would it embarrass you very much if I told you that I love you..."

The young college men who worked for him too came under his influence. Jim Larkin wrote, "I have never really told you what a large role you have played in shaping my life. Somebody asked me not long ago what person or persons have made the greatest influence on me, and four people immediately came to mind—Jesus Christ, Gandhi, Thoreau, and John Allen Adams. That's pretty heavy company, huh! But it is true. You have an independent, practical philosophy of life that is in tune with the universe. . . ."

John Allen Adams was a man of contradictions. Although almost totally paralyzed, he was the strongest man I've ever known, a man who found freedom while bound to a wheelchair and independence while almost totally dependent on

those around him. He made his way in the world as a businessman dealing in the products he loved most—books; and
though confined for forty-six years to two houses two blocks
apart, his influence reached across the country and beyond
and enriched the lives of many people. This amazingly gifted
son of a carnival fortune teller whose promising future was
shattered by an accident on a high-school football field found
within himself the resources to build a life that made a difference, a difference reflected in the testimonies and memories
of those whose lives he touched.

* * *

On a cold, raw February day in 2007, I visited once more
the Horton graves in Rose Hill Cemetery. After completing
my tour of the eastern section I drove down the hill on Main
Street to the adjoining section of the graveyard where John
Allen is buried. There, just over the fence beneath a great
spreading water oak tree, I found the Salisbury tombstone. On
Joy's right is Tom, her first husband. Engraved on a small flat
marker at his feet is, "Daddy," and "Papa Bear." On her left
with a separate headstone is the grave of John Allen. Beneath
his name, as he had requested, are the words, "A Bookseller
and Poet." At the top is the peace symbol adopted by protesters of the Vietnam War and widely recognized in the 1960's
and 70's. For John Allen, however, the symbol represented,
not a single protest movement, but the commitment of a
lifetime. Since he had not mentioned it in his burial instructions, Joy must have had it engraved on the stone. He had
been loved by many women, but Joy was the last, and while
caring for John Allen had been a demanding responsibility

she had done so gladly and believed herself privileged to have had the opportunity.

A cold wind was blowing. I had been in the cemetery a good while now and my fingers were getting puffy with chilblains; I needed to go. It had rained over the last several days and water had washed red mud over the small flat marker at the foot of the poet's grave. With my foot I wiped the dirt from the stone and uncovered Joy's last words to John Allen:

"Beloved Husband."

* * *

Works Cited and References

Adams, John Allen. *Papers and Correspondence.* Donated by Mrs. John Allen Adams.

Barry, John M. *Rising Tide: The Great Mississippi Flood of 1927 and How It Changed America.* New York: A Touchstone Book, Simon & Schuster, 1997.

Bledsoe, Bennie G. *Henderson State University: Education Since 1890.* Houston, TX: D. Armstrong Co., Inc., 1986.

Brands, H. W. *The Age of Gold: The California Gold Rush and the New American Dream.* New York: Anchor, 2003.

Butler, Laura W.S. "A Tribute to Mrs. Elizabeth Scott Horton." *Confederate Veteran.* p.425 (unk. Date).

Camus, Albert. *Lyrical and Critical Essays.* New York: Vintage Books, 1970.

Christ, Mark K., ed. *"All Cut to Pieces and Gone to Hell": The Civil War, Race Relations, and the Battle of Poison Spring.* New York: August House, Incorporated, 2003.

Clark County Arkansas: Past and Present. Ed. Wendy Richter. Clark County Historical Association, Arkadelphia, Arkansas, 1992.

Cole, Jonathan. *Still Lives: Narratives of Spinal Cord Injury.* New York: MIT P, 2006.

DeBlack, Thomas A. *With Fire and Sword: Arkansas, 1861-1874.* Fayetteville, AR: University of Arkansas Press, 2003

Emerson, Ralph W. *Essays and Lectures.* Ed. Joel Porte. New York: Library of America, The, 1983.

Encyclopedia of Arkansas. http://www.encyclopediaofarkansas.net/

Faust, Drew G. *Mothers of Invention : Women of the Slaveholding South in the American Civil War.* New York: University of North Carolina P, 1996.

Fox-Genovese, Elizabeth. *Within the Plantation Household: Black and White Women of the Old South.* New York: University of North Carolina P, 1988.

Gandhi, Mahatma. *The Essential Gandhi : An Anthology of His Writings on His Life, Work, and Ideas.* Ed. Louis Fischer. New York: Vintage, 2002.

Goodspeed Biographical and Historical Memoires of Southern Arkansas. Goodspeed Publishing Co., 1890

Gresham, William L. *Monster Midway.* New York: Rinehart, 1953.

Hall, John G. *Henderson State College: The Methodist Years.* Kingsport, TN: Kingsport P, 1974.

A History of Arkansas: In Stories and Pictures. New York: August House, Incorporated, 1998.

Johnson, Ben F. *Arkansas in Modern America, 1930-1999.* New York: University of Arkansas Press, 2002.

King, Gertrude Horton. "Horton Family History." Unpublished Manuscript.

Knaebel, Nathaniel. *Step Right Up: Stories of Carnivals, Sideshows, and the Circus.* New York: Carroll & Graf, 2004.

Manas. http://www.manasjournal.org/index.html

Ouachita River Foundation. http://www.ouachitariver.org/main.htm

Randolph, Vance. *Ozark Magic and Folklore.* Minneapolis: Dover Publications, Incorporated.

Reeve, Christopher. *Still Me.* New York: Ballantine Books, 1999.

Steward, Diana, ed. *A Rough Sort of Beauty: Reflections on the Natural Heritage of Arkansas.* New York: University of Arkansas Press, 2002.

Thoreau, Henry D., and Robert Sayre. <u>Thoreau.</u> *A Week on the Concord and Merrimack Rivers, Walden, The Maine Woods, Cape Cod.* New York: Library of America, The, 1989.

Thoreau, Henry D. *Walden and Resistance to Civil Government.* Ed. Owen Thomas and William Rossi. Boston: W. W. Norton & Company, Incorporated, 1992.

Tolstoy, Leo. *The Kingdom of God Is Within You.* New York: Wildside Press, 2006.

Twain, Mark. <u>Mark Twain:</u> *Mississippi Writings Vol. 1: Tom Sawyer; Life on the Mississippi; Huckleberry Finn; Pudd'Nhead Wilson.* Ed. Guy Cardwell. New York: Library of America, The, 1982.

Wells, Linda. Notes on John Allen

We Were There: Clark Countians In World War II. Arkadelphia, AR: Clark County Historical Association, 1995.

* * *

Index

4901396R0

Made in the USA
Charleston, SC
02 April 2010